T
i
c

Gl
Li
n

WHEN
WE WERE
LIONS

WHEN
WE WERE
LIONS

EURO 96 AND THE LAST
GREAT BRITISH SUMMER

PAUL REES

Aurum
Press

Quarto is the authority on a wide range of topics.

Quarto educates, entertains and enriches the lives of our readers—enthusiasts and lovers of hands-on living.

www.QuartoKnows.com

First published 2016 by
Aurum Press Limited
74-77 White Lion Street
London N1 9PF
www.QuartoKnows.com

A catalogue record for this book is available from the British Library.

ISBN 978 1 78131 508 8
EBook ISBN 978 1 78131 550 7

10 9 8 7 6 5 4 3 2 1
2020 2019 2018 2017 2016

Typeset by SX Composing DTP, Rayleigh, Essex

Printed and bound in Great Britain by CPI Group (UK) Ltd, Croydon, CR0 4YY

This one's for Martha Rees who
never failed to be glorious

CONTENTS

PROLOGUE

As darkness ran to dawn on the morning of Thursday, 27 June 1996, Paul Gascoigne could be heard sobbing himself to sleep. During the previous three weeks a more uproarious sound would have been booming out from his room at Burnham Beeches Hotel, a grandiose whitewashed pile near Slough where the England football team were billeted. On any given morning or afternoon, 'Gazza' would crank up his portable CD player, throw open the door and windows and let the adopted anthem of England's Euro 96 campaign reverberate down the corridors, across the landscaped lawns and out to the supporters thronging the leafy approaches to the hotel. The crowds would then pick up the song's triumphal chant and send it rolling back to Gascoigne with gusto. 'It's coming home, it's coming home, it's coming, football's coming home,' they sang, their voices raised in exultation.

To be sure, the summer of 1996 was an extraordinary time to be in Britain and to be British, and most especially English. It was the summit of a halcyon period in the country's modern history, both socially and culturally. The cresting of a boundless mood of optimism and patriotism that had bubbled up during the preceding two years and swelled through sport, music, art, fashion and even politics. The mid-1990s were when Tony Blair and New Labour emerged, Oasis, Blur and Britpop boomed, Kate Moss was turned into a fashion icon and *Trainspotting* revived the British film industry with an electrified jolt. Through that sun-baked month of June, Englishmen strove to win the Wimbledon tennis championship, the Formula One world drivers' title and The Open golf tournament. There, though, at the very centre of things were Euro 96, the Three Lions and Gazza, rallying points for all England's hopes and dreams.

England started the tournament slowly but gained momentum and swept the country along with them. As Euro 96 unfolded, thirty years since the national football team had won its last and only major honour, it seemed increasingly as if the side moulded by head coach Terry Venables, and blessed with Gascoigne's magical touch, was going to repeat the feat. The euphoric scenes that accompanied Venables's men to, during and from each of their games were now etched in the national consciousness, indelible and definitive of the era. If that euphoria could be distilled into a single image, it would be of the old Wembley Stadium, its crumbling terraces packed and turned to a sea of red and white St George's flags. This was England that June, revelling in the moment when thrilling and powerful forces collided, on the cusp of promised glory.

At the witching hour on that Thursday, however, the grounds of Burnham Beeches, like the country as a whole, were silent and still. Towards midnight the England team bus had rumbled up the hotel's tree-lined avenue, returning them to rural Berkshire from the hustle, bustle and noise of Wembley. The hotel staff and a small retinue of locals lined up on the driveway to greet them. Gascoigne, his team-mates and Venables were cheered into the lobby. They smiled back dutifully, but their faces were frozen in a kind of disbelieving, dead-eyed shock. Among them were the stoical Alan Shearer, the tournament's top goalscorer, and his strike partner, Teddy Sheringham; the two full-backs, young Gary Neville from Manchester United and the veteran Stuart Pearce, who had informed the coaching staff and his team-mates during the journey that he meant to retire from playing for England; the captain, Tony Adams, who looked as if he would run through a brick wall; Paul Ince, Gascoigne's partner in midfield and such a swaggering presence he christened himself 'The Guv'nor'; and the Liverpool duo, Steve McManaman and Robbie Fowler, whose antics had amused and irked Venables in equal measure.

Each one of them had anticipated coming back victorious, triumphant, with one more spell-binding night in North London still ahead of them. On the evening of 30 June they meant to lay to rest thirty years of hurt by winning the Euro 96 final and securing for themselves the sporting immortality enjoyed by Sir Alf Ramsey and his boys of '66. That much had seemed to them pre-destined ever since their second game of the tournament when Gascoigne lit the fuse with a breath-taking act of impudence and sheer brilliance against England's oldest football rivals, Scotland.

Saturday, 15 June, twenty-five minutes to five o'clock on a roasting summer's afternoon at Wembley. At that precise moment, Gascoigne collected a hopeful forward punt from Darren Anderton. In a single, fluid movement, running between two Scottish defenders on the edge of the opposition penalty area, he lifted it over their heads and met it on the volley. The shot speared into the Scottish net, winning the game for England and sending into raptures the thousands of English supporters in the stadium as well as millions more watching on television at home and in countless pubs and clubs across the country. After a stuttering start, it was Gascoigne's intervention that sparked England and the tournament into life. It also restored Gascoigne to his exalted position as the finest English player of his generation and a national treasure.

Going into Euro 96, Gascoigne had been written off, his mental and physical fitness in serious doubt and his powers perceived to be waning. On the eve of the tournament, notably after the team returned from a disastrous warm-up trip to China and Hong Kong, he was singled out, demonised in the press and faced a growing movement to have him kicked out of the squad. The prodigiously talented boy-man who had first enraptured the nation by shedding tears as England crashed out on penalties to West Germany in the semi-final of the Italia 90 World

Cup appeared now, at just twenty-nine, to be broken and spent. A fallen hero wrecked by his own ill-discipline on and off the pitch and beset by demons. The awesomeness of his goal against the Scots reversed that notion at a single, dazzling stroke. It was as if he had somehow been able to roll back time and recapture the essence of himself. From that point on the England team moved to Gascoigne's beat: a dextrous, conjuring rhythm. His displays at Euro 96 returned him to the pinnacle of his sport.

Gazza was especially influential in England's next match against the Dutch, one of the pre-tournament favourites and among the powerhouses of world football. Revelling in having the ball at his feet, and using it with the precision of a surgeon's scalpel, Gascoigne was the team's fulcrum, the pivot around which they were able to confront and crush the Dutch at their own cultured game. Collectively, it was a performance for the ages, the highest point of Venables's tenure. That had begun after England failed to qualify for the finals of the 1994 World Cup and were left mired in the doldrums of international football. But in much less than three years they had reached this giddy point. Cavalier and canny, Venables had restored self-belief and a sense of pride to English football, building a team of equal parts strength and skill, with leaders such as Adams, Pearce, Ince and Shearer and artisans like Gascoigne, Sheringham, Anderton and McManaman.

England advanced to a semi-final against the Germans. That meeting took place on the grey, humid evening of 26 June and proved to be a gripping battle of wills. It pitted the two best teams in the tournament, its heavy-weights, against each other and they stood toe-to-toe, trading blows across the lush expanse of the Wembley pitch. England were looking to avenge their cruel defeat in Turin. Their opponents were seeking to exorcise the ghost of 1966 when Ramsey's team put a strong West German side to the sword. Before the encounter six years earlier, England's then-manager, Bobby Robson, had told a callow Gascoigne that he would be facing the world's best midfielder, the Germans' imperious schemer Lothar Matthaüs. 'No, Bobby,' Gascoigne shot back, 'you're wrong – he is.' Now, Gascoigne was once again as confident and bullish, assured of his status as the game's pre-eminent playmaker. He strutted through the battle, England's lightning rod, the channel through which the ebb and flow of the match was set and controlled. He was so sure of his moment and looked certain to seize it.

Gascoigne's chance came towards the end of the game, and in an instant. The ball flashed across a gaping German goal with him rushing to meet it, his leg stretched out to turn the ball into the net. All of England was ready to roar his name as he grabbed the 'golden goal' that would claim a place in the final. Agonisingly, unfathomably, he came up a step and a beat short. In a blink the ball and history sped past Gascoigne, the team and the country.

Afterwards, Gascoigne tried to put a brave face on things. When Venables suggested one last hurrah back at the team hotel, he was among the most determined to drink to another heroic English footballing failure. As the party-wake got into full swing, and the England team and staff set about drowning their sorrows, he commandeered a vat of tomato ketchup from the hotel kitchen and emptied it over Fowler, still playing the part of the company's ringleader and its resident clown.

Yet the booze and bonhomie did not numb the creeping, clawing fear that plagued Gascoigne that night. It was the realisation that it would not be his feats against Scotland, Holland and during that last epic game with Germany that would be his defining moments, but rather that last-gasp miss. It was only then that he had failed to shine. But he must have wondered if this was how it was going to be for him from now on. That whenever he reached for the heights of old, he would find himself instead clasping at air and crashing to earth. He fled upstairs to his room and there in the dark wept until sleep and a fragile peace came upon him.

The hotel bar at Burnham Beeches had come alive into the early hours after England defeated Scotland, Holland and then Spain in the quarter-final. On these occasions, Venables let his players off the leash and led them in jubilant sing-songs on the karaoke machine. No one slept much on such heady nights when pure adrenaline pumped through their veins and the drink flowed. These were the best of times. No one would sleep much on this night, either. But now the atmosphere was more forced, the mood not so riotous, since the prospect of writing their names in the lexicon of English sport had been wrenched from them. While Gascoigne was crying in his room upstairs, there were other haunted souls downstairs in the bar, tending their wounds and nursing their fears.

In one corner sat Venables and Gareth Southgate, who had missed the decisive penalty in this latest shoot-out with the Germans, the two of them talking in hushed voices. For Venables this was the end of his time in charge of England, the role he believed he had been born for, but from which he had been removed. It was not football matters, but his extracurricular business dealings that had led to his downfall. His employers, the Football Association, perhaps fearing revelations from a spate of court cases that Venables was fighting in an attempt to clear his name, had refused to renew his contract beyond Euro 96. Back in January Venables had announced he would step down after the tournament, and there was no going back on that now. Southgate's miss had robbed the departing head coach of a lasting legacy. Venables had said on the eve of the match that victory, and getting England to the final, would provide the greatest moment of his life. Not only was he leaving his job reluctantly, but also now unfulfilled and with a sense of disappointment that was so great and so heavy that it made him feel he was going to be sick. He had, though, retained the loyalty, admiration and respect of his players. It was Venables who was the first to rush to console Southgate on the pitch and then afterwards in the dressing room.

As he sipped at his regular tipple, an orange juice, the sober, studious Southgate was still despondent. Venables told him that he had been one of the stars of the tournament. That he should not, need not, feel ashamed and must instead be proud of his performances. Southgate looked as if he was listening but not hearing. Venables was interrupted when Southgate received a phone call from his mum, Barbara. Her counsel to her stricken son was rather less prosaic. 'Why didn't you just belt it?' she asked him.

Tony Adams, outwardly towering, domineering and forthright, came over to their table and thanked Venables for dragging English football out of its dark ages. The defeat had also hit Adams hard. He was slurring his words and battling his own inner demons. For years a binge drinker, he had sworn off the booze for the duration of Euro 96, willing himself to greatness. But now he was cutting loose. Directly after the match, he had helped himself to a can of lager in the dressing room, sinking it in one greedy gulp, grabbed another and dived headlong for the abyss. He was a further five pints of Guinness into his descent when he approached Venables. More would follow in quick succession before oblivion.

The party finally wound down at six in the morning, the stragglers managing a last chorus of 'football's coming home' before sloping off to bed. It sounded tired, worn out and beaten. Gascoigne, Venables and most of the rest of the England squad were up and gone by the time Adams surfaced. Adams stumbled across the last remnants,

Southgate and Pearce, in the process of checking out. He suggested a drink for the road, but they declined. Undeterred, Adams had one of the team's security staff chauffeur him to his local, the Chequers Inn, a mock-Tudor pub in the Essex commuter town of Hornchurch. Upon arrival he handed his England kit bag to the landlord, Bill, to stow behind the bar and hit the bottle again. By the time he came up for air seven weeks later, Adams had dropped half a stone in weight and was in a ruined state.

Adams ignored the acclaim that followed England's loss. The morning after the semi-final, the same newspapers that had questioned, even scorned the team in the aftermath of their pre-tournament tour to the Far East, hailed their gallantry in defeat and admired their achievement in reclaiming England's place at the top table of international football. The ultimate prize might have been lost, but there was now a depth of feeling that England could take on the best teams in the world and beat them; that if nothing else, Euro 96 had made English football, and football in England, seem great again.

PART ONE:
APRIL

CHAPTER ONE

'Everyone at the FA was worried about Terry'

At the beginning of April Terry Venables flew out to Spain for a short holiday. It would be his last chance to catch his breath before the build-up to Euro 96 began in earnest with a friendly fixture against Croatia at Wembley on 24 April. Two things were most occupying his mind. The first was the mounting number of injuries to key players in his squad. He was already missing Blackburn's Alan Shearer, Darren Anderton of Tottenham, and Aston Villa's Gareth Southgate, who had damaged knee ligaments in his club's FA Cup semi-final defeat by Liverpool on 31 March and would be absent for ten weeks. Now he discovered that Tony Adams's planned comeback from a cartilage operation had been aborted by Arsenal's club doctor. His leader on the field, Adams had managed just two competitive games in three months.

The other thing troubling Venables was his imminent departure from the job he had coveted for so long and held for little more than two years. At the end of the previous year, after England had beaten Switzerland at

Wembley, Venables anticipated the FA would extend his contract past Euro 96 and through to the 1998 World Cup finals in France. He received a rude awakening. The whip-hand at the FA was held by Liverpool director Noel White, head of the International Committee and who had opposed Venables's appointment from the outset. White had set Venables a minimum target of reaching the semi-finals of Euro 96 and told him that only then would his performance be assessed. Venables countered that he did not do auditions and in January announced that he would stand down at the end of his existing contract.

As Venables boarded his flight to Spain, the English press were speculating on who the FA were head-hunting as his successor. Among the names thought to be in the frame were Howard Wilkinson, who had won the league title with Leeds United in 1992, and three former England captains: Gerry Francis, the Spurs manager, Kevin Keegan at Newcastle and Bryan Robson, who was now managing Middlesbrough and was a member of Venables's England coaching staff. Unbeknown to Venables, the media and almost everyone else, the FA had in fact already offered the job to Alex Ferguson, the Manchester United manager. Ferguson had led United to two Premier League titles but was a proud Scot. He was amused by the approach and politely declined. At all events, England would be going into their most significant tournament in thirty years under the stewardship of a man whom his employers seemed eager to be rid. But then, when Venables was first linked with England in 1993, FA chairman Bert Millichip was reported as saying he would be installed 'over my dead body'.

Few figures in English football straddled the divide between its old-school traditions and the new era being ushered in since the founding of the Premier League in 1992, as assuredly as Venables. Even fewer divided opinion like the England supremo. There were no greys in terms of how Venables was perceived, only black and white. Depending on which side of the fence you sat, he was either an astute, inspirational coach and far-sighted entrepreneur, or a spiv with questionable ethics and a fatal weakness for chasing easy money. It was generally agreed, however, that in person he was charming, charismatic and entirely engaging.

Back in December 1993 the FA enlisted the widely respected Jimmy Armfield to take soundings from people within the game to help them appoint a replacement for Graham Taylor, who had resigned as England manager following the ignominious failure to qualify for the 1994 World Cup finals. Armfield, capped forty-three times by England between 1959 and 1966, and formerly manager of Bolton and Leeds, reported back that the unanimous choice of the professionals was Venables.

Venables ticked all the boxes for the job bar one. Put simply, he was carrying more baggage than all of the other prospective candidates put together. Most specifically there was a nagging question about the probity of his business dealings. The previous May he had been dismissed from his position as chief executive of Tottenham Hotspur by chairman Alan Sugar amid claims of financial malpractice. These were investigated in a damning *Panorama* documentary broadcast on the BBC as recently as 4 October 1993. Venables responded with the threat of legal action against both Sugar and the BBC. A department of Trade and Industry investigation into the activities of four of his companies was still looming as Euro 96 approached.

A four-strong panel subsequently assembled at the FA's Lancaster Gate headquarters to debate Venables's credentials and quickly split in two. The FA's chief executive, Graham Kelly, was Venables's strongest advocate and had even persuaded Millichip on to his side. White and his fellow northern businessman, Oldham Athletic chairman Ian Stott, were steadfastly against. In a febrile atmosphere, the question of Venables's candidature even reached the House of Commons. Using parliamentary privilege, Labour MP Kate Hoey, an Arsenal supporter, warned the FA against appointing him. Quite how the otherwise urbane Venables was brought to this point is a story in itself.

An only child, Terence Frederick Venables was born in the east London suburb of Dagenham on 6 January 1943. The drone of Luftwaffe planes was still then a familiar sound in the skies over the capital as the war ground on. Not long after they moved out, the Venables's first family home was razed by a German bomb. Among the other war babies to have been brought kicking and screaming into the world in close proximity to the Essex town were three members of Alf Ramsey's World Cup-winning squad: the captain Bobby Moore, Martin Peters and Jimmy Greaves. A laconic midfielder, Venables, captain of Chelsea at nineteen, was one of the thirty-three-strong provisional squad Ramsey announced in advance of the competition, but did not make the cut. In fact, he did not add to the two full England caps he won in 1964. However, these were enough to secure him an unbreakable record of being the only player to represent the country at every level from school-boy, through the FA's now-defunct amateur team and up to the full side.

It was also true of Venables that he never fulfilled his early promise as a player. He left Chelsea for Spurs in 1966, but ended up being no more than a cog in a machine built around such formidable figures as Dave Mackay, Alan Mulley and Greaves, and presided over by the taci-turn Bill Nicholson. Venables won the FA Cup with Spurs in 1967, but it never suited him to play a supporting role and he left two years later for Queens Park Rangers in the Second Division and then Crystal Palace in the Third. An ankle injury ended his career in 1976. Venables, though, had been canny enough to plan ahead. He had been inspired by the example of the enterprising young coach he played under at Chelsea, Dave Sexton, and he took his coaching badges while at Spurs.

In this respect at least, fortune favoured Venables at Palace. He was signed by the club's charismatic new manager, Malcolm Allison. 'Big Mal' may have been characterised as a flamboyant figure with his wide-brimmed Fedora hat, accessorised with ostentatious jewellery, a fat Havana cigar and a bottle of bubbly, but he was an inventive coach. He had first met Venables in the late-1950s, when as captain of West Ham he was detailed to call at the young prospect's home to persuade him to sign schoolboy forms with the club. Allison failed in that instance, but seventeen years later succeeded in persuading Venables to join his Palace coaching staff.

Allison schooled his protégé throughout the 1975–76 season, when master and apprentice would talk about training drills, tactics and playing systems from first thing in the morning until late at night. Allison, however, was reckless and prone to self-destruct. Increasingly, he absented himself from training to sleep off the effects of the night before, leaving the day-to-day running of the club to Venables. It was better for everyone that he did. On one of Allison's rare midweek visits to the club's Selhurst Park ground, he turned up with a well-known glamour model, Fiona Richmond, and a photographer in tow. This unlikely trio proceeded to the dressing room where the shy, retiring Miss Richmond shed her solitary item of clothing, a fur coat, and leapt naked into the communal bath with Allison, sending the stunned players scattering. The publicity photographs from the escapade may not have done for Allison with Palace's appalled directors, but his failure to get the club promoted did. At the end of the season Allison was sacked and Venables appointed in his place.

The pattern of Venables's managerial career was set from the beginning. At Palace, he nurtured an attractive, enterprising young side, guiding them to the First Division in just three seasons, and earning them the premature tag of 'Team of the Eighties'. Palace topped the league table for one starred week in 1979, but Venables could not sustain their momentum. He bought in expensive new recruits and the team lost focus and direction. In October 1980, and with Palace bottom of the First Division after a run of nine defeats in ten games, Venables left to take over at one of his other former clubs, Queens Park Rangers. Back at Loftus Road, Venables was able to indulge his wider ambitions. He had fancied himself as a business and renaissance man ever since his time at Chelsea when he ran around swinging London with the actor Adam Faith and fashion photographer Terry O'Neill, a wide boy on the make with his Beatles haircut and pearl-white smile. In his first spell at QPR, he befriended a Booker Prize-winning author and dedicated *bon vivant*, Gordon Williams. Together they created the character of wide-boy cockney private detective James Hazell, co-authoring three books about their titular anti-hero and giving rise to a briefly popular television series in 1978.

Second time around Venables was indulged by QPR's irascible chairman, Jim Gregory, who had made his money trading cars. Gregory eventually promoted Venables to managing director and the club's second largest shareholder. The two men conspired to initiate a revolution in the game from their modest west London base. Intent upon maximising revenue, they plotted the development of an all-seat, multi-purpose stadium with a retractable roof. As a concept it was a decade ahead of its time and impossible for them to realise. Ultimately, the only fresh ground they broke came in the summer of 1981 when the first artificial pitch in English football was laid at Loftus Road. It did not prove a watershed. The surface caused the ball to bounce erratically and the players to suffer carpet burns. Venables and Gregory's 'plastic' pitch was appropriated by just three other clubs in the Football League, Luton, Preston and Oldham, before being banned by the FA in 1985.

Venables's success in winning promotion to the First Division and qualifying QPR for the UEFA Cup in 1984, though, made an impression that extended beyond England's borders. On 23 May 1984, and at the age of forty-one, Venables was appointed head coach of the Spanish giants Barcelona. At the time Barcelona had not won a *La Liga* title for ten years and Venables was their eighth coach in five seasons. He had an unpromising introduction to the job. The club's star player, Diego Maradona, had run up such ruinous debts through gambling and indulging his extravagant lifestyle that he required a big money transfer to make him solvent. Yet Venables never lacked self-belief or sheer force of personality. Once again he made a galvanising start, Barcelona romping to the league title in his first season in charge, losing just two games. He would have secured his reputation had the Catalan club won its first European Cup the next season.

He led Barcelona to the final in Seville, but he and his team froze, losing a dour game to the Romanian champions Steaua Bucharest on penalties. Venables eventually left Barcelona in 1987, wealthier and worldlier, but not having made his name.

He spent the next four seasons as manager of Tottenham, winning the FA Cup in 1991, but despite spending big he could not elevate the club above being also-rans in the league. However, one of Venables's most notable achievements was signing the twenty-one-year-old Paul Gascoigne from Newcastle in the summer of 1988, ahead of Alex Ferguson at Manchester United, and then polishing the rough diamond into a jewel.

Gascoigne was never more impish nor, until Euro 96, better than he was when playing under Venables for three years at White Hart Lane. Venables believed the richness of Gascoigne's talent more than compensated for the quirks and excesses of his obsessive compulsive behaviour. On one occasion, Venables excused Gascoigne from training so that he could return to his hotel room to straighten out the towels. Gascoigne rewarded Venables's tolerance by almost single-handedly carrying Spurs through to Wembley in 1991, pulling the strings of a side that was no more than average without him, but which his influence made dangerous and devilish. 'We had acquired a genius,' said Venables. 'Of all the great players I managed for the club, none had his sublime talent or a greater winning attitude, and none did I feel more warmth towards. He never caused me trouble I couldn't cope with at Spurs. He was never perfect and his behaviour could be in poor taste, even anti-social, but we just learned to accept him as he was and hope we could control his awkward days. He was so committed to the game that after training he would join up with the reserves. He would even turn up to work with the kids. Everybody else would be knackered, but not Gazza.'

Venables was eventually forced to sell Gascoigne to Lazio in Italy. The cost of building a new stand at White Hart Lane, disastrous stock-market investments by the board and his own largesse on players, had left Spurs in a parlous financial state. The club's chairman, Irving Scholar, began casting around for investors to bail them out. Venables viewed the crisis as an irresistible opportunity. Seizing it would allow him to progress from being a mere football manager to becoming an owner and impresario. The trouble was that he did not have the estimated £6 million required to buy Spurs. Fatefully, to do so he needed a co-conspirator and the loan of a small fortune. He found his man in Alan Sugar, an east London wheeler-dealer who had made his millions running an electronics company, Amstrad. In July 1991, Venables and Sugar took control of Spurs. Venables was installed as chief executive and Sugar as chairman. They were on a collision course from the start. Sugar believed he could run a football club with the same efficiencies as his other business and Venables wanted to go on splurging on top-quality players. Sugar became convinced that his money was being misspent by Venables on an under-achieving team. On 14 May 1993 he fired his business partner.

Initially, Venables was portrayed in the press as a dutiful football man fallen victim to a ruthless tyrant and he sued for wrongful dismissal. However, a different narrative gradually began to emerge. The pieces of it were leaked out to Sugar's favoured journalists by his publicity manager, Nick Hewer, later to attain a kind of fame as his deadpan henchman on TV's *The Apprentice*. One of Hewer's main contacts was Mihir Bose, then of the *Sunday Times*. Hewer directed Bose to investigate Eddie Ashby, who Venables employed as his financial advisor and personal assistant at both Spurs and Scribes West, the private members club he owned in Kensington.

Bose discovered that, unbeknownst to Venables, Ashby was a serial and undischarged bankrupt who was legally forbidden from holding a management position. In due course Bose also gained access to the affidavit Sugar had filed in the case Venables had bought against him. This opened up a nest of vipers. In it, Sugar alleged that there was a long-established culture of illegal payments, or 'bungs', in English football and implicated Venables, claiming he had told him that Nottingham Forest manager Brian Clough 'likes a bung'. In his affidavit Venables denied this, and a police investigation into the matter was susequently dropped in May 1994. Bose broke the story on the front page of the *Sunday Times*. His allegations – denied by Venables – were quickly followed up by the *Panorama* exposé, *The Manager*.

* * *

The FA panel prevaricated for weeks over appointing Venables, but finally offered him the job on 25 January 1994. There were caveats attached. His title would be head coach rather than manager. This was a sop to Noel White and his International Committee and carried with it the suggestion that Venables would be kept on a tighter leash than his predecessors. Likewise, he was handed a short-term contract that took him up to the finals of Euro 96. 'Noel White was from a solid working-class northern back-ground,' says sports writer Ian Ridley. 'He had originally been chairman of Altrincham. I don't think he ever trusted Terry. But then, everyone at the FA was worried about Terry.'

Venables was given just over two years, and less than twenty friendly games, in which to revitalise a deflated England team and get the country dreaming. It was a daunting challenge, but he saw a bigger picture. He would go down in history if he could emulate Ramsey's achievement and lead England to victory at a home tournament. After two years of internecine warfare with Sugar, and having mud slung at his name, it was the prospect of immortality that had Venables's blood pumping again. He was also gripped by the conviction that he could institute a daring revision of English football's DNA and fashion an England team that was flexible, adaptable and mobile; one that could keep hold of the ball and move opponents around. 'I knew exactly what I wanted to do and how I wanted to do it,' Venables said. 'Ever since my England youth team days, when we would go to the Netherlands and win 5–0 or even 10–0, I have had a strong interest in

Dutch football. I admired the determination of their clubs to formulate a coaching strategy and stick with it, no matter how long it was going to take, [and] they played without restrictions. With exceptions, we English were terrible plodders. Even when we were brought to our senses, when the Hungarians made us look like prehistoric dinosaurs in football terms in the 1950s, we had been slow to react to new ideas. One of the main deficiencies in the English game was our players' failure to understand what was expected of them and what their role was in the team. This was not a case of lack of individual ability, though that could be a factor, nor their fitness or character. I wanted each player to have a specific role and to know exactly what it was in a system that was distinctly not what the world recognised as England's.'

To help him institute his masterplan, Venables appointed Don Howe as his right-hand man. Howe had coached Arsenal to the Double in 1971, and during the 1980s worked under a previous England manager, Ron Greenwood. Venables also brought in his old Chelsea coach, Dave Sexton, to mould the under-21 team in the seniors' image, and Bryan Robson to be a conduit between the management and players. This was, says Matt Dickinson, chief sports writer for *The Times*, 'by anyone's estimation a heavyweight set-up. A very constructive, adult environment developed where Venables might say stuff and Don Howe was able to disagree, and it would be acted upon. That is very different to the way England dressing rooms have operated ever since.'

Progress was measured, but tangible. Beginning with a 1–0 victory over the reigning European champions Denmark at Wembley on 9 March 1994, England suffered just one defeat in the fifteen games Venables had presided over before the visit of Croatia, and that to the world champions, Brazil. He tried out different formations, but with an emphasis on fluidity and possession. There had been at best a muted response to England's goalless draw with Colombia the previous September, but Venables derived great satisfaction from the fact that England had kept the ball from their skilful South American opponents for long periods of the game.

Venables had also whittled his squad down to its essential elements. He began working with a list of forty-five potential players, but soon discarded those who could not adapt to his more refined approach, the traditional English workhorses. Goalkeeper David Seaman and his Arsenal team-mate, David Platt, Paul Ince and Alan Shearer were certainties from the start. The Premier League had an abundance of English goalscorers, such as Les Ferdinand at Newcastle, Manchester United's Andy Cole, and Robbie Fowler and Stan Collymore at Liverpool, but Venables soon became convinced to pair Shearer with Teddy Sheringham of Spurs as the spearheads of his attack. An often underrated but intelligent footballer, Sheringham offered England something different: guile. Undemonstrative and unselfish, he had an acute appreciation of the shape and movements of a game and was able to deftly link play to Shearer.

Gascoigne and Tony Adams were the other key components of Venables's team, but less stable. The longest run of games Gascoigne was able to complete at Lazio was six. He missed most of Venables's first season in charge after hurtling into a training-ground tackle with team-mate Alessandro Nesta and breaking his leg. Toying with the idea of making Adams his captain, Venables invited him to lunch at Scott's, a swanky seafood restaurant in London's Mayfair. Unaware of the extent of Adams's drink problem, Venables offered him a glass of white wine with his meal. The taste of it was enough to send Adams careering off on a four-day bender.

'As a man, Venables was slippery and streetwise, but what he was preaching as England coach was smart, clever stuff and a breath of fresh air,' says Ian Ridley. 'It was clear from the training sessions that the players were enjoying what was going on, but more important that they were learning. I think they thought they might at last be able to compete with the Hollands and Germanys and not be made to look outdated. That being said, one could never see Venables staying put for more than a few years, if that. It was almost as if he got bored. Irving Scholar coined this wonderful phrase about him, that he had a butterfly mind.'

Gary Neville, the up-and-coming Manchester United full-back, said: 'I know there was a massive clash of personalities with Noel White, but only at the FA could it be the elite coach who packs his bags and the blazer who wins the day. It was a massive cock-up, but that was the trouble with the FA: too many suits, too many guys with agendas, too many people listening to the press and panicking at the first sign of controversy.'

The matter of Venables's departure and his succession rumbled in the background. But two months ahead of kick-off, England was not being stirred by a Euro 96 fever. The drip-drip succession of friendly fixtures had done nothing to fire the public's imagination. Just twenty thousand had turned up at Wembley to see the midweek clash with Colombia. The old stadium had also been barely a third full for the most recent match against Bulgaria on 27 March. Such was the apathetic reception the game was afforded, it was almost immaterial that England ended up beating the World Cup semi-finalists 1–0.

Ticket sales for the tournament itself were proving sluggish as well. This was especially true of the group games that would be staged outside London and not feature the hosts. It was looking increasingly likely that there would be banks of empty seats for games at venues such as Manchester's Old Trafford, Liverpool's Anfield, Elland Road in Leeds, Villa Park in Birmingham and Sheffield's Hillsborough. This might have been anticipated for fixtures involving relatively uncelebrated nations such as Switzerland, Turkey and Romania, but Europe's superpowers, Germany, Italy, Spain and Holland, would also be touring the provinces. The root cause was not so much disinterest as the escalating cost of attending football matches in England. The supporter base was still the working classes, and they were in the process of being priced out of the game. But a bigger, more affluent replacement audience had not yet been tempted. On 2 April, *The Times* reported the FA's media spokesman, Steve Double, responding to the fact that ten thousand tickets had gone unsold for the Liverpool versus Aston Villa FA Cup semi-final at Old Trafford. These had been priced between £30 and £38, at the time a tenth of the average Britons' entire disposable income for a month. 'We have no plans to review our prices,' Double blithely asserted. 'However, our ticket structure may need to be addressed.'

Double's attitude was reflective of the new reality dawning on the game. Since its launch in 1992, the Premier League revolution had appeared slow-moving and relatively benign, but it was being driven by outside forces. The Australian media tycoon Rupert Murdoch had paid an unprecedented £304 million to secure exclusive television broadcast rights to the nascent league for five years for his BSkyB operation. It was this injection of cash, rather than the match-day ticket money from supporters, that was now the top-flight clubs' primary source of revenue.

Before Murdoch pitched up, live football was a rarity on British television and almost exclusively restricted to World Cups, European Championships and the annual FA Cup final. Armchair football fans were instead accustomed to getting their fix from the BBC's long-running, staid highlights show, *Match of the Day*. BSkyB swept in offering a glut of games and presented them with a hitherto unseen sense of breathless excitement and technical bravura. Coinciding with the Graham Taylor-era slump in England's fortunes, the net result was that the appeal of club football was now much greater than that of the national team. It was also the case that the race for the 1995–96 Premier League title was proving to be a gripping drama.

It pitched together Alex Ferguson's Manchester United, Kevin Keegan's Newcastle and Liverpool, under Roy Evans. On Tyneside, Keegan had built an adventurous, buccaneering team in his own image. They raced into a twelve-point lead over United, but were beginning to falter on the run-in. Ferguson's side reeled them in and Liverpool were coming up on the rails in third place as dark horses. The defining game of the campaign proved to be at Anfield on a warm 3 April evening when Liverpool played Newcastle. The visitors started the game three points in arrears of United and requiring a three-goal margin of victory to return to the top of the table with seven matches to play. The game was televised live and what unfolded was a thrilling, topsy-turvy contest that not only decided the fate of the title but also cemented the idea in even the most casual fan's mind that the Premier League and Murdoch's interlopers were now synonymous.

Typically, the game was played at a furious, relentless pace and Liverpool won 4–3. It was a classic contest of its kind, but one that was ruled by the huff and puff, up-and-at-'em ethos that had sent English football charging up a blind alley. The frenzy at Anfield masked the game's many technical deficiencies, but Venables would not have failed to see them. He would have also considered the more sobering evidence provided by that season's European club competitions where the English participants had been ruthlessly ejected. In the Champions League, Blackburn failed to progress to the knockout stages, finishing bottom of their qualifying group. Everton were beaten by the Dutch side Feyenoord in the second round of the Cup-Winners' Cup. Manchester United, Liverpool and Leeds all crashed out in the early stages of the UEFA Cup. Nottingham Forest did progress to the quarter-finals of that competition, but were then dismantled 7–2 on aggregate by Bayern Munich. Perhaps this stark evidence had also tempered public anticipation for the Euros. It certainly emphasised the scale of the task facing Venables as he contemplated his final days with England.

CHAPTER TWO

'God, please tell me what I have done wrong'

In Terry Venables's mind he was attempting to put to rights decades of systematic failure and wrong-headedness in English football, and most especially with regard to the national team. For years underachievement had been endemic. Ever since 1966 England had stood static as the likes of Brazil, Germany, Italy and Argentina stole a tactical march on them. England went on playing in rigid lines with sweat and toil but little panache. Too often outwitted and outgunned by more deft opponents. It was not until Italia 90 that they again made the latter stages of a major tournament, having failed to even qualify for the World Cup finals of 1974 and 1978 as well as the 1984 European Championship.

In large part, their run to the semi-finals in Italy was more the result of good fortune than design. Bobby Robson's team had failed to get out of the group stages at the 1988 Euros and the England manager had lost the confidence of the FA as a result. Like Venables, he went into the World Cup with the FA having declined to renew his contract, a dead man walking. Robson, though, was no visionary, but rather an old school football and company man. He set up his England teams to play in a straight, unbending four–four–two formation, up and down the pitch. Restricted and functional, Robson's England struggled in the group matches in 1990 and were outplayed for long periods of their knockout ties against Belgium and Cameroon, neither of them elite nations. Robson could count his blessings that he was able to call upon the precocious talent of Gascoigne and had a natural goalscorer in Gary Lineker.

His successor, Graham Taylor, was not so fortunate in either respect. During the course of Taylor's ill-starred reign, Gascoigne was beset by injuries and Lineker reached the end of his career. His preferred choice to replace Lineker, Alan Shearer, also proved vulnerable to strains and knocks. Taylor's own credentials for the job were open to question. Following a playing career with Grimsby Town and Lincoln City, he was handed his first management job by Fourth Division Lincoln in 1972. Taylor moved on to Watford in 1977 and took the club from the bottom division to the top one in just five seasons, and into the 1984 FA Cup final. He went on to manage Aston Villa to a runners-up finish in the old First Division in 1989–90. But when he took over from Robson, Taylor had not won a major trophy in club football and had no first-hand experience of the international game.

Taylor was a traditionalist like Robson and his view of the game was based upon simple, practical principles. He believed in getting the ball forward quickly and into dangerous areas of the pitch. A great part of his ideology was shaped by two men, Charles Reep and Charles Hughes, both of whom had a profound influence on thinking about football in England. A former wing-commander with the RAF, Reep was encouraged into football theory by the example of Herbert Chapman's all-conquering Arsenal teams of the 1920s and 1930s. Developing a thesis that most goals were scored as a result of three passes or fewer, Reep was employed in the 1950s as an analyst by Brentford, Wolverhampton Wanderers and Sheffield Wednesday. Hughes, a former school teacher, was made the FA's director of coaching in 1990, working alongside both Robson and Taylor. He was still in the post when Venables took over, though the two men had a more distant, less collaborative relationship. In his writings on the game, Hughes stressed the importance of set-plays and of bombarding the opposition penalty area with crosses. He emphasised what he termed 'Positions of Maximum Opportunity' – the areas of the pitch where goals were most likely to be scored. Together with Reep, Hughes was viewed as the architect of the long ball game. It was widely adopted in the English domestic leagues and proved effective. However, as more evolved systems sprang up in the world game, it was made to look like a blunt instrument, meat and drink to the best international teams.

Taylor unwittingly proved this point. Yet he began his new posting well. He steered England to the 1992 European finals with ease. Retaining a clutch of experienced internationals from the 1990 World Cup, such as Platt, Pearce and Lineker, Taylor mixed in a group of hard-working, but often limited players. The football wasn't pretty, but Taylor bonded his team with a strong spirit. Central to this was the presence of his long-serving coach, Steve Harrison. The antithesis of Howe, Harrison was a bubbly, effervescent character who pepped up squad get-togethers with high jinks such as bursting into team dinners naked but for an old raincoat and a strategically placed rubber chicken.

England headed for the 1992 Euros in Sweden with the expectation of being genuine contenders, only to crash out at the group stages without winning a game. Taylor's next mission was to pilot England to the 1994 World Cup finals. The roof began to cave in on that venture when England flopped to a humiliating 2–0 loss to Norway in Oslo on 2 June 1993. The irony of that defeat was that the opposing head coach, Egil Olsen, was also a student of Charles Reep. The Norwegian FA even flew the then eighty-nine-year-old Reep out to watch the game as their guest.

'I thought [Taylor] was a very intelligent man and I liked him personally,' said Tony Adams, a regular in Taylor's teams. 'He thought about things deeply and tried to make things interesting and lively. Whenever we met up as a squad there was Champagne on the table. I had respect for his methods, which included extra iron as part of a diet designed to help maintain a quicker-paced game, [but] I did have reservations. His way of playing was short-sighted, because if you did reach the finals of a major tournament, you would not be able to sustain the effort right through if you had ambitions of winning the trophy.

'He also made himself look foolish, I think, because he didn't surround himself with the best people. With Phil Neal, his assistant, you almost felt as if he was making you stand to attention whenever Graham was approaching. "Come on, lads, the boss is coming," he would say. You can't have respect for someone like that. What can I say about Steve Harrison, Graham's warm-up man? Or perhaps entertainments officer might be a better description. He was probably the funniest, or daftest, bloke I have come across in football.'

The Norway defeat left England requiring a draw from the penultimate group match in Holland to retain a realistic hope of reaching the finals. The match at Rotterdam's compact De Kuip stadium on a mild 13 October evening turned on an incident in the sixtieth minute as David Platt advanced on the Dutch goal. He was hauled to the ground on the edge of the penalty box by the last Dutch defender, Ronald Koeman. It looked a penalty and by the rules of the game Koeman should have been dismissed. However, the German referee, Karl-Josef Assenmacher, decided against inflicting either punishment on the home team. Rubbing salt into England's wounds, barely a minute later Koeman scored the first of the two unanswered Dutch goals that all but condemned Taylor to his fate. Taylor and England limped on to the concluding match of their campaign against the minnows of San Marino a month later. Played before a paltry crowd of two thousand in the Italian city of Bologna, it offered the beleaguered Taylor a cruel, forlorn hope of redemption. In the unlikely event of England winning by seven clear goals, and the Dutch slipping up in Poland on the same night, his team would still make it to the United States. Eight seconds was all it took for that hope to crumble. From the kick-off, the usually dependable Stuart Pearce fluffed a back-pass to David Seaman, and Davide Gualtieri, a computer salesman by trade, ran on to score. Taylor looked to the heavens and mouthed a silent prayer: 'God, please tell me what I have done wrong.'

England went on to win the game 7–1, but Holland also beat the Poles and Taylor was forced to fall on his sword. Even then his suffering was not at an end. With a hopelessly misplaced sense of hubris, he had agreed to let a documentary film crew shadow him during the last months of his tenure. The resulting film, *An Impossible Job*, was broadcast on Channel 4 on 24 January 1994 and watched by six million people. It went on to win a Royal Television Society award, the only tangible success Taylor could be said to have had as England manager. Looking haunted and hunted, Taylor was caught on camera uttering the helpless refrain that was to become his unwanted catchphrase: 'Do I not like that.'

Venables had repaired much of the damage left by Taylor and reconstructed the England team. The transition was as great a leap in pure footballing terms as that from the Industrial Age to the Digital. Venables tutored his players in a more cultured version of the game out on their training grounds at Bisham Abbey where he could affect and conjure his schemes. He had a crane set up by the practice pitch so the sessions could be filmed from an elevated vantage point. 'He would go back over the video to show you your movements on the pitch,' said Gary Neville. 'At the time it was a novel approach and very educational to me. As a defence, we were drilled with military precision by Terry and Don Howe.'

'Venables had England playing a modern style of football,' says Ian Ridley. 'Looking back, his was a really talented England side – we would kill for that calibre of player now. There was very much a sense of optimism before Euro 96 kicked off and a feeling of possibilities. But it was England, so you always had this reservation that it would end in tears.'

By the middle of April, the domestic season was drawing to a close and the race for the Premier League title was effectively over. Newcastle lost again at Blackburn and Liverpool slumped to a 1–0 defeat at perennial strugglers Coventry. Manchester United, meanwhile, rolled on, beating local rivals Manchester City, Coventry and Leeds. They could even afford a slip-up at Southampton where they were humbled 3–1 on 13 April. After that game, Alex Ferguson offered a bizarre excuse for the below-par performance of his team, blaming it on their change of strip. They had worn a new grey-coloured design for the match and Ferguson claimed that his players had found it difficult to pick each other out on the pitch.

United's strip was designed and manufactured by

Umbro, who also held the England contract. The following week the company unveiled the national team's new away kit as Venables's squad gathered at Bisham Abbey for the Croatia game. It was instantly dismissed by the FA's commercial director, Trevor Phillips, apparently viewing it for the first time. Phillips, who had drummed up the idea of hawking the England team to sponsors, and had signed a £4 million contract with the insurance company Green Flag, was particularly aggrieved by David Seaman's multi-shaded goalkeeper's jersey. He seethed that Seaman 'looked like a tube of Refreshers sweets'.

Venables, though, was more concerned with the fitness of his key players. The previous week he was told that Alan Shearer required an operation on his troublesome groin injury and watched Darren Anderton play his first competitive game in seven months for Spurs at Arsenal. Anderton managed just twelve minutes. It meant England's head coach would not be able to field his preferred eleven against Croatia. Nor had the FA resolved the matter of anointing his successor while he had been in Spain, although the fact that Glenn Hoddle was stalling over a new contract offer from Chelsea had the press speculating that he was now the preferred choice. At his first press conference at Bisham Abbey, Venables archly noted that it was a good job he had given his dithering bosses such an extended notice period. Normally a relaxed operator in front of the media, Venables cut a distracted, frustrated figure. It was not part of his plan to be talking about who the next man to fill his shoes would be. Euro 96 was meant to be the pinnacle of his career and he wanted it to be his and his alone.

Dark clouds hung over the country as England prepared to face Croatia. On 11 April, the UK government had announced plans to slaughter up to thirty thousand cattle a week in an attempt to contain a food crisis that was spiralling out of control. In March, scientists had advised the government of a potential link between so-called Mad Cow Disease and its human variant, Creutzfeldt–Jacob Disease. The repercussions from this were now threatening to drive Britain's £20 billion beef industry into financial meltdown.

Internally, Prime Minister John Major's government was being wrenched apart by a damaging division over the extent of the UK's role in the European Union. Caught between two warring extremes, the pro-Euro MPs and a smaller, but aggressive tranche of renegade right-wing Euro-sceptics, the Prime Minister was fatally compromised. Since 1993 Major had also had to deal with a series of sex scandals brought about by the colourful extra-marital activities of three of his ministers, Stephen Norris, Tim Yeo and David Mellor, which had encouraged a sense that the government had lost its moral compass.

On 15 March, two days after sixteen children aged five or six, and one of their teachers, were shot dead at a primary school in Dunblane, the Prime Minister visited the pretty Scottish town alongside the man poised to inherit his office, Tony Blair, the leader of the opposition. Blair had revitalised the Labour Party in the aftermath of its fourth straight General Election defeat by the Tories in 1992. His rise to the forefront of British politics since then had been an almost direct counter-balance to Major's abrupt fall from grace. A private school-educated Scot with an English Home Counties accent, Blair had created New Labour, neutralising the party's left-wing, muting its socialist rhetoric and burnishing it to appeal to the mass of Middle England voters who determined General Election results.

That April, there was the strongest measure yet of Blair's success in re-branding his party. On 11 April, Labour won a by-election for the Stafford South-East seat, brought about by the death of the sitting Tory MP, Sir David Lightbown. In the process of overturning a Conservative majority of seven thousand, Labour also reduced the government's majority in the House of Commons to just one seat. At the end of the month, Labour also routed the Tories at council elections across the country, enhancing the impression of Blair as Britain's Prime Minister-in-waiting.

The mood of the nation was lifted by a series of British sporting victories. On 7 April, English racing driver Damon Hill won the Argentine Grand Prix in Buenos Aires. Hill had now triumphed in the opening three races of the season and had a commanding lead in the drivers' championship. The following week, in the final round of the US Masters golf championship in Augusta, Nick Faldo clawed back a six-shot deficit to the Australian Greg Norman to land his sixth major title. The Scot Liz McColgan won the London Marathon on 21 April in the hottest temperature recorded in the race's sixteen-year history. It was not just McColgan's battle with the 21°C heat that made her triumph so impressive. After suffering knee and back injuries, the thirty-one-year-old former 10,000 metres world champion had been told by a specialist that she would never be able to run again.

England's friendly against Croatia was not about to attract the same delighted attention or rouse such heady emotions. The prospect of yet another meaningless fixture, even against a team as adventurous as the Croats, had meant that barely thirty thousand tickets had been sold for the game. Wembley was once again going to be less than half full. Often as not, what atmosphere there was inside the creaking old national stadium was also laced with a drop of poison. 'Being a United player at the time was to be a target for some terrible stick at Wembley,' said Gary Neville. 'People either loved or hated us now that we were winning trophies every year. There would be groups of West Ham and Chelsea supporters, lads who had not come to cheer England but to get pissed and hammer a few United players on a Wednesday night. You could hear every shout. "Munich bastard! Red bastard!"'

One of Europe's emerging teams, with an abundance of technically accomplished players, Croatia had qualified for Euro 96. At Wembley they paraded a brace of deft midfielders, Robert Prosinečki and their captain, Zvonimir Boban, an imposing centre-forward, Alen Bokšić, and his elusive, mercurial foil, Davor Šuker. Venables fielded an experimental formation with Neville and Stuart Pearce flanking Liverpool's Mark Wright in a three-man defence, and Steve McManaman and Nottingham Forest's Steve Stone operating as raiding wing-backs. Gascoigne, Ince and Platt marshalled central midfield, with Stan Collymore filling in for the absent Shearer as Teddy Sheringham's strike partner. Collymore's team-mate, Robbie Fowler, who was rumoured to be the subject of an imminent £10 million bid from Johan Cruyff at Barcelona, made his second consecutive appearance from the substitutes' bench.

England contained and pressed their dangerous opponents, but the game itself was dull and uneventful. It finished goalless, the third such stalemate in six matches under Venables. Afterwards, his opposite number, Croat coach Miroslav Blažević, criticised England's performance as 'sterile and predictable'. Venables countered that it was his side who had carved out the game's scant clear-cut chances. Writing the next morning in *The Times*, Rob Hughes noted that Venables had 'withstood almost two years of scepticism over his attempts, now coming into bud, to turn Englishmen into continental footballers', but concluded: 'When, however, he says, "We just have to finish things off, it will be all right", it still demands a spectacular leap of faith.'

Returning to his eyrie at Lancaster Gate, the head coach would have pored over the spate of downbeat headlines and match reports. Venables was outwardly assured, but away from prying eyes, he fretted and obsessed over how he was being portrayed in the media. 'At eleven each night, Terry sent someone out to King's Cross station to get the first editions of the newspapers,' reveals Henry Winter, now senior football writer at *The Times*. 'He would have them brought back to him at the FA or taken to Scribes West. He wanted to know everything that was being written about him and also who he might have to sue next.'

The very next month, Venables would face a glut of stories relating to him and his team, none of them positive, and all of them as a result of another lucrative deal struck by Trevor Phillips at the FA.

CHAPTER THREE

'I hardly thought about death and other awful things'

The Saturday afternoon after the Croatia game, Paul Gascoigne won the Scottish Premier League title for Glasgow Rangers. Playing against Aberdeen in the penultimate match of the campaign, and at a broiling Ibrox Stadium, Gascoigne scored a hat-trick in a 3–1 win that moved Rangers out of reach of their closest challengers, Celtic. Following the match, Gascoigne told reporters that he had thanked the Rangers manager, Walter Smith, 'for giving me my life back'. He added: 'I've had fourteen operations so I've deserved this more than anyone. I've come through and answered my critics.'

It was Smith, as tough and unyielding as Glasgow steel, who had rescued Gascoigne from his three-year odyssey in Italy. Gascoigne was originally supposed to have joined Lazio at the end of the 1990–91 season, his most productive for Spurs, but tore the cruciate ligaments in his right knee tackling like a madman in the FA Cup final against Nottingham Forest. He spent a year out of the game. Lazio hung on for him and he finally signed for the Rome club in the summer of 1992, agreeing terms of £22,000 a week. At his best, and when the demons were at bay, he was good value for such a king's ransom, the rare and unpredictable kind of footballer who can turn and win games by his own actions alone. The hard truth, though, was that he was not at his best often or for anything like long enough at Lazio.

Holidaying after his first *Serie A* campaign, a bout of binge eating took his weight up to fourteen stone. In order to shed the excess pounds before reporting back for preseason training, Gascoigne subjected himself to what would become his regular, self-prescribed crash-diet: he consumed nothing for four days but water, lemon juice and the occasional dose of maple syrup for energy. His behaviour was just as erratic and unbecoming when he was on club duty. Among a catalogue of incidents, he appalled the buttoned-up Italian press by belching into a microphone during a live television interview before a game against Juventus. On another occasion, Gascoigne casually informed Lazio's president, Sergio Cragnotti, that his daughter had 'big tits'. Appraising Gascoigne as he recovered from the broken leg he had sustained in training, Lazio's new head coach, Zdeněk Zeman, a Czech of military bearing, told him he was two stone overweight and marginalised him. Gascoigne went through his final months in Rome like an apparition, written off at twenty-eight by commentators in Italy. By the time Lazio finally cut their losses, he had scored just six league goals for the club at a cost of almost a million pounds each.

At first, Glenn Hoddle at Chelsea offered to come to his rescue and the two men met in London to discuss terms. However, Gascoigne was otherwise preoccupied with nursing a rotten tooth and barely listened to Hoddle's pitch. Smith swooped instead, enticing Gascoigne to Rangers with a lucrative contract and the more forgiving environment of the Scottish Premier League. Under the stewardship of Smith, another understanding, tolerant manager, Gascoigne flourished again. He made forty-two appearances and scored nineteen goals for Rangers that season, once more becoming the beating heart of his team. At the end of it he was voted Scotland's Player of the Year by both his fellow professionals and the Scottish football writers.

Not that it was all plain sailing for him north of the border. Nor was it when it came to his on-off relationship with Sheryl Failes. The two of them had first met in a wine bar in Hertfordshire in 1990. Gascoigne was dancing on a table at the moment their eyes locked. Failes was blonde, attractive, had done bits of glamour modelling and, like him, came from a working-class background: her father was a welder, his a building labourer. At the time she was married with two children, but in the process of getting a divorce. Failes was Gascoigne's first serious girlfriend and their coupling was tempestuous and interrupted by regular volcanic eruptions. On one occasion, when Gascoigne was playing for Lazio, Failes fled the Italian capital after he tore off in his car to confront her when she was late arriving home from visiting a friend. It was not so much

Gascoigne's possessiveness that had sent Failes running as the fact he had driven the wrong way down the motorway and into oncoming traffic to meet her.

Failes had nonetheless returned to him at Rangers and they settled into a new £500,000 house on the outskirts of Glasgow. However, they picked up where they had left off in Rome. That February, Gascoigne missed the birth of his son, Regan, after a flare-up with Failes. However, he was now able to focus on football, his anchor to the world, and to revel in his own instinctive brilliance. Accordingly, he was, he noted, 'sleeping okay, having no twitches and I hardly thought about death and other awful things'. In short, Gascoigne was as fit and ready as he was ever going to be for the demands of Euro 96. Speaking to English reporters at the time, his former Lazio team-mate, Dutch international midfielder Aron Winter, predicted that Gascoigne was going to be the star of the tournament. 'I know Paul well and, believe me, he can be anything he wants to be at Wembley this summer,' insisted Winter. 'If he plays as I know he can, he'll be the big figure of the tournament. I know for sure he is an outstanding footballer for your country right now.'

That month, with the domestic season drawing to a close, the FA released details of an encouraging report showing that the number of arrests for football hooliganism in England was down for the second consecutive season. The scourge of the game for the previous two decades, football violence had not been entirely driven from the sport. Indeed, its full ugliness was all too visible at

Terry Venables's aborted seventh game in charge of the national team. On 15 February 1995, England travelled to Dublin for a supposed friendly against the Republic of Ireland. Shortly after David Kelly had given Ireland the lead in the twenty-second minute, trouble flared among the four thousand England supporters inside Lansdowne Road. With seats and missiles raining down on the pitch, Dutch referee Dick Jol took the two teams to the dressing rooms. The riot intensified as Irish police fought with the marauding English and the game was abandoned. Before kick-off a pocket of English supporters had made Nazi salutes during the playing of the Irish national anthem and members of a far-right, neo-Nazi group, Combat 18, were later found to have incited the trouble. This was a grotesque reminder of an era presumed to have been left behind, recalling as it did the ghost of the National Front and the hooligan gangs of the 1970s and 1980s.

In the aftermath of the Hillsborough tragedy of 1989, when ninety-six Liverpool supporters were crushed to death at their team's FA Cup semi-final against Nottingham Forest, and the subsequent publication of the Taylor Report into the events surrounding it, the realities of watching top-flight club football in England had changed. Pre-1990, English football stadiums were by and large rotting, dilapidated ruins with the most vociferous supporters congregating on great concrete terraces like the last remnants of an embattled army. Attendances had tumbled as football fans found themselves buffeted by economic recession and the spectre of hooliganism. Lord Justice

Taylor's recommendations signalled the beginning of the end of supporters being herded like cattle into these decrepit monuments to graze upon the barren fields of the national game.

From 1994, all clubs in the top two divisions were required to have an all-seat stadium. The sight of massed, seething ranks standing on such famed 'ends' as the Stretford End at Old Trafford, the Kop at Anfield and the Shed at Chelsea's Stamford Bridge, followed the minimum wage, quagmire pitches and the half-time cup of Bovril into the mists of history. All of those grounds had been modernised and theoretically made safe. Other clubs were moving into brand new arenas. Middlesbrough had begun this exodus at the start of the 1995–96 season, departing Ayresome Park, their home since 1903, for the thirty thousand-capacity Riverside Stadium. A state-of-the-art, but charmless edifice on the banks of the Tees, the Riverside made apparent the looming gentrification of the English game. Soon, Boro's neighbours, Sunderland, would trade in Roker Park for the Stadium of Light which initially accommodated forty-two thousand seated spectators. Bolton went, too, exiting crumbling old Burnden Park for the Reebok Stadium, sited adjacent to a ring road on the outskirts of the town like a superstore. It looked like one, too.

These new football venues also housed restaurants, bars and plush corporate facilities. Little more than a decade after he dreamt it at QPR, Terry Venables's vision of multi-purpose stadiums had become a reality. That April,

Chelsea floated nine million shares on the Alternative Investment Market for the Chelsea Village leisure and retail complex that was to surround Stamford Bridge. In 1985, Chelsea chairman Ken Bates threatened to erect electric fences to deter hooligans from invading the pitch. Thirteen years later he would open a four-star hotel on the site. These new, sanitised facilities would soon encourage both the chattering classes and families to Premier League football, cooling down the tribal warfare.

A growing social and cultural movement had also cast its influence over the game. It had spurned the inflammatory record that was just then number one in the pop charts and prompting questions to be raised in the House of Commons. The Prodigy had released their 'Firestarter' single on 19 March. A sparse, percussive track built over a guitar loop that buzzed in the background like a wasp, it was accompanied by a striking black-and-white video filmed in an abandoned London Underground tunnel at Aldwych. In it, the group's distinctive singer, Keith Flint, who had shaved his head bald down the middle and sculpted the remaining tufts of hair into devil horns, leered into the camera and proclaimed: 'I'm the trouble starter, fucking instigator.' The sight of the twitching Flint flashing his pierced tongue and promising to raise merry hell was enough to get the video banned from *Top of the Pops* following a record number of complaints. Meanwhile, the combined forces of the tabloid press, the

Fire Service and a gaggle of MPs decried the song itself as an incitement to commit arson. The controversy, of course, conspired to do nothing so much as make 'Firestarter' the must-hear record of the moment. It vaulted to number one on 30 March and remained there for three consecutive weeks.

Formed in 1990 by a hip-hop fan and budding DJ, Liam Howlett, in Braintree, Essex, the Prodigy was completed by dancers Leeroy Thornhill and Keith Palmer [aka Maxim Reality]. They had all become embroiled in the rave and Acid House movement that sprung up in Britain in the summer of 1987. Acid House's roots lay deep in the black and gay urban underground club scenes that fermented in the United States in the 1970s. It was at clubs in cities such as New York, Detroit and Chicago that its pulsating, trance-inducing sound was first cooked up from the embers of disco. At the turn of the next decade it was exported to the Balearic island of Ibiza, which had been transformed by Spain's booming tourist trade from rural backwater to a hedonist's paradise.

By the mid-1980s, Ibiza was a destination point for thousands of young Brits desperate to escape to the sun from the drabness of Thatcher's Britain. Joining this rush were two London-based DJs, Paul Oakenfold and Danny Rampling, who returned home to open their own versions of the island's heaving clubs. Oakenfold's Future night on Charing Cross Road and Rampling's Shoom, launched in a gym near Southwark Bridge, set the agenda for Britain's Acid House era. Their regulars adopted the

Ibiza uniform of T-shirts with shorts or voluminous jeans and began daubing their faces in Day-Glo colours. Announcing Acid House's coming of age in 1989, the so-called 'Second Summer of Love' marked the point at which it exploded from the capital's clubs and out across the country via warehouse parties and huge outdoor raves. The fact that it was the hottest British summer in a decade enhanced the mood of communal well-being and wild abandon sown by the apparent wonder 'love drug' that accompanied Acid House, Ecstasy. Bringing together people from all social and ethnic backgrounds, the period was perhaps the first time such a bright light had been shone on the diverse, multicultural nation that Britain had become. And among those lured in and most affected by Acid House's breaking down of barriers were young football supporters.

'The only working-class kids who travelled around Britain before Acid House were football fans, and they were going to fight the people they met, not dance with them,' says Sheryl Garrett, then-editor of style bible *The Face*. 'There was a lot more social mobility after Acid House. There was also a different feeling of all the walls that separated us coming down. A Spurs fan would meet someone who was a Chelsea fan on the steps of, say, Shoom and realise they had more in common than they thought.'

Garrett wrote a cover line at the time hailing a core of the new Acid House generation as 'football thugs with flowers'. However, its impact on softening supporters' attitudes and reducing incidents of hooliganism was not quite so clear-cut, and took another, less utopian turn. 'A lot of the people who were the high-level football hooligans basically turned into drug-running gangsters,' says Garrett. 'They realised there was a lot more money to be made in dealing some of the chemicals that were flooding into the country at the time.'

By the mid-1990s, though, the shifting sands of popular culture had moved back to a more traditional sounding form of music and the crash of this wave resounded even louder. Britpop brought together boys – and girls – with guitars and in a spirit of patriotic cultural revivalism, reaching back to such archetypal British bands as The Beatles, The Who, The Kinks and the Sex Pistols for inspiration. There were numerous foot soldiers in the Britpop camp, but its undisputed generals were Blur and Oasis.

Blur began life as Seymour in 1989, the brainchild of three students from Goldsmiths College in New Cross, south London: singer Damon Albarn, his schoolboy friend from Colchester, guitarist Graham Coxon, and louche, foppish bassist Alex James, who came up from Bournemouth. Drummer Dave Rowntree, also from Colchester, completed the line-up soon after and the foursome subsequently changed their name to Blur. It was with their third album, *Parklife*, released on 25 April 1994 and assembled from a patchwork of vintage British pop forms, that Blur established themselves as the pre-eminent British pop group of the time. It also opened the floodgates for a retinue of bands in thrall to one strain of British pop or other to come pouring through: the likes of Sleeper, Echobelly, Supergrass, Dodgy and Elastica, who were fronted by Albarn's then girlfriend, Justine Frischmann.

Blur reigned unchallenged as the leaders of the pack until a motley assortment of football-loving scallies burst out of the Manchester suburb of Burnage. Oasis were fronted by brothers Noel and Liam Gallagher, a pair of cocksure ne'er-do-wells born into an Irish family presided over by a domineering father, Tommy, a builder and part-time DJ, and nurtured by mum Peggy, who worked in a biscuit factory and was one of seven sisters from County Mayo. Inspired by the example of two local heroes, Johnny Marr of the Smiths and the Stone Roses' John Squire, Noel Gallagher taught himself to play an acoustic guitar bequeathed to him by his belligerent father when his parents separated. He started writing songs and, finding himself at a loose end in 1991, accepted his younger sibling's offer to join the fledgling band he had put together with three pals for a trial rehearsal. Determining that the tunes he had been squirrelling away for years were 'fucking brilliant and miles better than theirs', Noel Gallagher effectively took charge of the band from that point.

In 1993, Oasis signed to iconoclastic indie label Creation Records, owner Alan McGee, a livewire Glaswegian, convinced that he had unearthed the most exciting band since the Sex Pistols. The following year, their grandstanding debut album, *Definitely Maybe*, stormed into the charts at number one, challenging Blur's hegemony and beginning a bitter rivalry between the two bands that came to a head in August 1995 with the so-called 'Battle of Britpop'. Building up to their respective new albums, Blur and Oasis had each scheduled their taster singles for release on the same day, 14 August. What ensued was a race for number one that pitted Blur's 'Country House' against Oasis's 'Roll With It', self-styled southern intellectuals against northern hoodlums, and was afforded such saturation coverage that it was even a lead item on evening television news bulletins. Blur won the battle, edging Oasis out to claim the top spot, but they lost the war.

A mere shadow of its stellar predecessor, Blur's *The Great Escape* album was shunted aside by Oasis's oncoming juggernaut, *(What's the Story) Morning Glory?* Oasis's record was a flag-waving compendium of seminal British rock moves, and by that April had been to number one in sixteen countries and sold more than 6.5 million copies. This was ubiquity on a scale not seen since The Beatles were in their pomp. Now entering their own imperial phase, Oasis had lined up two homecoming shows at their beloved Manchester City's Maine Road stadium on 27 and 28 April. On both days an air of menace pervaded the streets of the surrounding Moss Side area as local youths touted stolen tickets and tried to intimidate the crowds teeming into their neighbourhood. Inside the stadium, though, the atmosphere was uproarious. 'Wonderwall', perhaps Oasis's defining song, had been adopted by City's supporters ('. . . and after all, we've got Alan Ball') and, in general, their flag-waving anthems made an easy transition to the football terraces. The guest-list for the gigs included most of the City first-team squad as well as David Beckham, Gary Neville and Ryan Giggs from United. The previous year, when Oasis played a show at the Nynex Arena in Manchester, Giggs had rung the band's office to beg tickets. Liam Gallagher happened to be there, snatched up the phone and told United's star winger to 'fuck off'.

At Maine Road, Oasis were greeted on stage like returning cup-winning heroes: Liam Gallagher, glowering and still as a statue; Noel Gallagher brandishing a guitar emblazoned with a Union Jack flag, a gift from his girlfriend, Meg Matthews. Both brothers soaked up the adulation and were in their element as the massed ranks of their fans picked up and sang every word of Noel Gallagher's rousing songs with unfettered delight. A little more than a month ahead of kick-off, this was the essence of the jubilant, roaring spirit and unabashed display of nationalistic iconography that would peak at Euro 96.

Terry Venables's preferred England captain was in peril of missing the tournament altogether. A knee injury had kept Tony Adams out of the Croatia game and left him on the sidelines for most of the second half of the domestic season. Though it was not apparent even to those closest to him in the Arsenal dressing room, Adams was walking a precarious mental tightrope in his attempt to lead his country at Euro 96. At the start of the season, team-mate Paul Merson had gone public about his addictions to alcohol, cocaine and gambling. Merson's problems were made to appear an extreme case. However, a drinking culture thrived at the club, indeed was endemic to English football in general, and Adams had also wallowed in and then been consumed by it. However, his boozing bouts were passed off among the Arsenal first-team squad as being typical of the game's play-hard-drink-hard culture.

Adams had graduated to the England team in February 1987, becoming the country's youngest centre-half since Bobby Moore. But for the first time since he began kicking a ball against a wall, Adams took time to settle as a full international. He was caught off guard to begin with by Bobby Robson's habit of addressing him as 'Paul'. Robson, who gave off the air of a genial but bumbling uncle, had tutored a young apprentice named Paul Adams when he was manager at Ipswich and was forever confusing players' names. More damagingly, Adams was singled out for particularly virulent criticism as a member of the England team who slumped to three defeats at the 1988 European Championship finals in West Germany. In their second group game at the tournament, England were beaten 3–1 by the eventual champions, Holland, and Adams was brutally exposed by the quicksilver Marco van Basten, who helped himself to a hat-trick. 'The more experienced players kept their heads down and escaped relatively unscathed,' Adams said later, '[while] I felt humiliated and inadequate.'

The ordeal brought him an unwanted sobriquet, 'Donkey Adams'. During the ensuing seasons, he grew used to his every touch of the ball being met with a derisive braying chant from opposition supporters. Adams bounced back on the pitch, captaining Arsenal to the league title in 1989. However, he was by then already battling a debilitating alcohol problem. Sunday was his big drinking day when he would booze until he blacked out, waking up the next morning with the haziest of recollections of the night before and often having wet the bed. On such occasions, he would wear an extra layer of kit for training and sweat the alcohol out of his system. Adams hit the buffers on a spring day at the end of the 1989–90 campaign. Hours before he was due to fly to Singapore on a post-season club tour, and having been drinking since the previous night, he accepted an invitation from a stranger in a pub in Rayleigh, Essex, to attend a barbecue at a house nearby. Adams chipped in for a crate of beer, topping up the five pints of lager he had sunk in the pub. He left the soirée intending to drive the sixty miles to Heathrow Airport to meet up with the Arsenal party, but managed to travel just sixty yards, mounting the kerb, clipping a telegraph pole and then ploughing his 4x4 Ford Sïerra through a garden wall.

'On impact, the car windscreen shattered, which was fortunate as my head was thrown forward towards it,' he recalled in 1999. 'The driver's door had come off and I staggered out, picking glass out of my hair. By now, the lovely old couple whose front wall and garden I had just demolished had come out of their house. They were probably shocked, but were more concerned for me.' Found to be four times over the legal drink-drive limit by police officers attending the scene, Adams was charged with driving recklessly and drunk. The following December he was sentenced to nine months in Chelmsford Prison, though his term was subsequently commuted to fifty-eight days for good behaviour. Among the letters he received during his incarceration was one from Glenn Hoddle, a born-again Christian. Hoddle expressed a belief that Adams had demons in his soul and that drink was poisoning his spirit. 'It seemed to me at the time the last thing I needed to hear,' Adams mused.

To all intents, Adams appeared to put the incident behind him and settled down. He married in 1992 and fathered two children, a son and daughter. In 1993 he led Arsenal to victories in the finals of the FA and League cups. In reality, he went on being the first of his teammates to the bar, and the last to leave. On one occasion while on England duty under Graham Taylor, Adams got blind drunk at Burnham Beeches and rampaged upstairs to his room, whereupon he crashed through the oak door, removing it from his hinges, and collapsed into a stupor. He was discovered amid the wreckage the next morning by a visibly shocked Taylor, who informed him that he would be dropped from the squad if the papers got hold of the story. Adams, though, was spared and carried on in the same vein, unchecked, unabashed and as if he believed he could escape another day of reckoning. However, a harsher, more unforgiving reality was slowly dawning on him. That April, he separated from his wife, Jane, and started seeing a counsellor.

Changes at Arsenal, and a challenge on the pitch, had also helped to focus his mind. At Highbury, a new manager, Bruce Rioch, had begun the season picking up the pieces left by George Graham's abrupt departure in February 1995. Graham had been the sole casualty of the much-trumpeted FA investigation into the issue of bungs, and was found guilty of pocketing £425,000 from illegal payments. Nothing was proven against Venables or others accused. Preparing for the campaign, Rioch coaxed David Platt back from Sampdoria in *Serie A* and also splashed out a club record £7.5 million to lure the Dutch striker Dennis Bergkamp from Inter Milan. With his beguiling range of movement, magnetic hold of the ball and the cold, appraising eye of an assassin, Bergkamp was the type of exotic footballer who, to that point, had largely been absent from the English game. He was a rarity to the Premier League in another key aspect, too: the manner in which he conditioned himself for the game. 'I can remember going along to see Arsenal in pre-season training at their London Colney complex,' says Henry Winter. 'Bergkamp came out after the session and he was cradling armfuls of fruit: a couple of apples, four bananas, a bunch of grapes and a melon. The press guys had to tell him that we really weren't used to seeing that kind of thing.'

Watching Bergkamp demonstrate his repertoire on the training ground, Adams was struck by the same feelings of inadequacy he had felt facing his compatriot Van Basten in 1988. 'Seeing a counsellor, I was making a start on understanding myself,' he considered afterwards. 'I certainly knew that once I started drinking, I had to carry on until I was drunk – and beyond. So I decided that the only way for me to function properly through Euro 96 was to stay away from drink altogether.'

PART TWO:
MAY

CHAPTER FOUR

'Everyone had to have a pint poured
over them and their shirt ripped'

After months of speculation, the FA confirmed on 1 May that Glenn Hoddle was their choice to take over as England coach from Terry Venables following Euro 96. Hoddle was reported to be sleeping on the offer. He was, in fact, holed up in a Thames Valley hotel with Chelsea's vice-chairman, Matthew Harding, who was making a last-ditch attempt to keep him at the club. Meanwhile, Chelsea's bullish chairman, Ken Bates, derided the cloak-and-dagger manner in which the FA had courted his manager, describing it as 'anarchy'. Bates, who had served as an FA council member for the previous ten years, added for good measure his belief that Hoddle would be an 'idiot' to subject himself to the scrutiny that went with managing England.

At just thirty-eight, Hoddle would be England's youngest manager, if nothing else a statement of intent from the FA that they meant to progress English football. 'The very fact that the England call has come to a man with no coaching badges,' wrote Rob Hughes in *The Times*, 'is testimony to the way Hoddle is perceived as being in tune with foreign ways.' As a player Hoddle had shown as much. Such was his technical command of the game, and so elegant was he on the pitch, he was like an alien figure amid the hustle and bustle of the English league.

A Londoner, Hoddle joined Spurs as an apprentice and made his full debut for the club at nineteen. He marked the occasion with a goal, and of a type that would come to be characteristic. Struck from distance, it left Stoke City's then England goalkeeper, Peter Shilton, for dead. Hoddle was idolised at Spurs, the embodiment of the fans' belief in playing the beautiful game. He progressed to the England team, but though he went on to win fifty-three caps, he never quite fitted into the national set-up. He was a craftsman, not a labourer, and a succession of England managers struggled to accommodate him in their straitjacketed systems. No matter that he could land the ball on a penny from any distance, Hoddle was thought to be work-shy, to not tackle back or run till he dropped as was expected of the archetypal English midfielder at the time.

Inevitably, Hoddle was more appreciated on the continent, and in 1987 joined France's glamour club, AS Monaco. He was playmaker as the club won the title in his first season on the French Riviera. Hoddle spent three years by the Mediterranean, helping to dismantle the notion in Europe that all English players were artless, before a serious knee injury forced him home in 1990. He became player-manager at Swindon Town and helped them escape relegation to the third tier of English football. Hoddle brought along with him the fresh ideas on training and conditioning that he had absorbed in France. He stabilised the club and in 1993 led them to promotion to the Premier League, scoring the first goal in a 4–3 play-off final victory over Leicester City at Wembley. Within days of that game, Hoddle left Swindon to take over at Chelsea. During three years at Stamford Bridge, the club reached an FA Cup final, a European semi-final and attracted top-class players like Dutch captain Ruud Gullit to west London. However, he was still to win a major trophy as a manager and had not succeeded in taking Chelsea higher than eleventh in the Premier League.

'With hindsight, Hoddle's elevation does seem crackers,' says Matt Dickinson of the *Times*. 'Obviously, he had serious clout as a player, but his CV as a manager wasn't *that* good. It was a classic case of how English football was run: getting rid of Venables, never mind the fact that he was the best coach we could have had. It was all down to this English, and English football's, obsession with morality, whereby people don't just have to be good at their job, but they also have to be symbolic of something right and proper.'

Back in February, after leading Chelsea to a 5–0 victory over Bryan Robson's Middlesbrough, Hoddle had responded to the first dribbles of speculation linking him to England. 'I really feel that Terry Venables is still the right man for the job,' he said, 'and no one else is ready for it.' Apparently, he changed his mind in the interim period, and on 2 May the FA called a press conference at a west London hotel to unveil him.

It proved to be a stiff, uncomfortable occasion. Facing a room packed with more than one hundred reporters and thirteen television crews, a tired and drawn-looking Hoddle was flanked by Graham Kelly to his right and Venables to his left. If anything, Venables appeared even more ashen than Hoddle, a rueful expression on his face. He could not have failed to have noted that the FA had restored the title of 'Manager' to Hoddle. Nor that his successor was being handed a four-year, £1.2 million contract, double the time and money he had been allowed. Venables expressed the opinion that the job should have gone to an older, more experienced man. Hoddle countered: 'I wouldn't have taken it up if I didn't feel I was ready for it in my heart. Sometimes experience is judged by grey hairs, but I've been abroad, I've played abroad, and those are the experiences I hope to bring in.'

Having fired these shots across each other's bows, Venables and Hoddle then settled into a wary kind of bonhomie. Hoddle suggested Venables had been a significant influence on him accepting the job. 'The way Terry has been playing has been very brave at times,' he offered. 'For me it is very exciting. The last two performances have been superb.' Tip-toeing back from his initial assertion, Venables welcomed Hoddle as 'a good appointment. I coached him when he was in the under-21s and he was always keen to look at new things even then. I've not had much contact since, but it was obvious we thought along the same lines.' Even a question to Venables about whether he would consider an approach to manage England again in the future failed to draw blood. Yes, he said, smiling over at Hoddle, 'but not for four years'.

Kelly visibly relaxed, but there was a sting in the tail. As Kelly tried to bring proceedings to a close, Venables was asked if he would welcome a visit from Hoddle to England's pre-Euro 96 training camp. A cloud passed over Venables's face, a clue to the storm that was raging inside him. 'It will not help to have one manager on the training field and another watching from the touchline,' he responded, tight-lipped. 'The players would not know where to look.'

Hoddle was not due to take up his post for a month, but he nevertheless put in a call to his former manager at Monaco, Arsène Wenger. Charles Hughes was approaching retirement and Hoddle intended to persuade Wenger to take on the role of the FA's new director of football. Wenger's scientific approach to the game had left a lasting impression on Hoddle. At Swindon and Chelsea he had consulted Dr Yann Rougier, a nutritionist Wenger employed at Monaco, about prescribing high-performance diets for his players. Wenger was now managing Nagoya Grampus Eight in Japan. He asked for time to think over the offer and the two men agreed to speak again in August.

Venables returned to Lancaster Gate to continue his planning for Euro 96. Not for the last time that month, the FA mandarins around him were soon thrown into a state of panic and confusion. Just as Hoddle was being announced, police were raiding eleven premises across the country, including those of the National Sporting Club, as part of an investigation into the sale by unlicensed agencies of Euro 96 hospitality packages. Believing it had sanctioned just two outside agents to sell corporate tickets, the FA endorsed the raids to recover ten thousand missing tickets and eighteen arrests were made.

However, within days it transpired that Trevor Phillips's commercial department had encouraged other parties to apply for the ticketing business. An aggrieved spokesman for the National Sporting Club, which had had its supply of tickets seized, thundered: 'I cannot believe that one department in the FA instigated a raid when they were clearly not aware of the actions of another department.' Phillips was summoned to a showdown meeting with Kelly. His resignation was announced on 8 May, a curt statement from the FA claiming he had left over a number of issues not all connected to the ticketing fiasco. They did make it clear, though, that there was no suggestion he had profited from the ticket sales.

There was no such drama surrounding the end of the Premier League season. There was relief, though, for Venables who watched Tony Adams, Alan Shearer and Gareth Southgate return to action with Arsenal, Blackburn and Villa. Suggesting teams tried harder against his Manchester United than their title rivals, Alex Ferguson spooked Kevin Keegan into a wild-eyed outburst before the Sky TV cameras. Keegan's Newcastle team, though, still ended up rolling over, drawing their last two games and handing the title to United. Ferguson's team finished up thumping Nottingham Forest 5–0 and put three past Middlesbrough. The scent of a league and cup Double was now in their nostrils.

The FA Cup final went ahead at a sunny Wembley on Saturday, 11 May, and less than twenty-four hours after Chelsea had confirmed Ruud Gullit as their new manager. United met Liverpool in a forgettable game more notable for the injuries to Liverpool's Stan Collymore and full-back Rob Jones that ruled them out of contention for England's Euro 96 squad. The contest was settled by a solitary Eric Cantona goal in the eighty-fifth minute.

Dull as the Cup Final was, it was nevertheless a symbolic occasion. With a young generation of English footballers parading across the Wembley turf, it heralded a decisive breaking point from the game's unsophisticated past, for better and worse. Nothing telegraphed this more clearly than the sight of David Beckham, as well-groomed as a matinée idol, lining up next to his captain, the veteran defender Steve Bruce, thirty-five, his broken nose splayed across a face that was also a mess of scar tissue. Or the appearance of the youthful Liverpool team out on the pitch during the build-up to the game: Steve McManaman, Robbie Fowler, Jamie Redknapp and the rest of the squad were attired in cream Armani suits more tailored to the cat-walk. Fresh-faced and well-scrubbed, they were among football's new breed and on the cusp of becoming celebrities.

Redknapp, in particular, was emerging as the proto-typical modern Premier League footballer. Born into a footballing family, dad Harry and his maternal uncle, Frank Lampard Senior, both having played for West Ham, he signed for Liverpool at seventeen in 1991 and made his England debut four years later. The young Redknapp was set to establish himself as a full interna-tional at Euro 96, but above that, it was his male-model looks and the fact he was dating a pop star that lay at the root of his broader appeal.

The pop star in question was twenty-one-year-old Louise Nurding, who for three years from 1992 had been one-quarter of a somewhat successful girl group, Eternal. Nurding was on the point of releasing her first solo album, *Naked*, which as the title implied was meant to make her seem more risqué. That May Nurding peered out coquet-tishly from the cover of the men's magazine *FHM*, stripped to her underwear and next to a grammatically challenged headline: 'She Rocks! Louise. Singer. *Seriously* Sexy.' At the same time, her blossoming relationship with Redknapp was attracting the attentions of a salivating press pack also pursuing the Gallagher brothers and Princess Diana. Momentarily, the rising footballer and the country's pop pin-up *du jour* were transformed into one of Britain's first celebrity golden couples, viewed as being as much of an aspirational commodity as a sports car or Rolex watch. 'As money flooded into football, all these young guys were going out and buying loads of clothes and Bentleys,' says Tim Southwell, co-founder of *Loaded* magazine, another among the spate of publications then cashing in on the broadening interest in the game. 'They were good-looking, rich and let off the leash. It's no wonder they ended up getting into trouble.'

Venables received a taste of what was lurking for him and his squad on 20 May. Poring over his daily copy of the *Sun*, Venables would have happened across an 'exclusive' kiss-and-tell interview with Amy Kilfoyle. The twenty-year-old was the tearaway daughter of Labour's shadow education spokesman, Peter Kilfoyle, MP for Liverpool Walton and an Everton supporter. Earlier in the year she had dropped out of a politics degree course at Glasgow University and seemed set upon rebelling against her father in every possible sense. In the *Sun*, Kilfoyle related the salacious details of a 'night of passion' she and a student pal had enjoyed with Robbie Fowler. Admitting to being a 'bit drunk' at the time, Kilfoyle claimed to have met the Liverpool and England striker at a nightclub in their mutual hometown. She and her friend, she said, had accompanied Fowler from there to his house. 'It was an unbelievable night,' Kilfoyle added. 'He might be disappointed about Liverpool losing the FA Cup final, but at least he's had one double this season.' The tabloid also devoted its back page to the revelation that Venables intended to allow his players time off to see their wives and girlfriends during the course of Euro 96. The headline was better than a low-key story: 'Bonk of England.'

Two days earlier England played their final Wembley warm-up. Thirty-four thousand spectators, less than half the number who watched the Cup Final, turned out to see them face Hungary. Venables again fielded a back-three of Pearce, Neville and Wright, flanking them on this occasion with Darren Anderton and Blackburn's Jason Wilcox. With Gascoigne playing for Rangers in the Scottish Cup final, Newcastle's Rob Lee slotted into midfield and his team-mate Les Ferdinand partnered Teddy Sheringham up front. Shearer and Southgate came off the bench and England won 3–0. But the modest opposition kept the ball from them for long periods of the first half. The atmosphere inside Wembley was subdued, sullen even, and press reaction to the win was muted. Questions were asked of Venables's tactics and of England's chances of competing with the better teams at Euro 96. 'It seems that some people don't recognise progress when they see it,' Venables retorted. 'When I started, England had lost some international respect. We've regained some of that now and I think teams will fear us [in the tournament]. We believe it's coming good at the right time.'

Venables also did his best to put a positive spin on why his squad were being sent halfway around the world, to China and Hong Kong, to prepare for a home tournament. He told his players and anyone who asked that travelling five thousand miles would get them away from the pressure building in the press about him and also Euro 96.

The truth was that they were fulfilling a commercial deal negotiated by the departed Trevor Phillips. Venables's reasoning seemed to placate the team at least. However, the portents for the trip were ominous.

At the start of the month Venables had flown out to Beijing on a fact-finding mission. He took issue with the state of the pitch at the Workers' Stadium, where England were scheduled to face the Chinese national team, and asked that it be re-laid. Arriving back in England, Venables told reporters that negotiations over the matter had been cordial, but that 'the language barrier was a bit awkward. I asked for a roller and they bought out a Rolls Royce.' Fearing the beginnings of a diplomatic incident, the FA dispatched Venables's genial chief scout, Ted Buxton, to the Chinese capital to act as a go-between. The matter of Buxton's war record was somehow overlooked. He had served as an infantryman in the jungles of Malaysia, hunting down Chinese insurgents.

The full England party flew out to Beijing on 19 May. Gascoigne hooked up with the squad worse for wear after celebrating Rangers' Scottish Cup win over Hearts. He approached the trip as if it was an end-of-season jaunt and of a mind to let his hair down, which usually spelt trouble. This, coupled with his acute fear of flying, was enough to ensure that England's misadventure started as it would go on.

The plane had not even left the runway at Heathrow when Gascoigne began to beseech a male flight attendant for a drink to calm his nerves. He was given a bottle of

Budweiser, sank it and demanded another. Since the cabin crew were now preparing for take-off, the flight attendant asked Gascoigne to wait and carried on with his other duties. Gascoigne kept begging. 'The steward was starting to get quite irritated,' said Stuart Pearce. 'He was standing just ahead of Gazza, looking after the row in front of him. So Gazza reached forward and to attract his attention patted him on the bum. The steward turned round and punched him straight in the face. He caught him a classic. I was sitting close by with Steve Stone and we just fell about laughing.'

Shocked, Gascoigne was on the point of tears, his bottom lip quivering just as it had done on that fateful night in Turin. The pilot intervened and broadcast a warning to Gascoigne that if there was any more trouble he would stop over in Moscow and have him thrown off the flight. Gascoigne sat in silence for the rest of the journey, brooding. He had, however, been fortunate. Henry Winter and the scrum of journalists covering the trip had been booked on a separate outbound flight and the story never made the papers. Neither Gazza's, nor the rest of the squad's luck would hold out, though.

Upon arrival in Beijing, the mood lightened. The players were escorted around Tiananmen Square and to the Great Wall, or otherwise whiled away their time in card schools or idling. Venables had taken along both Neville brothers, with Phil, nineteen, on his first England call-up. Like peas in a pod, they were both full-backs who had joined Manchester United from school in their hometown of

Bury. Gary made his first-team debut in 1992, aged seventeen, and Phil during the 1993–94 season. Wide-eyed at being in China, they comported themselves like eager boy scouts, rushing to help the corps of press photographers haul their gear up the steep inclines of the Great Wall and generally bursting with enthusiasm.

The game against China took place on 23 May before a crowd of sixty-five thousand on a hot, humid afternoon. In spite of all the dialogue about improving the playing surface, it was rock-hard and like a rutted field. England breezed to a 3–0 win with two goals from Middlesbrough's Nick Barmby and one from Gascoigne. Shearer returned to the starting line-up, but failed to score for the ninth successive time in an England shirt. That fact would soon become an issue in the English papers, but for now Venables was able to enjoy some rare upbeat notices. *The Times* match report cooed: 'Nobody, for once, could begrudge the officials of the FA their smiles nor the mixture of joy and relief on the face of Terry Venables whose side showed admirable composure in an atmosphere of noise and passion long forgotten in the echoing mausoleum of Wembley. This was how it used to be: England travelling to far-flung corners of the earth to administer a sharp lesson to willing pupils.'

A more familiar colonial note was struck when the England party landed in Hong Kong ahead of their second game. On this occasion Venables decided to forego an invitation for his squad to train at the quaintly named Happy Valley Stadium. He awoke the next morning to find the local papers fulminating about how the arrogant English thought themselves too good for Hong Kong's facilities.

The match itself, meant as a low-key training exercise, took place on 26 May against a Hong Kong XI select side made up of local players and a handful of imported British professionals. Most of the latter group were in the twilight of their careers. Among them was an ex-Manchester United full-back, Michael Duxbury, now thirty-six, and thirty-four-year-old Carlton Fairweather, who had spent nine years with Wimbledon up to 1993 before drifting off through football's outlands. Their goalkeeper, Iain Hesford, was also thirty-six and a former England under-21 international put out to pasture in Chinese football after spells at Blackpool, Sunderland and Hull. Hesford encapsulated the overall tone of the game: with his hang-dog moustache and bulging jersey, he had the appearance of a Sunday-morning footballer.

The contest, such as it was, proceeded at a pedestrian pace in front of twenty-six thousand spectators more diverted by trying to find shelter from a torrential downpour. A further touch of the surreal was added by the nominal home team's strip, a lurid pink affair. England's performance was as drab as the weather. On one occasion, Tony Adams found himself left floundering for pace by Lee Bullen, at the time a journeyman Scottish striker deemed surplus to requirements by Dunfermline Athletic, Meadowbank Thistle and Stenhousemuir. Venables was more pre-occupied with his own strikers. In that respect the match did at least provide him with an important marker. Bringing Shearer on as a forty-seventh-minute substitute, he was at last able to pair him with Sheringham again in his ideal attack.

The two of them came from typical football backgrounds. Shearer, twenty-four, grew up on a council estate on the outskirts of Newcastle. His father, also Alan, was a sheet metal worker and the young Shearer stood out among thousands of hopefuls playing junior football in the North East. He joined Southampton as a schoolboy trainee and was in their first team at seventeen. He made his England debut under Graham Taylor in 1992, and at the end of that season joined free-spending Blackburn. He had been their top scorer in both of the two seasons leading up to Euro 96.

Sheringham was born in the London suburb of Higham's Park and was picked up by Millwall aged fifteen. He helped fire the south London club into the top division in 1988 and moved on to Nottingham Forest in July 1991, signed by the incomparable Brian Clough. At their first meeting, Sheringham asked his new manager if he would be allocated his preferred number nine jersey. 'Just make sure you're wearing a shirt with a number between one and eleven on it, son,' Clough shot back at him. The adroit Sheringham was Clough's sort of footballer, but like so many others before him, the Forest manager underestimated his influence on a team and sold him to Venables's Tottenham. Sheringham scored twenty-one goals in his first season at White Hart Lane. Forest were relegated.

The first time Venables paired Shearer and Sheringham for England was against the United States at Wembley on 7 September 1994. Shearer scored both goals in a 2–0 win, Sheringham his foil. On the pitch the two of them were contrasting personalities, chalk and cheese. Shearer, a more conventional centre-forward, threw himself into the heat of battle, a warrior leading the line. Sheringham was cuter, more cerebral, his languid bearing sometimes causing him to be mistaken as uncommitted or just plain lazy. Off duty he was just as smart and self-assured, but with a more extravagant air, so that one might think him something of a playboy. By contrast, Shearer appeared to the casual observer to be poker-faced, dour, as if he had accelerated towards middle-age. Asked by a reporter how he planned to celebrate winning the league title with Blackburn in 1995 and being crowned Player of the Year, he had replied: 'By creosoting the fence.' Yet a different Shearer lurked behind this public façade. Within the tight-knit confines of the dressing room he was also very much one of the lads, a practical joker with a fine-tuned sense of humour.

Shearer drew another blank in Hong Kong. His deputy, Les Ferdinand, spared England's blushes with a first-half goal. As far as conditioning them for the rigours of tournament football, the match was of no consequence, nothing more than a kick-about. However, the travelling press contingent were still divided on their opinion of Venables's suitability for the job and the naysayers were waiting for any opportunity to pounce like jackals on fresh meat. Foremost among them was Harry Harris, chief football writer for the *Daily Mirror*. Harris's damning match report was headlined 'Honkers 0, Plonkers 1'. Dismissing Venables's rationale that the stadium's long grass was ill-suited to England's passing game as 'the most pathetic excuse ever', Harris concluded: 'He now has only twelve days to restore England's pride and spirit.'

'To begin with I hadn't been quite able to work out Venables,' says Henry Winter, covering the tour for the *Daily Telegraph*. 'Was he the shady wide boy who spent all his time holding court at Scribes or the King of Barcelona? As ever, the truth probably lies somewhere between the two, but he was certainly tough. Going into his press conferences at the time, it was like a wedding where the two families are split down the middle and not talking. On the one side of the room were his friends, those he would invite down to Scribes for a drink. On the other you had Harry Harris and all those who were hammering Venables. That group would rip him apart and he took it head on.'

For all his truck with the latest coaching methods, Venables held firm to the enduring belief that there was no harm in allowing players to let off steam; that nights out bonded them together. Before the match, he had agreed to release the squad from their barracks that evening. He, of all people, was not about to renege on that promise now. Back when he was Chelsea captain, towards the end of the 1964–65 season, manager Tommy Docherty had told his squad they would be let loose after their game at Liverpool, but rescinded the offer when they lost.

Venables and seven other players went out regardless. The next morning Docherty ordered them home from the team hotel in Blackpool. 'When we arrived back in London, the world's press was waiting for us,' Venables said later, perhaps exaggerating slightly. 'It was the big football scandal of the year.'

Back at their Hong Kong hotel, Venables imposed a curfew of two o'clock the next morning and warned the players to be careful if they left the premises. The squad gathered for a meal and afterwards a number of them retired to their rooms. Among these was Tony Adams, off the booze, and his fellow centre-half, Gareth Southgate, who was teetotal. In his first months at Manchester United, Alex Ferguson had broken up the team's hardened drinking club, shipping out some of its ringleaders, marginalising others. Reared under this regime, and at the beginning of their England careers, the Neville brothers also opted out. David Platt had also told them, along with Nicky Barmby and Jason Wilcox, that the night out could be 'one to miss'. Likewise, Stuart Pearce counselled his Nottingham Forest team-mate, Steve Stone, against going out into the city, but Stone ignored him and went off with a group of other players. Also included in this outbound party was Teddy Sheringham, Robbie Fowler, Steve McManaman, Paul Ince, Chelsea's Dennis Wise, Spurs goalkeeper Ian Walker, and Gascoigne, who was limbering up for his twenty-ninth birthday the next day.

Venables dispatched Bryan Robson to go with them as chaperone. The players, conspicuous in their England tracksuits, made for a well-known local nightclub called China Jump.

'There was an agreement that night among the football writers and players that we would go one way and they another,' says Henry Winter. 'You wouldn't get that these days, but to be honest, nor would the players even go out now. At the time, there wasn't a big issue being made of the dangers of refuelling, and that if you did have three or four pints, it would set your training back by a week or however long. Euro 96 was the last tournament where that was the case for England.'

'I got drinking with Robbie Fowler at the bar,' recalled Gascoigne. 'He saw this girl and said to her, "Hi, what's your name?" I said, "What an awful line!" So, of course, we started pushing and shoving each other. Nothing serious, but it led to me picking up a pint and pouring it over Robbie's head. Then Teddy Sheringham arrived. I poured a pint over his head as well. Steve McManaman came over and he, too, ended up wearing a pint. At the same time, I somehow managed to rip his T-shirt. The evening's game then became that everyone had to have a pint poured over them and their shirt ripped.'

Robson, who was wearing an Armani suit, a gift from his wife, had his designer shirt ripped off at the collar by Gascoigne. Sheringham and Wise spied a pair of boxing gloves hanging up behind the bar, pulled them down and began sparring with each other. English tourists in the club were taking photographs of the proceedings, but no alarm bells went off among the players. One of the party noticed that there was a dentist's chair stationed by the dancefloor and suggested they investigate. It proved a simple enough premise. Willing participants prostrated themselves in the chair and a barman poured spirits from the bottle down their throats. On this particular evening tequila and Drambuie were on the menu. Gascoigne, Sheringham, Ince, Fowler and McManaman all took up the challenge. More cameras clicked and whirred.

Shearer was a late arrival on the scene, but by that time the night was winding down and the mood less raucous. The group left the club soon after, hailing taxis back to the hotel. Gascoigne paired with Robson, who was trying to maintain his dignity in his shirt collar. Gascoigne recalled thinking that it had been 'a quiet night, nothing wild'. He was still going strong the next day, bleary-eyed but celebrating turning twenty-nine. 'I walked into the dining room for lunch and Gazza was lighting a cigar with something that looked like a Bunsen burner from a chemistry class,' Gary Neville recorded. 'The flame must have been three-feet long and Gazza, in the dining room of a five-star hotel, was almost setting fire to himself. If anyone had done that at United you wouldn't have waited for the bollocking from the manager, you would have packed your bags and gone.'

The fallout from the events in China Jump began even before the England party returned to London. Pictures of the booze-soaked players roistering at the club, and of

Sheringham and Gascoigne guzzling in its dentist's chair, were splashed across the tabloids. The accompanying headlines and editorials were united in moral outrage, the brunt of which was targeted at Gascoigne. 'Disgracefool,' roared the *Sun*. 'Look at Gazza, a drunken oaf with no pride.' The *Daily Mirror*, meanwhile, quoted Sir Alf Ramsey stating that he would not attend any of England's Euro 96 fixtures if the errant Gascoigne was selected to play. The affair even stirred a sense of disquiet among other members of the squad. Stuart Pearce, in particular, took exception to such public displays of ill-discipline. 'Teddy Sheringham came out of the incident looking more like Ollie Reed than an international footballer,' he ventured. 'It was naïve, the lads should have known better. It's not a lot to ask to keep your heads down for two weeks. There were times with England when I looked at players and wondered how they managed to get that drunk. I don't have much sympathy with the drinking stakes. Whenever I went away for a tournament I could never understand why players needed to go for a drink during that period. In six weeks' time they could drink themselves silly.'

Venables was furious, too, if more sanguine. 'It was only six or seven of the total squad who went out, and they returned before the curfew I'd given them,' he said. 'If there was a punishment, it was the pictures. They looked ridiculous, to me, to the rest of the squad, and to their families back home.'

Worse, though, was to follow. Gascoigne had kept on drinking right through his birthday and up to the time the squad boarded their return Cathay Pacific flight. On the Boeing 747, the players were allocated seats apart from the management and other FA officials in the upstairs first-class cabin. Wary of further trouble, Venables sent up the team doctor, John Crane, specifically to keep an eye on Gascoigne, who had at last passed out. 'The thing was, Doc Crane liked a tipple himself and fell asleep,' related Gary Neville. 'Alan Shearer then came down to our row to play cards. As he was walking past Gazza, he slapped the back of his head – a big clout. Gazza woke up with a start and thought it was McManaman or Fowler, because they were sat a couple of rows behind.'

Whatever Gascoigne had pent up inside him erupted to the surface and he rampaged up the aisle, kicking seats and bellowing his frustration. In spite of their protestations of innocence, he took revenge on the Liverpool pair, unleashing his furies and smashing their in-flight TV monitors. 'While I was going around shouting at everyone, an FA official came up the stairs from the lower deck and told me to stop all the noise, sit down and go to sleep,' Gascoigne recalled. 'I told him to fuck off. "We do all the playing, you do fuck all," I told him. It was a bit out of order, I admit, but then, I was a bit tipsy. During the ten days or so we'd been away, I had only actually been drunk on two nights. I didn't think that was so bad. Plus, of course, on the plane home.'

Unlike the outbound journey, the bare details of this in-flight incident were picked up by the press, with Cathay Pacific claiming that £5,000 worth of damage had been done to their aircraft. However, the identity of the vandal was unknown to both the press and those on the lower deck, who were only aware of Gascoigne shouting. It nevertheless gave rise to a second wave of appalled headlines. Less than two weeks before they began their tilt at Euro 96, the host team flew home as pariahs.

CHAPTER FIVE

'What's this guy saying? We're going to get stuffed?'

While England's Far East trek was unravelling, back home there were further complications surrounding the preparations for Euro 96. Councils in London refused a request from the FA to arrange for more camp-sites to be set up on green land across the capital to help accommodate the anticipated additional quarter of a million visitors from overseas. Between them the two designated sites on Hackney Marshes and near the prison at Wormwood Scrubs had just four hundred vacancies. The opening of the official Euro 96 telephone ticket hot-line was also attended by farce. Close to twenty-thousand callers besieged the fifty staff working out of its Stoke-on-Trent office on the morning it was launched, instantly jamming the lines.

However, the pervading gloom hanging over the tour-nament was lifted by a simple pop song. Released on 17 May, 'Three Lions', written and performed by Ian Broudie, Frank Skinner and David Baddiel, was commis-sioned by the FA for its official Euro 96 compilation album,

The Beautiful Game. The album also featured contributions from the likes of Blur, Supergrass and Bristol trip-hop collective Massive Attack, but it was the wistful 'Three Lions' that stood out. Evoking sepia-tinted memories of 1966 ('Bobby belting the ball and Nobby dancing'), and mourning the 'thirty years of hurt' that had ensued for English football, it was certainly trite and twee, but ingratiating, too. It also had the additional bonus of an uplifting chorus. This was a single, oft-repeated line: 'It's coming home, it's coming home, it's coming, football's coming home …'

Songwriter Broudie, thirty-seven, had cut his chops on the post-punk scene that flared up in his native Liverpool in the late-1970s and spawned bands like Echo and the Bunnymen and The Teardrop Explodes. His own first, short-lived group, Big in Japan, also featured the talents of future Frankie Goes to Hollywood singer Holly Johnson and Bill Drummond, later co-founder of the KLF, one of the biggest-selling groups to emerge from Acid House. Even Broudie admitted Big in Japan were 'pretty rubbish', and he went on to form a second band, Original Mirrors, whose cult did not extend much beyond the odd John Peel radio session. Broudie was better appreciated as a producer and for his work with the Bunnymen, fellow Liverpudlians The Icicle Works, and a band of bellicose Mancunians, The Fall.

Broudie had established his current band, the Lightning Seeds, in 1988 and had gone on to have a degree of success. Essentially a one-man operation with Broudie as the sole full-time member, the Lightning Seeds enjoyed a top-twenty hit with *Pure* in 1989. Their most recent album, 1994's *Justification*, had also sold well in Britpop's slip-stream, but it would still be hard to pick out the bespectacled Broudie in a crowded room, so low-key was his public profile. Nevertheless, he had form when it came to football: the Seeds' 1992 track, 'Life of Riley', had provided the background music for *Match of the Day*'s Goal of the Month segment. That was enough to convince the FA to approach him to write a song for the Euros.

Broudie was at the time working on a fourth Lightning Seeds album at Eel Pie Island Studio, which was based on a Thames houseboat and owned by Pete Townshend of The Who. Taking a break from the sessions he began sketching out 'Three Lions'. He had an idea to open the track with the sound of a roaring crowd that he had taped at Anfield the previous October during a UEFA Cup clash between Liverpool and the Danish side Brondby. Fittingly, given the bittersweet tone Broudie was fashioning as the musical backdrop to 'Three Lions', Liverpool lost both the match and tie to a late goal.

As the music track took shape, Broudie approached two comedians, Skinner and Baddiel, to pen the accompanying lyrics. Real-life flatmates, the pair of them presented the popular *Fantasy Football League* television show, which took a sardonic but affectionate view of the game and was broadcast from a mock-up set of their front room. It was then in its second series and was watched by up to six million viewers a week. Skinner, thirty-nine, was born Christopher Collins on a council estate in the West

Midlands and had come up on the local stand-up circuit. He took his stage name from a member of his dad's pub dominoes team and was an avid West Bromwich Albion fan. Baddiel, a Spurs supporter and seven years his junior, was a Cambridge graduate who made his name during the alternative comedy boom of the late-1980s and early-1990s working in a duo alongside Rob Newman. Aside from their shared love of football with Liverpool fan Broudie, The Fall also happened to be Skinner's favourite band.

Given free rein by the FA, the three of them agreed that the finished song should resonate with genuine football fans and reflect the highs and lows of following the national team. They surely accomplished that, but ultimately *Three Lions* tapped directly and more generally into the musical mood of the time. Broudie's 1960s beat-pop-inflected tune and the song's surging, optimistic refrain set it in the same Britpop line as such everyman anthems as Oasis's 'Wonderwall', Blur's 'Parklife' and 'Common People' by Pulp, and as such it was destined to find a much wider audience.

Three Lions was completed by March and before England faced Bulgaria at Wembley that month, Broudie, Skinner and Baddiel were invited by the FA to preview their creation to Terry Venables and his squad at Bisham Abbey. 'It was nerve-wracking,' Skinner told the *Independent*. 'We were having lunch with the players and, when we got to the cheesecake, Gazza couldn't wait any longer and went to put the song on. Fortunately, he was unable to use a cassette player.'

The composers were particularly anxious about how the song's first verse would be received by its audience. Meant to establish the fatalistic mindset of England supporters, it ran: 'Everyone seems to know the score, they've seen it all before. They just know, they're so sure, that England's gonna throw it away.' According to Broudie, officials at the FA had blanched when hearing the song for the first time just days earlier and 'hated it'. There was also a dead-eyed response from the England players when it was played to them. 'It was a funny moment,' Broudie recalled to the *Guardian* in 2009. 'As soon as those lines came on I was looking at the ghetto blaster and looking at them. I could see them thinking, "What's this guy saying? We're going to get stuffed?"'

'At first, the players showed no more enthusiasm than occasionally tapping a fork against a plate,' Baddiel added in the *Independent*. 'Then we explained the song as if to a group of three-year-old children and they got it. Terry Venables was particularly positive about it. "Roll on 8 June," he said.'

After lunch, the squad, along with Broudie, Skinner and Baddiel, headed out on to the training pitches, trailed by a film crew. Scenes of the players mouthing the words to the chorus of the song, and its writers joining them for a supposedly impromptu kick-about, were filmed for the video to accompany the track. The remaining scenes were shot on a chilly Saturday morning in late-April at a spit-and-sawdust pub, the Queen of the Isle in London's Docklands. In these, the three performers were shown watching a compendium of England's most enduring moments on the pub's television set: Gordon Banks saving from Pele in the 1970 World Cup; Lineker scoring against the Germans in Turin; the toothless Nobby Stiles skipping across the Wembley turf with the Jules Rimet trophy. The punchline was the closing shot. As the three of them walked out of the pub, coming in the opposite direction was Geoff Hurst, England's 1966 hat-trick hero.

Hurst was also at the centre of a pre-Euro 96 campaign being launched by *Total Football* magazine to recover the match ball from the 1966 final. It was by rights Hurst's after his three goals, but West German striker Helmut Haller had instead raced off to the Wembley dressing rooms with it at the final whistle. *Total Football* was urging its readers to lobby the German Ambassador to Britain to have the ball located and returned to Hurst. Subsequently, the magazine tracked Haller down to his Bavarian hometown of Augsburg and he admitted that he had given the ball to his son, Jurgen. The *Daily Mirror* then stepped in, paying the younger Haller £80,000 for the ball and bringing it back to England, where it now resides at the National Football Museum in Manchester.

The history of songs associated with England teams was as chequered as their results. It began at the 1970 World Cup finals when Sir Alf Ramsey's defending champions went off on their ill-fated mission to Mexico singing the brainless 'Back Home'. Credited to the England Squad, it nonetheless went to number one. The erstwhile West Bromwich Albion and England striker, Jeff Astle, had revived the song on *Fantasy Football League*, singing a tuneless version of it to herald his weekly cameo appearance. With England failing to qualify for the next two World Cups, there was a pause until 1982 when Ron Greenwood's Spain-bound team served up 'This Time (We'll Get it Right)' with misplaced confidence. Written for them by Chris Norman and Pete Spencer, mainstays of grizzled 1970s rockers Smokie, it charted at number two, which was three places higher than Smokie's best-known hit, 'Living Next Door to Alice', had managed.

'We've Got the Whole World at Our Feet', an entirely asinine concoction, followed for the 1986 finals staged again in Mexico. Diego Maradona's 'Hand of God' goal tipped England out of that tournament and the song also crashed, stalling at number sixty-six. Pop hit-makers Stock, Aitken & Waterman were then called in to bolster England for the 1988 European Championship. Forced to sing the execrable 'All the Way', Bobby Robson's men could almost be forgiven for going on to lose all of their games and not progressing beyond the halfway mark. Then came Italia 90 and an England song that broke with all precedent by actually being half-decent. 'World in Motion' was co-written by the critically adored Manchester electro-pop quartet New Order and an actor, Keith Allen. It included a rap from England winger John Barnes and stormed to number one, transcending its otherwise inglorious genre.

'Three Lions' did not break the same ground as 'World in Motion' and might not have been as good a song, but it had a big hook. Just as the England team flew in from Hong Kong, under siege, this began to sink in. 'Football's coming home' resounded from car radios and pub juke-boxes up and down the country. A would-be anthem to both sing along and cry into a beer to, it also found an entirely receptive audience among a male stereotype who emerged in the mid-1990s: the Lad. An inverse reaction to the feisty feminism and caring, sharing 'new man' of ear-lier decades, being a Lad allowed British men an outlet to reclaim their maleness and revel once more in the simple pleasures of birds, beer and football.

Like the new man, the Lad was essentially a media construct, and as patronising a one at that, but it epito-mised the giddy, euphoric spirit of the times. Upbeat and celebrating the communal experience, this ran counter to the grey, downtrodden image of Britain perpetrated by John Major and his government. It was turned loose at outdoor raves, found a voice in Liam Gallagher, and would soar to a crescendo at Wembley that June. The Lads' bible was *Loaded* magazine. This was the brainchild of Tim Southwell and James Brown, both former *NME* writers and Leeds supporters. Their joint inspiration was a jaunt to see Leeds play a Champions League tie at Camp Nou in October 1992. Strolling down Barcelona's teeming Las Ramblas thoroughfare after the match, Brown decreed that there should be a magazine that evoked the same feeling of an unforgettable night out.

'*Loaded* was a massive celebration of what it was like to be a man in the 1990s,' Southwell opines. 'The existing men's magazines like *GQ* and *Esquire* were full of five thousand pound suits and didn't say anything to me about what my life was like. I was a twenty-seven-year-old football fan, which was kind of frowned upon at the time. The whole perception of men at that point was that you were either a new man or a lout, with nothing in between. Men were almost being asked to re-invent themselves as sort of multi-dimensional and socially caring. Completely stupidly, it was presumed that you would be embarrassed to have natural impulses and do what men do, which is to loaf around and have a laugh.'

Loaded set out its stall from the start. Announcing itself as the magazine 'For Men Who Should Know Better', the cover of its first issue in 1994 proffered a defining two-word headline: 'Super Lads'. The inside pages were crammed with homages to such Lad icons as Paul Weller and Eric Cantona and a feature on the joys of hotel sex. As *Loaded* evolved, so Lad culture billowed out around it. *Fantasy Football League*, the premise of which was ostensibly two blokes loafing around and having a laugh about football, was just one among a spate of Lad-friendly television shows to be commissioned. At the same time, *Loaded*'s sales grew incrementally from one month to the next. By the summer of 1996 its readership had risen above three hundred thousand. On its most recent issue, a black and white portrait of Kevin Keegan peered out from the cover. Following on from an earlier Paul Gascoigne cover, this cemented the magazine's relationship with football and was diverting for the simple reason that someone had scribbled a pair of spectacles and a moustache on to Keegan's face.

'Footballers and football people were the ultimate heroes for us,' says Southwell. 'You might not be able to sing, but you could still be successful as a singer. With football, there's nowhere to hide – you're either brilliant or you're not, and you've got to play to that level every game. Keegan, though, was in a bad mood on the day we had to photograph him and there wasn't a single picture of him not looking pissed off. We stood around the office considering this thoroughly underwhelming image on the cover when James just picked a pen up and drew on Keegan's face. It ended up being nominated as one of the hundred best magazine covers of all time.'

Two weeks after it was released, 'Three Lions' climbed to number one in the charts. In doing so, it eclipsed the official theme tune of Euro 96, 'We're in this Together', a flaccid effort from pop balladeers Simply Red. It gave a boost to Ian Broudie's career. The Lightning Seeds' next album, aptly named *Dizzy Heights*, was certified Gold soon after it was released the following November. The immediate rewards for Frank Skinner and David Baddiel were rather less glittering: both of them pocketed £35,000 apiece in royalties. Moreover, 'Three Lions' served to wake the country up to England's imminent quest for football glory and also helped encourage the nascent movement in the country back towards unashamed displays of patriotic symbolism.

'It seems mad now,' Broudie reflected in the *Guardian*, 'but I think before that record if you'd asked people what was on the badge of the England shirt, no one would have been able to tell you. If I went into a pub anywhere in the country that summer, everyone would start singing it at me. It was nice, really, but a bit surreal.'

'"Three Lions" is perhaps the most striking memory of Euro 96 that everybody has, because it was identified with the tournament over and above all else,' considers Henry Winter. 'It became the soundtrack to all of our lives for a month.'

PART THREE:
JUNE

CHAPTER SIX

*'Only in England could you have an opening
ceremony that almost kills an animal'*

Located a mile from the Berkshire town of Marlow, and
on the banks of the Thames, Bisham Abbey was built
in the thirteenth century. During its colourful history
both Henry VIII and Elizabeth I used the old manor house
as a bolthole for their courts outside London. Its rolling
grounds now housed state-of-the-art sports facilities and
it was here, on the morning of Sunday, 2 June, that Terry
Venables and his England squad reported to begin their
final preparations for Euro 96. They had been blown back
from the Far East by the ill-wind that was still causing a
storm in the press.

Stories about the incidents in Hong Kong, and on the
Cathay Pacific flight home, had been running in the papers
for three consecutive days. The team was being portrayed
as a national disgrace, but particular opprobrium was
reserved for Paul Gascoigne. In a poll published in the *Sun*
that Saturday, 'disgusted' readers were reported to have
voted by a margin of six-to-one for Gascoigne to be kicked

out of the squad because of his antics. The bookmakers William Hill were running a sweepstake on what Gascoigne might do next to embarrass the country. They offered odds of eighteen-to-one on Gascoigne having 'I am a complete prat' tattooed across his backside, and twenty-five-to-one against him walking out for England's first match of the tournament with a plant pot on his head.

In *The Times*, meanwhile, a matter of drunken horse-play was being blown up into an issue affecting the entire country. 'Euro 96: a question of sport, or something of much deeper importance to the English nation?' wrote Rob Hughes. 'We must know, after the furore of Paul Gascoigne's birthday party in the skies, that the values of British society as a whole, never mind what happens on the pitch, are about to be judged by the world at large.'

Returning from Hong Kong, Gascoigne at first attempted to flee the clamour by checking into a secluded health farm located in the village of Measham in rural Leicestershire. However, on arriving he was met by a phalanx of pressmen and photographers. 'I immediately turned round and went to Newcastle instead and had a quiet time there,' he said later. 'I can when I put my mind to it.'

Before leaving the sanctuary of his hometown for Berkshire, a distraught Gascoigne had nonetheless rung the FA's director of communications, David Davies, and begged to know why he was being picked on. Trailing Venables, Gascoigne was the first of the players to arrive at the England team hotel, sweeping up Burnham Beeches' expansive driveway in a Range Rover driven by his former Newcastle captain, Glenn Roeder, and in a pensive mood. Once the rest of the squad turned up, Venables gathered them together and asked that someone come forward and claim responsibility for causing the damage to the Cathay Pacific plane. No one did and the next morning Venables summoned a fretful Davies to the hotel for an emergency contingency meeting over breakfast. Venables told Davies he was being pressured by FA officials to make Gascoigne a scapegoat for the whole mess and throw him out of the camp. 'God, if only they had known how fragile Gazza was,' Davies told the *Daily Mail* in 2008. 'All of the players were quieter than usual, chastened even, I sensed, a little frightened.'

To try and blunt the press attacks and shift the focus from Gascoigne, Davies suggested Venables put out a line that the squad was taking collective responsibility for what had occurred on the flight. The two men drafted a statement in which the team boss was quoted as stating: 'Three of the players [Gascoigne, McMamanan and Fowler] were very angry that they had to take the blame publically, and without justification, they believe.' Venables then went off and called the players to a second meeting to thrash out the terms of this approach. The upshot was an agreement that each member of the squad would hand over two match fees to pay for the damage to the aircraft. Any outstanding monies would be donated to charity. It was not a solution that went down well with all the players.

'Our match fee was £1,500, which was a fortune to me at the time,' Gary Neville said later. 'I had a moan to my brother. We hadn't been on the piss-up or caused any of the damage. The truth was that the players were willing to make allowances for Gazza because they knew what he could do for the team.' Stuart Pearce echoed that: 'I didn't think the solution was fair. But for the sake of squad harmony I kept my lip buttoned and put my hand in my pocket.

'Gazza was fortunate to have the ideal manager in Terry Venables. Terry was very shrewd: he knew he could not squeeze the best out of his enigmatic player if he put constraints on him. He let him have his head and then reined him in with a few well-chosen words. Gazza also has a heart of gold. Ask him for anything and if it was in his power, he would do it. He was kind-hearted and always wanted to please. That's why he does stupid things, to make people laugh. All the time I was in the squad, it was Gazza who provided light relief.'

Outside the camp, the solution dreamt up by Venables and Davies was welcomed even less. The *Sun* and other newspapers branded it a whitewash. MP David Wilshire joined the chorus suggesting to journalists that 'this is a splendid cover-up'. However, out on the lush pitches at Bisham Abbey, the sense of a veil being drawn over the matter lasted less than twenty-four hours. It took that long for FA chairman Bert Millichip to get cornered by a reporter from the Press Association, Rob King, wanting to know the finer details of the squad's supposedly noble stand. Panicked, Millichip blurted out the inconvenient truth that it had, in effect, been forced upon them.

Venables's blackening temper would not have been lightened by an ill-timed interview Glenn Hoddle gave to the

Sun and published on 3 June under the headline: 'Gazza and co on trial – Hoddle raps out World Cup warning'. Hoddle, who two days earlier had officially taken up his office at FA headquarters, told the tabloid he would be focused during the next month on assessing the England players' respective characters. 'That is fifty per cent of any player, character and mental strength,' he opined. 'It felt like we had been under siege at Burnham Beeches,' Alan Shearer wrote afterwards. 'It almost seemed as if the nation, whipped up by a hate campaign in the media, wanted us to fail. In effect, the hostility made us all close ranks.'

Forced back on to the offensive, Venables insisted there had been no whitewash and scorned Cathay Pacific's claim of £5,000 damages. 'It has gone incredibly out of proportion,' he told reporters. 'There was very little problem in the upstairs section of the plane, but it has been made to sound like there was a party. Actually, they were playing cards all night,' he added, erroneously. The sense of wagons being circled around the England camp was soon enforced by the presence of burly security guards patrolling the approaches to the hotel and Bisham Abbey. Furthermore, out at the squad's training facility a towering tarpaulin was rigged up around the pitches to keep them off limits and ensure Venables and his team could go about their business away from prying eyes.

'Those were an awful few days leading up to the Switzerland game,' recalls Henry Winter. 'At the time, the players absolutely loathed those of us in the press because of the battering we'd given them. We knew them all, it wasn't as if you were detached from them like you are now, so the fall-out seemed quite spectacular. We couldn't get them to come out and talk to us. Gazza was going absolutely crazy. Actually, Gazza was in quite a bad place then, as is sort of his wont, but because he was so popular, the players rallied around him.

'At Bisham, the FA also erected this huge media tent that was made to look like a mini-Camelot. The first time we all went down there was for a press conference with David Davies. Lining the walls of the entrance, there were these great floor-to-ceiling photographs of all the players in action. The first three you saw as you went in were those most associated with the Cathay Pacific trouble: Gazza, Fowler and McManaman. When Davies came out a great shout went up from the back of the tent to get a picture of Southgate moved up to the front.

'I've always had this theory, though, that the England players are at their best when they're getting hammered by the press. It had happened in advance of Italia 90, too, when Bobby Robson and his team were getting killed in the papers. Also, football itself was changing. Television was starting to make footballers celebrities – it was more like pop stardom. In fact, footballers like Gazza were the first true characters since the rock stars of the 1970s.'

In London, a second vast press and hospitality marquee was pitched on the concourse outside Wembley Stadium and tournament banners dotted the route of the orbital

North Circular road. However, these were scant and silent totems, apologetic and almost invisible when compared to the manner in which the capital was subsequently saturated in advance of it hosting the 2012 Olympics. In respect of the capital at least, it was the tabloid press who took it upon itself to bang the English drum for the fast-approaching Euro 96. The *Sun* launched a 'Roar for England' telephone hotline for supporters to call with their good-luck messages for the team and printed the most effusive on a daily basis.

'Three Lions' was ubiquitous and Frank Skinner and David Baddiel beamed out from the cover of that month's *Loaded*. Across the country, a general feeling of well-being was inflated by forecasts of a glorious summer. Football was set to come home bathed in sunshine and with a song in its heart. The scale of the challenge facing the host nation, though, was emphasised on 4 June when the Dutch, their most ominous-looking group opponents, brushed aside the Republic of Ireland 3–1 in a warm-up game in Rotterdam. Dennis Bergkamp was among the Dutch scorers and looked his side's most potent weapon. After the match, Mick McCarthy, the newly installed Ireland manager, told reporters: 'Mark my words, Holland will win the group. That side is just sheer quality.'

The next morning, police officers raided homes in London, Manchester and elsewhere in an attempt to round up suspected hooligans before the tournament kicked off. In London, fifty officers with police dogs raided seven suspects' homes. One arrest was made in Manchester and three members of Combat 18 were detained in neighbouring Oldham. Among the items police seized were tickets for England matches and weapons, including three knives, a knuckleduster, a sword and a bayonet. That same day, officers and a police dog in Warwickshire recovered the Scotland squad's Euro 96 kit. It had been stolen two days earlier from a van parked outside their team hotel on the outskirts of Birmingham.

Against this backdrop Venables bunkered down to the task of pruning his squad to twenty-two. Given his own omission at the hands of Alf Ramsey thirty years earlier, it was one to which he was particularly sensitive. He had already lost Mark Wright to injury and now had to cut five more players. The ones to go were Newcastle's Rob Lee and Peter Beardsley, a veteran of Italia 90; Aston Villa defender Ugo Ehiogu; Jason Wilcox; and Dennis Wise, who Venables believed had tried too hard to impress as opposed to singling him out for the China Jump debacle. The final twenty-two were: goalkeepers David Seaman, Ian Walker and Tim Flowers of Blackburn; defenders Tony Adams, Gareth Southgate, Stuart Pearce, Gary and Phil Neville, Sol Campbell of Arsenal and Steve Howey from Newcastle; in midfield Paul Gascoigne, Paul Ince, David Platt, Steve McManaman, Jamie Redknapp, Steve Stone, Darren Anderton and Nick Barmby; and four strikers in Alan Shearer, Teddy Sheringham, Robbie Fowler and Les Ferdinand.

Within a day Venables lost another player. Howey injured himself jogging and with the deadline for submitting the tournament squads gone, UEFA refused to allow England to call up a replacement. Venables also had to confirm the issue of the captaincy. Platt had filled in during Adams's extended injury lay-off, but Venables always viewed this as a temporary arrangement. Platt, it transpired, had other ideas. 'It was a decision that David surprised me by taking badly,' Venables reflected. 'To me, it was simple – Tony was the dominant figure in the squad and, as I reminded David, his captain at Arsenal. Why would he accept it in one situation and not the other? There was no answer to that.'

Venables also had to contend with the Gascoigne issue. His most high maintenance player was not cowed for long. Gascoigne was hyperactive, barely slept, and soon began a routine at Burnham Beeches that would endure for the next four weeks: rising at the crack of dawn, turning on the portable CD player in his room, and blasting awake the rest of the England party by playing 'Three Lions'. One evening, having decided he had not yet marked his birthday on home soil, Gascoigne left the hotel in search of redress. He pitched up at the bar of a smaller hotel nearby. Since he had bleached his hair blond and was wearing his England tracksuit and a pair of Doc Martens boots, he could not fail to be the centre of attention. Having sunk a few beers with the locals, Gascoigne then made his way back to Burnham Beeches in high spirits and brandishing a fat cigar. He headed to the dining room, where a gaggle of high-ranking FA brass had assembled for dinner, and ordered Champagne all round. 'That,' he recalled sometime after, 'was an occasion when Terry did tell me to calm down.' In this instance it was not only Venables who was moved to act. 'I saw David Seaman confront Gazza,' revealed Tony Adams. 'He told him to sort himself out, that he was letting the boys down. But I don't think you can cage a tiger like him.'

Venables always felt he could handle Gascoigne, but he was more taxed by yet another conundrum he now found himself facing: the increasing, hovering presence of his successor. Glenn Hoddle had agreed a deal to moonlight during the tournament as an analyst for ITV. In this guise he would be covering England games, which irked Venables considerably. Stewing in the background, Hoddle also made entreaties at Lancaster Gate to have some involvement with the England squad during the tournament. Pressed to accommodate him, Venables begrudgingly extended an invitation to Hoddle to come along and watch a training session. Venables, street smart, a scrapper, and Hoddle, who thought himself more of a thoroughbred, were as unalike as they were wary of each other. Kept apart, the two men had been able to maintain cordialities for the sake of appearances, but when Hoddle forced the issue that fragile state ended.

'I've got a picture from the day Hoddle turned up at Bisham Abbey,' recounts Henry Winter. 'It shows him halfway up a tree and watching over the players as they go through their paces. Terry was very polite to Hoddle, but he gave him short shrift. There was a lot of bitterness on

Venables's part. It hurt him that he wasn't going to be able to take that team on.'

Relations between the two men deteriorated. The very next day, Hoddle rang Venables and asked to be allowed to make further visits to Bisham Abbey and be granted more access to the team. Venables hit the roof. 'Terry made it clear he didn't want me around and I wasn't made particularly welcome,' Hoddle admitted four years later. 'The FA might have done more to help – perhaps they should have insisted I was allowed some involvement with players who I was soon expected to take to the World Cup finals. I've never really got close to Terry, despite working with him on TV. I don't think managers should make life more difficult than it already is for their successors.'

'I agreed to [Hoddle's initial visit] only to stop the situation developing into a major media row, but I was not happy,' Venables expanded in 2014. 'Glenn infuriated me after I opened the door for him to see the squad in action. We looked after him. He met the players, watched us train and had lunch with us. I was stunned when he phoned, basically wanting an observer's role for the tournament. To me, that was so damned arrogant. I said to him, "Glenn, these are my finals, you get yours next time". Until then he was to stay away from my squad. It seemed so unprofessional of him, and it carried the danger that it could confuse or distract the players. He should have known better.'

* * *

Before Venables's coronation, England had slumped to twenty-fifth in Fifa's world rankings, down in the boondocks of international football. Credibility had been restored under him, but Euro 96 was going to be the first, and only, true test of his mettle at England's helm. He promised his team would tackle the tournament playing with 'quality, versatility and flair', and above all with self-belief. The presence of the Dutch aside, the draw for the group stages had been kind, pairing England with Switzerland, a team they had beaten 3–1 at Wembley the previous November, as well as Scotland, also rank outsiders. Nonetheless, on the eve of the tournament, the sense out in the country was more of hope than expectation. The press were also still sharpening their knives. Previewing England's opening game with the Swiss in the *Sun*, John Sadler wrote: 'I do worry what awaits us over the next three weeks. I even worry about the implications should Terry Venables's team pull it off and win the European Championship: quite an advert for boisterousness, boozing and vandalism . . . [though] the very least that the country demands is that they be walking from the Wembley tunnel on Sunday, 30 June as finalists. Rarely has so much been owed to so many by so few.'

Sadler was certain of the key to England's success. 'For all his immature daftness off the field . . . Gascoigne remains one of the most eloquent footballers on earth,' he stated. 'Maybe not as quick as he used to be before putting his career in jeopardy through his own recklessness. Not quite, but he still has the ability to produce something unexpected and different to win a game. Don't worry,' Sadler confidently concluded, 'England will beat Switzerland, not least because the Swiss are sounding like non-qualifiers before a ball is even kicked.'

The Swiss squad had indeed endured a troubled build-up to the tournament. It was a different, seemingly weaker proposition to the one England had seen off seven months earlier. The impressive Roy Hodgson had been their coach that evening, but since then had been replaced by Artur Jorge, a well-travelled Portuguese with a moustache like a sweeping brush that gave him the appearance of a silent movie villain. Jorge was not a popular appointment in Switzerland. He had compounded this animosity with his apparently wilful approach to team selection, dropping from his squad the country's two most accomplished players, Alain Sutter and Adrian Knup. As his side laboured to a 2–1 defeat by the Czech Republic in their final Euro 96 warm-up game in Basel on 1 June, Jorge was barracked by sections of a fourteen thousand crowd, pockets of whom were waving banners reading: 'We want Hodgson back.'

Things did not improve for Jorge when the Swiss arrived at their London base for the tournament. He had expected his team to be able to train on the Wembley pitch forty-eight hours before they faced England. However, the FA put a block on this session, informing the Swiss that the venue would instead be hosting a dress rehearsal for the opening ceremony. 'We thought everything was fixed up until two days ago,' Swiss FA vice-president

Guido Cornella moaned to English reporters. 'When we phoned the FA they said they had sent us a fax some weeks ago to tell us, but we didn't receive it. That just isn't very good. Surely football is more important than something like a dress rehearsal?'

Euro 96 finally opened at Wembley on the sun-dappled afternoon of Saturday, 8 June. More than seventy-six thousand spectators flocked to the stadium early to watch the opening ceremony. Bringing a sense of occasion and colour to the event, ranks of English and Swiss supporters turned out with their faces painted the colours of their respective national flags, a new phenomenon in England at least. From lunchtime onwards the thronged approaches to the stadium were consumed by a tumult of noise, tournament fever uncorked and breaking out at last. 'On the coach going to the stadium, I phoned a friend I knew was already at Wembley to ask him if there was a buzz there,' Venables said afterwards. 'I was told we would be stunned by the support we would receive. He had seen nothing like it that he could remember for an England match.'

Given the events of the last few days, though, it was perhaps appropriate that the game was preceded by something that mixed low farce with unintended drama. Conceived as a glorious pageant celebrating an idealised version of England's medieval past, the opening ceremony incorporated a cast of hundreds variously attired as knights in shining armour along with Robin Hood and his merry men. The climax was a fly-past by the Red Arrows aerial display team, red, white and blue smoke trails billowing behind them. However, by the time the distinctive red jet aircraft flew into view, the whole affair had descended into an undignified scrabble that resembled nothing so much as a children's fancy dress party, but with added chaos.

'I remember thinking when the knights on horseback rode out that they were bound to churn the pitch up,' says Henry Winter. 'A horse got spooked and we subsequently discovered that Paul Ince's young son, Thomas, was one of the mascots during the pageant and that he was hurt in the melee. He hadn't been looked after very well and Paul got to hear about it. Only in England could you have an opening ceremony that almost kills an animal and upsets a key player before a crucial game.'

There was a palpable air of relief and a corresponding ratcheting up of the tension inside Wembley as kick-off neared. At ten to three, the England and Switzerland teams emerged from the Wembley tunnel, the brightness of the red, white and blue of their strips accentuated by the sunlight, the noise of the crowd amplified in the stadium bowl. After months of playing friendlies before sparse, apathetic Wembley crowds, the sight and sound of this eager mass of people was a positive shock to the England players. 'I shall never forget as long as I live the sense of expectancy before the game,' Teddy Sheringham recorded. 'The long walk out through the tunnel, the explosion of affection and support that hit us as we entered the stadium.'

Bolstered by this fanatical home support, and faced with workmanlike opposition, England began brightly and with purpose. Venables had been able to select his strongest side: Seaman in goal; Neville, Adams, Southgate and Pearce strung across the back; Gascoigne and Ince patrolling the central midfield areas and Anderton and McManaman stationed wide of them; Shearer and Sheringham up front. Platt, still sore about the captaincy, was dropped to the bench. It was the first time this eleven had played together.

Before the match there had been a chorus from football writers for Shearer to be dropped for Fowler. It took just twenty-three minutes for Shearer to hit back. Ince slipped a ball through to him on the right-hand edge of the Swiss penalty area. Sheringham moved into space to Shearer's left, but was ignored, as Shearer lashed the ball instead into the roof of the net from an acute angle. Shearer's blank façade dropped and he let out a scream of unbridled delight.

'It was brutal what had been happening to Shearer in the press, but he never complained,' says Henry Winter. 'I can remember a couple of occasions leaving Wembley with him after supposed friendlies and walking towards his car. Most footballers can out-walk a running journalist, but he was absolutely battered from playing with his back to goal for ninety minutes. He took the hits on and off the pitch. There were some strong characters in that England dressing room, but Shearer was very much among the leaders.'

'All the frustration of the last twenty-one months went into that shot,' Shearer said. 'I had my own reasons for wanting to do well. I had put my England future on the line by declaring I would score when it really mattered.'

Wembley exploded as much in relief as exultation. Ten minutes later, Shearer had a second opportunity, a header, but steered the ball wide. Up to that point, England had a grip on the game, the initiative seized through the midfield areas where Ince was a diligent barrier and Gascoigne a blur of kinetic energy. One of the things that set Gascoigne apart from other players was his ability to find space in even the most frenzied situations. He was doing so now in all areas of the pitch, and was distributing the ball with craft and cunning, opening up avenues for his team-mates and shifting the Swiss defenders out of their comfort zones.

Yet in the instant Shearer missed, it was as though all at once the drive and belief started to seep out from England. Gascoigne began to tire. The Swiss were galvanised. English passes were soon going astray, doubt creeping into the players' minds and uncertainty weighing them down. The Swiss were ascendant and should have equalised as half-time approached, their central striker Kübilay Turkyilmaz stealing in between Adams and Southgate, but hitting the crossbar with the goal at his mercy.

The second half continued in the same vein: England nervy and indecisive, the Swiss growing in conviction and menace. Venables withdrew Sheringham and McManaman with twenty minutes to go, and then Gascoigne, sending on Platt, Stone and Barmby to try and coax his team to life and wrest back the initiative. Still, though, England capitulated, giving up possession of the ball and bettered by the one team in the group they were expected to roll over. 'The game was a duffer,' Venables said later. 'Perhaps some of the players were nervous. We played well on the back of Alan's goal, but then it was as if our legs had been drained of energy. It was so frustrating, as it had been one of the issues that I had identified right at the start of my tenure.'

It was the Swiss who seized the last chance of the match. With just seven minutes remaining, Pearce tried to guard against an awkward ball into the England box, and was struck on the hand. Spanish referee Manuel Díaz Vega had no hesitation in awarding the Swiss a penalty. Turkyilmaz stepped up and redeemed himself, rifling his spot-kick past Seaman. The mood inside Wembley deflated like a punctured ball and the game ended drawn. What had looked on paper to be England's most routine game had stretched and troubled them.

Afterwards, the Swiss captain, Alain Geiger, told reporters that his team had expected England to burn out and had sat back and waited for them to do so. 'I was not surprised Gascoigne got tired,' Geiger elaborated. 'In the first half he was going to the left, right, backwards and forwards . . . It was too much for him. If you contain Gascoigne, you just have to wait for him to fade [and] without him the England team do not have much to offer.'

The result did little to quell the rancour being directed at Venables and his squad from the press battalions lined up outside England's Berkshire HQ. Coming down from his moralising pulpit, Rob Hughes wrote in *The Times* that Venables had been outwitted by his Swiss counterpart, the hapless-seeming Artur Jorge. 'The draw was as much as faded England deserved,' Hughes concluded. 'Venables snapped, "You don't just get given the points. It's not fantasy football." No, sir, not even close.' In the *Sun*, Martin Samuel struck an even more downbeat note. 'Unless this semi-detached England performance can be put right before next weekend's game with Scotland,' Samuel considered, 'football will not so much come home as take up temporary lodgings while it looks for somewhere more suitable to live – somewhere with a bit of class, in fact.'

CHAPTER SEVEN

'Where's Hendry? Has he gone to get me a pie?'

With a full week stretching out between the Swiss game and England's next group match, Venables decided to give his squad two days off. Since he would have rested them anyway, Venables naïvely believed his players would be better for having a break rather than being cooped up at Burnham Beeches. He was, in fact, releasing them into a hostile environment which their performance against the Swiss had done nothing to calm.

That Saturday night, Teddy Sheringham, Jamie Redknapp and Sol Campbell went out together to Faces, a popular bistro and nightclub in Ilford, Essex. Sheringham was also accompanied by his girlfriend, Nicole Smith, and another couple. The group stayed out until after two the next morning. According to Sheringham: 'We had a meal and a moderate amount to drink with our food.' The *Sun* presented a rather different view of their evening in the following Monday morning's issue. 'England aces back on booze!' screamed a splash headline in the paper. The accompanying report went on: 'Three England stars went boozing in a nightclub . . . as fans mourned their pitiful 1–1 draw with Switzerland.' Tory MP David Evans was wheeled out to strike an even more righteous note. 'It's a disgrace,' fumed Evans, who had been on Aston Villa's books in the 1950s and chairman of Luton Town for five years from 1984. 'The whole team, including the manager, should be sacked. This is not some great side that we can't do without.'

Back at Burnham, Venables continued his habit of getting the first editions of the papers delivered to him. He came down to breakfast that morning, unshaven and in his training kit, brandishing a copy of the tabloid and in a grim mood. In Venables's mind, the constant press hounding of him and his team was now bordering on traitorous and meant to hijack their tournament. 'There were no restrictions on the players, other than their own good, common sense,' Venables insisted later. 'Once again, we had to go through the inquisition of explaining the actions of these "bad boys". I knew that having a few drinks, even at two-thirty in the morning, would have no effect on their fitness to play six days and numerous training sessions later . . . Not only was so much of the criticism shocking and abusive, it was wrong. The press had turned it into a huge witch-hunt.'

Further north, in Cheshire, the actions of the German squad were also causing a stir. Fellow guests at the team hotel in Wilmslow were reported to be shocked by their players' habit of taking a daily sauna and then plunging into the hotel pool naked to cool off. Following a spate of complaints, the manager of Mottram Hall had asked that the Germans cover up but, claimed the *Sun* with a not even barely concealed xenophobic edge, 'the kooky Krauts refused, saying they always go skinny-dipping back home'.

Facing the Czech Republic at Old Trafford in their opening match on 9 June, the Germans had seemed daunting, menacing even, as they eased to a 2–0 victory. 'They look so big, so physical and threatening,' the beaten Czech goalkeeper, Petr Kouba, told reporters afterwards. 'They are a very formidable side.' The Germans had, though, lost their experienced defender and captain Jürgen Kohler, who injured knee ligaments in the first half and was subsequently ruled out of the tournament.

There were few surprises or fireworks generally during the opening round of fixtures. By and large, the games were cautious, unadventurous affairs with goals at a premium. In England's group, Scotland fought out a creditable goalless draw with Holland at Villa Park. There was also no separating Spain and an ageing Bulgaria team in Leeds, or Denmark and Portugal in Sheffield, both matches ending 1–1. As expected, France beat Romania in Newcastle and Croatia saw off Turkey at the City Ground, Nottingham, by the odd goal in each instance. The highest scoring contest was at Anfield where Italy edged past Russia, 2–1.

It fell instead to the supporters to bring Euro 96 to life. In Birmingham, thousands of Dutch and Scottish fans united to create a carnival atmosphere, the city centre and the streets around Villa Park being made resplendent in shades of orange and tartan. More than four hundred police officers bussed in to control the crowd were left idling as the opposing throngs mingled outside local pubs, smiling and good natured. Aston Villa secretary Steve Stride recalled the unique flavour of the contest for the BBC in 2010. 'I remember the Dutch supporters all marching from the city centre down to Villa Park,' Stride said. 'They all wore orange to a man, to a woman. Then they had got these funny hats on and trumpets. Everybody was in a great mood. There was such a mass of orange that they completely covered one half of the stadium. Coupled with the blue and white flags of the Scottish supporters, it was an awesome sight. It was one of the most incredible atmospheres I've ever witnessed at a football game.'

This was the scene being played out in cities up and down the country. Nottingham hosted thousands of Croat, Turkish, Portuguese and Danish supporters, the latter group using the city as a base from which to commute to their team's games in nearby Sheffield. One hotelier hosted four hundred Danish fans for dinner in a single sitting and marvelled to the *Nottingham Evening Post* that they were 'the best behaved football fans in the world'. Pubs, clubs and restaurants in the city enjoyed a boom in takings. By contrast, the Nottingham Civic Society recorded its worst month on record for customers booking on to its historical walks around the city. Sixty miles west of Nottingham, the sleepy Cheshire town of Alsager was roused by the presence of the Italian squad who were training on the Crewe & Alsager College campus and brought with them a retinue of Italian sports reporters and television crews.

The Italians were involved in the first really stirring game of the tournament on the evening of Friday, 14 June at Anfield. Hot favourites to beat the Czech Republic, and thereby secure their passage to the quarter-finals, the Azzurri were instead victims of an outstanding individual performance from Karel Poborsky, the Czechs' slight, long-haired right-winger who taunted their defence and led his team to an unexpected 2–1 win. Displaying shameless double standards, the *Sun* gleefully revealed that the Czechs' success was otherwise founded on 'a cocktail of drinking and bonking', their players allegedly revelling in five a.m. boozing sessions and conjugal visits from their wives and girlfriends. 'We came to this tournament with absolutely nothing to lose,' reasoned their veteran sweeper, Miroslav Kadlec, 'so we thought, "Let's just enjoy it".'

Across the country, other matters, both trivial and serious, were vying for attention. That same Friday, the BBC broadcast *Top of the Pops* in its new tea-time slot after an unbroken run of thirty-two years of recording the temperature of popular music in Britain on a Thursday evening. Though no one knew it yet, it was the beginning of a long, slow death for this British institution. The next morning, at eleven-thirty precisely, the IRA detonated a bomb outside the Arndale Shopping Centre in the heart of Manchester.

It was a three-hundred-pound device, the second largest that the IRA had let off on mainland Britain, but a blood-bath on the city's biggest shopping day was avoided. At ten o'clock that morning a coded warning was sent to a local television station. Police were quick to arrive on the scene, evacuating the Arndale and clearing the area of shoppers. Army bomb disposal experts were in the process of investigating a white van parked outside a Marks & Spencer store when the device secreted inside it was detonated remotely. Two hundred and twelve people, many of them standing behind the police cordon, were injured by flying glass.

It was the second devastating blow that year to the Prime Minister's attempts to broker an end to the Troubles in Northern Ireland. On the evening of 10 February, the IRA had exploded a bomb at Canary Wharf in London's Docklands, killing two people and causing £100 million worth of damage to surrounding buildings. It also brought to an end a ceasefire negotiated by Major and which had held for seventeen months.

England's second game of Euro 96 kicked off at Wembley just three-and-a-half hours after the Manchester bombing. It pitted them against their oldest and fiercest rivals, Scotland. At Burnham Beeches, Terry Venables had spent the week plotting the best way to navigate a game he knew would be more like a typical Premier League encounter, which is to say frenzied, messy and without time to draw breath.

'Terry's knowledge and appreciation of tactics was extraordinary,' says John Motson, the BBC's voice of football. 'I went down to see him at Burnham before the game and he told me exactly what he was going to do. He wanted to get this thing going between McManaman and Anderton. Everybody called them wing backs, but Terry said to me, "No, they are wide players in an attacking system". At that moment I thought, "Hello, he might just do this and go on and win the tournament".'

England versus Scotland was football's longest established international fixture, its roots stretching back to 1870. It was then that Charles Alcock, secretary to the FA and captain of the pre-eminent club team of the day, Wanderers, issued a challenge through several Scottish newspapers for a representative team from north of the border to take on England. An unofficial contest between the two nations duly took place on 5 March that year at the Oval cricket ground in London. Alcock was injured and not able to play, but nonetheless officiated as a perhaps not altogether impartial linesman in a spirited 1–1 draw.

A series of similar ad hoc matches between the two nations followed in close succession at the Oval, but the first England–Scotland encounter to be officially recognised did not take place until 30 November 1872, St Andrew's Day. This fixture was staged at a Scottish cricket ground, Hamilton Crescent in Glasgow. Four thousand supporters paid a shilling each to witness the match, which by all accounts went ahead in a relaxed, even convivial atmosphere. The Scottish team was entirely made up of players from the Queen's Park club in Glasgow, the strongest in the land, while the redoubtable Alcock led an English side comprising representatives from nine different clubs. Scotland came closest to breaking the deadlock towards the end of the game, Robert Leckie lifting the ball on to the length of tape strung between two goalposts and which then passed for a crossbar, but it finished goalless. England won the next meeting, 4–2 at the Oval on 8 March 1873, and for the next hundred years or so held the whip hand in what became an annual event.

In 1884, the Home International Championship was founded, with England, Scotland, Wales and Northern Ireland playing each other at the end of each season. The series endured until 1984. During the course of the championships, the temperature of the England–Scotland clashes rose and they boiled up into fervent, hostile affairs. England dominated, winning fifty-four titles. In 1961, they eviscerated the Scots 9–3 at Wembley, Jimmy Greaves helping himself to a hat-trick to secure the biggest margin of victory between the two sides. However, the Scots had their glorious moments, too. On 31 March 1928, their 'Wembley Wizards' routed England 5–1 at the Auld Enemy's home stadium. And England's first defeat after winning the World Cup was also inflicted on them by Scotland at Wembley, a 3–2 reverse in a European Championship qualifier in April 1967.

On occasion, both tragedy and a venal ugliness ran alongside the blood and thunder. Twenty-six Scottish spectators were killed and five hundred and seventeen injured at Ibrox on 5 April 1902 when terracing in the overcrowded west stand collapsed fifty-one minutes into a game against England. Seventy-five years later at Wembley, and after their team had beaten the English 2–1, thousands of Scots supporters rampaged across the pitch, digging up turf and tearing down the goalposts.

It was this rich history that burnished every England–Scotland game with added meaning and deeper significance. The Euro 96 clash was given an additional edge because it was their first meeting in more than seven years. Both sides also went into the game with the extra burden of knowing that Holland had turned over the Swiss 2–0 at Villa Park two days earlier. The losers were facing an early exit from the tournament. The build-up to the match was coloured by side issues and dramas. On 11 June, Scotland's commercial television station, STV, confirmed that it had edited the montage sister channel ITV was using to open its Euro 96 coverage. Specifically, STV had cut out the soundtrack, a rendering of the English hymn *Jerusalem*, and clips of the white cliffs of Dover and Bobby Moore lifting the Jules Rimet trophy.

South of the border, the question of Paul Gascoigne was again vexing the football press. On the eve of the game, *The Times*, fixated on the issue, ran a piece headlined: 'Why England must discard their joker now.' Urging England's head coach to drop Gascoigne, David Miller wrote: 'It was apparent Paul Gascoigne had become a liability long before the ill-fated Cathay Pacific flight . . .

Venables is at fault for not imposing a stricter regime.' Gascoigne, though, was revving up for the tournament, focused in the only way he knew how. 'We all used to grab a few hours' sleep before each of our games,' said Alan Shearer. 'Everyone that is, except for Gazza. He was so hyperactive he rarely sat still, let alone went to sleep.'

Out in the country, the prospect of the game was also exciting passions. In Wolverhampton, a twenty-four-year-old sports teacher, Andy Banberry, had intended hosting a beery get-together with his mates that Saturday afternoon with the England–Scotland clash as the main attraction. His plans were stymied the Friday before the match, though, when his football-sick partner, Fiona Pearse, hocked their television set to a local pawnshop for £90. 'We had words when Andy got home and found out what I'd done,' Pearse told the *Sun* with no doubt a degree of understatement. 'But when I explained the football was driving me nuts, he agreed to watch the game at the pub and I've promised him the telly back as soon as the whole thing is over.'

Staged in front of a packed, partisan Wembley, the game itself took on the hellfire intensity of battle. It pitted club colleagues against each other. Shearer later recalled his Blackburn team-mate, Colin Hendry, growling at him as the two sets of players lined up to shake hands before kick-off. The Scotland manager, Craig Brown, had assembled a hard-working side blessed with reserves of grit but also a dash of guile. Its rearguard was marshalled by Hendry and another rugged centre-half, Spurs' Colin

Calderwood. A trio of able midfielders pulled the strings in front of this barrier: the captain, Gary McAllister of Leeds, Gascoigne's Rangers club-mate, Stuart McCall, and John Collins of Celtic. At the point of their attack was Gordon Durie, also of Rangers, nippy and as irksome to defenders as a buzzing fly.

Venables retained the starting eleven from the Swiss game, hoping to finesse his way to victory, to turn McManaman and Anderton loose. But the Scots snapped and bit at them, pressing the spaces and keeping the game on a leash. The first half went by in a blur of perpetual motion, neither team able to assert control in advanced areas of the pitch. Gascoigne found himself engaged in trench warfare, Ince at his side, their opponents' tight attentions cutting off England's most reliable supply line at its source.

'I anticipated it would be tough and messy,' said Venables. 'As the game progressed in a brilliantly charged atmosphere, it became clear we could do with just a little more creativity. The half-time break is when you earn the right to call yourself a manager. You have fifteen minutes to sit the players down and calmly tell them what you have seen and what you want covered. I always preferred to emphasise the things they could be doing better, so they could sense I wasn't entirely happy. If they got com-placent, they might get sloppy.'

Just a minute into the second period, Venables sent on Jamie Redknapp for Stuart Pearce, flooding the midfield and intending to seize and then monopolise possession of the ball. The move paid off within seven minutes. Gary Neville found space to deliver a cross for Shearer to head into the Scottish net. Scotland, though, refused to yield and began to gain footholds further up the field, threatening England's goal. Ultimately, the contest pivoted on two minutes of high drama.

On seventy-six minutes, Durie raced into the England box and tempted Adams into a reckless tackle. McAllister stepped up to take the penalty, but the ball appeared to shift on the spot at the moment of impact, whether blown by a breeze or rolling into a divot. Seaman dived to save. Italian referee Pierluigi Pairetto spotted an infringement from the corner that followed and gave England a free-kick. It was arced out to Anderton on England's left-wing. He hooked it on in the general direction of Gascoigne.

'Gazza's temperament can reach a high pitch prior to any match,' Terry Venables observed in 2014. 'He was hyped up for this one, but nicely so, in control. [What followed] was testimony to one of the great football talents we have produced in this country.' In the short span of time between the ball arriving at Gascoigne's feet and what occurred next, mere seconds, it was possible to appreciate the divide separating truly great players from all others. It was as if in his mind Gascoigne was able to freeze the action, pick out the one route to goal available to him, and then have the total command of skill and nerve to follow it through. He guided the ball over the onrushing Hendry's head, took it on the bounce and sent it just beyond the despairing reach of the Scottish keeper,

Andy Goram. As an act, it was graceful, audacious and otherworldly.

'That will always go down as one of the great Wembley goals,' says John Motson. 'Like many others, I thought Euro 96 was going to be Gazza's last chance and he managed something amazing. He had that ability to make something out of nothing. The pity was that he never again produced a moment in international football that wrote his name across headlines like that one.'

'The whole complexion of the tournament, and the mood of the nation, hinged on those sixty seconds,' Anderton told the *Mirror* in 2014. 'Nobody loved a big stage like Gazza. Those occasions were made for him. If Euro 96 ended up being a great party, he was the one that got everyone on their feet.'

For a split-second, the Wembley crowd seemed suspended in collective disbelief. Then a thunderous roar rolled down on to the pitch. Gascoigne ran across the face of the Scottish goal and prostrated himself on the pitch, mouth agape, waiting for Sheringham to sprint over and squirt a bottle of water down his throat. So it was that the dentist's chair scene from Hong Kong was re-enacted under a blazing English sun. 'I will never forget Gazza as he got up,' Sheringham added in the *Mirror*. 'He asked Goram why he had bothered diving. Then he said, "Where's Hendry? Has he gone to get me a pie?"'

Afterwards, in the victorious English dressing room, Gascoigne was like a man possessed, shouting and screaming out his joy as he took piggy-back rides from his jubilant team-mates. English hopes were rekindled. Soon after his post-match press conference, Venables was walking through the bowels of the stadium when he was spotted by a gaggle of police constables gathering at the end of their shift. By his account, they took up a chant, 'England, England!', and threw their helmets in the air. It sounds an unlikely, apocryphal story, but it was nonetheless true that the tide of England's Euro 96 had turned. The shift was marked by an editorial in the *Daily Mirror*. Headlined 'Mr. Paul Gascoigne: an apology', it began: 'Gazza is no longer a fat, drunken imbecile. He is, in fact, a football genius.'

At around the time the papers rolled off the presses, Gascoigne was holding court at Burnham Beeches, celebrating his renaissance with a cigar and a bottle of brandy.

CHAPTER EIGHT

*'Wembley was rocking, celebrating like I had
never seen or heard it before'*

Paul Gascoigne's wonder goal appeared not just to lift
England, but also to have elevated the whole tournament to a higher plane. On the pitch, the shackles came
off the other competing teams over the course of the next
five days, up to the end of the group stage. Where disciplined defending and fear of defeat had ruled the first
wave of games, it was now the case that attacking football
and goals came to the fore as teams strived to reach the
knockout phase.

A day after the England–Scotland encounter, Germany
swept aside Russia 3–0 at Old Trafford and Croatia beat
Denmark by the same score at Hillsborough. This second
game witnessed a feat of individual brilliance to match
Gascoigne's. Croatia's Davor Šuker, tall and elegant, took
a raking pass in his stride and glided to the corner of the
Danish box, whereupon he chipped the ball with the outside of his left foot up and over the Danes' giant goalkeeper,
Peter Schmeichel. The precision, the deftness of it, took

the breath away. Both results were enough to assure the victorious teams' safe passage through to the next round. Like many of the other games, both were played out to banks of empty seats, the armies of visiting supporters joined by just smatterings of home observers, the English saving their attentions – and money – for their own national team.

France and Spain qualified for the quarter-finals on Tuesday, 18 June. At Elland Road, Spain saw off Romania 2–1, substitute Guillermo Amor snatching a late winner. The French beat the hapless Bulgarians 3–0 at St James' Park, Newcastle. *Les Bleus* were evolving into a formidable team. It was one based on the bedrock of such stalwarts as Laurent Blanc and Didier Deschamps, plus a sprinkling of a younger crop of more finessing footballers like Christian Karembeu and Christophe Dugarry. However, their new playmaker, Zinedine Zidane, who had inherited the role from Eric Cantona, was struggling for form and with him out of sorts they were like a ticking clock that could not quite keep time.

A drop of poison also laced the France versus Bulgaria match. Early in the game French defender Marcel Desailly was booked for a cynical foul on Bulgaria's talisman, striker Hristo Stoichkov. After the match, Desailly claimed that Stoichkov had responded by directing a volley of racist abuse at him and then at France's other black players as the contest progressed. Stoichkov was unrepentant. 'I did say that, but I hope [Desailly] takes it as a man,' he informed reporters the next day. 'It is normal. If you take a microphone around every player, they would all be say-ing things like that.'

Ever since the dark days of the 1970s, when the National Front viewed football stadiums as fertile recruiting grounds, English nationalism had been associated with the ugly stamp of racism. Adopting it as their own, the NF and other far-right organisations had tainted the English flag of St George, so that it had become an emblem of shame. In marked contrast to the Scots' cross of St Andrew, the Welsh dragon and the Irish tricolour, the English flag had barely been displayed in polite company, much less honoured. Indeed, just two months earlier, Richard Littlejohn, tub-thumping columnist with the deeply con-servative *Daily Mail*, had bemoaned its invisibility and the absence of any sense of collective national pride to mark St George's Day on 23 April.

Even before Euro 96 reclaimed the flag, though, the rise of Britpop had reflected and encouraged a growing feeling of patriotism among the English. This ran in tandem with the tail-end of Thatcherism, the crumbling of Tory rule and the class divisions that had festered, and an emerging sense of optimism being encouraged by Tony Blair and New Labour. The spectacle of Noel Gallagher's Union Jack guitar at Maine Road that April had brought this renewed sense of Englishness out into the open. It was given its name by a song written in 1968 by pop satirists the Bonzo Dog Doo-Dah Band and revived that May by American ice-cream makers Ben & Jerry's for their new vanilla, strawberries and shortbread concoction: Cool Britannia.

However, it was at Euro 96 that the fetters that had been shackling patriotism were truly turned loose, given wings and a very English dimension as the England team began to win. And win with panache. The St George flag had re-emerged for England's opening match, waved on flag-sticks and banners, painted on to faces. It now became increasingly prevalent at each successive England game at Wembley. The distinctive red cross on a white background was also being shamelessly hung up in the front windows of houses, shops and office buildings the length and breadth of the land. Managers at the House of Flags factory at Kimbolton in Cambridgeshire were forced to take on extra workers to keep up with demand as England supporters snapped up their £36 St George flags at a rate of three thousand a day.

'Flag-makers cannot produce enough red crosses,' noted columnist Brian Appleyard, writing in the more moderate *Independent*. 'A national identity, formerly cloaked by irony and self-loathing, has been resuscitated by football . . . The English have suffered because, since the War, they have been obliged to carry the entire burden of imperial guilt. Euro 96 has, among other things, produced a popular revulsion against bland globalism.' Matt Dickinson remembers: 'A number of columnists began writing about how this was a nicer form of patriotism we were seeing. It was certainly again possible for you to display the English flag in your window and not have someone automatically assume that you were a mad racist.'

At Burnham Beeches there was further evidence of this billowing, feel-good mood. Surrounded by ancient woodland, Burnham had been used by successive England squads for the relative peace and privacy it afforded. It had remained undisturbed during the first week of the tournament, especially after the anti-climax of the Switzerland game. Such noise as there was came from birdsong, the babble of a stream and, of course, Paul Gascoigne. However, in the days leading up to the Holland match, crowds of supporters and well-wishers began to throng the tree-lined avenues leading to the grand white hotel building. The clamour became so great that the FA had to organise a rota for the players to go out and sign autographs.

'It's such a difficult place to get to, but it was madness outside the hotel,' recalls Henry Winter. 'People were climbing up the trees and singing, "Football's coming home". The team coach going to Bisham Abbey or Wembley had to leave ten, fifteen minutes earlier just to get through the crowds. I remember the FA being very concerned that someone was going to get run over. In fact, David Seaman did drive over a fan's foot when he went off fishing one day. You really did get the feeling at the time that people were spilling out and celebrating England and being English. I was also acutely aware that this wasn't just a celebration of eleven men and football. It was a whole phenomenon and to do with our place in the world. There was a huge sense of national pride. It wasn't just kids strolling up to Burnham Beeches either, but fathers, grandfathers and three or four generations of families. Those were extraordinary scenes.'

Such was the scale and intensity of this upsurge that at least one high-ranking official believed it might have a more far-reaching influence. Alastair Campbell, Tony Blair's combative press strategist, recorded in his diary his fear that the exultant atmosphere being engendered by the England team would somehow rub off on the flailing Prime Minister and encourage him to call an early General Election. 'On the way out [of the England–Scotland game], you got a sense of just how much of a feel-good factor you could get going on the back of all this,' Campbell wrote on 15 June. '"Football's coming home", was being sung everywhere you went, plus the less melodious "Eng-er-lund …" The Manchester bomb was massive across all the media and yet there was no sense of fear in London, which was odd, and again presumably an effect of the football.'

English optimism was stoked further by the apparent absence of a genuinely dominant team at the championship. The ever-impressive Germans had looked typically strong and obdurate in their first two games, but with possible vulnerabilities in attack and defence they were not unbeatable. Spain and Italy, like France, had gifted squads but their stuttering starts had also exposed flaws in their make-ups. The Dutch were the other fancied side. Their pedigree was impeccable and founded upon the 'total football' principles introduced into their national game by Rinus Michels, a crusading coach whose methods Venables greatly admired.

A striker with Ajax and Holland during the 1940s and 1950s, Michels made his reputation as a brilliant strategist and team-builder. At Ajax, Michels honed an attacking style of football based on players interchanging positions and being fluid in possession. He took Ajax to two European Cup finals and groomed such world-class exponents of his idyll as Johan Cruyff and Johan Neeskens. Michels successfully transplanted his theories to international football and led an outstanding Dutch team to the 1974 World Cup final, where they were unlucky to lose to the hosts, West Germany. He was victorious, though, at the 1988 Euros with a side that featured the sublime talents of Ruud Gullit, Marco van Basten and Frank Rijkaard. In between Michels spells, the Dutch had also reached the 1978 World Cup final where they were once again unfortunate in facing the host nation, Argentina in this instance.

Dutch sides were conditioned to play with skill, flair and panache. However, the Euro 96 vintage, though capable enough and in spite of Mick McCarthy's gushing endorsement, was not a truly great or unified team. Coach Guus Hiddink was able to call on world-class footballers like Dennis Bergkamp, Patrick Kluivert and Clarence Seedorf, but perhaps the most telling measure of his team was its right-side midfielder, Jordi Cruyff. The young Cruyff was a polished footballer in his own right, but no more than a shadow of his father, the imperious Johan. Though seeded, the Dutch had been forced to navigate a precarious route to the finals, finishing behind the Czechs in their qualifying group and having to face Jack Charlton's Republic of Ireland in a closely fought play-off match staged at Anfield back in December.

Kluivert, the team's talismanic young striker, had scored both goals that beat Ireland that night, but was now entirely out of sorts. In September of the previous year, he had been involved in a car crash which resulted in the death of a fifty-six-year-old man. Kluivert was subsequently convicted of dangerous driving, but escaped a custodial sentence. He had, though, arrived at the Dutch training camp seeming so distracted that Hiddink had left him on the bench for their opening two games.

Hiddink's squad also had a second trait that was characteristic of Dutch teams, and this one more of a scourge. It was riven with factions and easily bruised egos, and as the game with England loomed, it was on the point of imploding. The core of the party was made up of eight players from an excellent contemporary Ajax side who, under head coach Louis Van Gaal, had won the Champions League in 1995 and been beaten finalists that May. Among them were the captain, Danny Blind, and four impressive young black footballers, Kluivert, Edgar Davids, Winston Bogarde and Michael Reiziger. A fifth, Clarence Seedorf, had left the club for Sampdoria just the previous year. As the tournament developed, allegations began to circulate about the Dutch camp of a damaging split opening up between this group and the contingent of white players. These were further fuelled by the publication of a photograph of the squad having lunch together in the grounds of their hotel. It showed the five black players hunkered down at one table, away from the others.

In fact, the division wrenching the Dutch apart was not exclusively about race, but prompted by a series of smouldering grievances. Another strong root of it was money. It was a condition at Ajax that young players coming into the team were paid less than their more experienced counterparts and this had fostered resentment. The slow-burning tensions erupted to the surface just three days before their date at Wembley with England. After the stalemate with Scotland, Hiddink dropped Davids to the bench for the match against the Swiss and only employed him as a late substitute. In the dressing room after the game, Davids confronted the coach, accusing him of being 'too deep in the ass of Danny Blind'. In response, Hiddink expelled Davids from the squad and ordered him home. The fragile threads that had until now bound the Dutch together were liable to snap under the slightest pressure.

By contrast, England spent the three days between the Scotland and Holland games in high spirits. FA officials informed Venables that good luck messages were flooding in to Lancaster Gate from across the country and he relayed them to his squad. At Burnham Beeches the players relaxed watching films, comedy videos, listening to music or playing cards. Gascoigne, Fowler and

McManaman interrupted Venables's television interviews by running around in the background with white sheets over their heads and making ghostly noises. The three of them had confused Burnham with Bisham Abbey, since it was the medieval manor house that was in fact supposed to be haunted.

Venables played his own practical joke on the over-fussy David Davies, summoning the FA man to the hotel one morning to inform him police had visited the previous night. Davies listened ashen-faced as Venables recounted how a local dignitary, one 'Colonel Saunders', had complained that his teenaged daughter was shocked to see a naked man running through their garden earlier that evening. The suspect, Venables proclaimed, had bleached blond hair. Almost hyperventilating, Davies was on the point of ordering Gascoigne to a kangaroo court before a guffawing Venables revealed his hand.

The head coach also kept chipping away at his players, working on their collective state of mind, telling them the Dutch match was the biggest of their lives while at the same time exhorting them to be fearless. The night before the game Venables held a pivotal team meeting at the hotel. He gave a rousing, impassioned speech meant to inspire and steel his charges, and then went on to pick apart their opponents in forensic detail. 'Tony Adams always tells me that they came out of that team talk knowing they were going to win the game,' says Ian Ridley. 'Venables had gone through every one of the Dutch players' strengths and weaknesses, then through the England players' strengths. He told them precisely how they were going to play and where they were going to put the ball in certain areas.' Adams added: 'Every player left convinced he was better than his counterpart and that the Dutch were simply there for the taking. There was no way we were going to lose.'

Venables intended to field the same starting eleven once again, but with a tactical tweak on this occasion. Since Hiddink preferred to set his side up with a flat back three, Venables meant to move McManaman into an advanced area to join Shearer and Sheringham at the point of England's attack. He anticipated this would force Hiddink to employ an extra defender, compromising the Dutch's capacity to mount sorties from midfield, a feature of their play.

The evening of Tuesday, 18 June was hot and sticky with London basking in its fifteenth consecutive day of sweltering temperatures. England went into the game knowing a point would be enough to take them through to the next round, but that victory was required for them to win the group and be able to play their remaining fixtures at Wembley. The fact it was England's first night match of the tournament seemed to have brought a heightened atmosphere to the old stadium. There was a tangible sense of anticipation and of euphoria bottled up and waiting to burst out. Long before kick-off, the now familiar chant of 'Football's coming home' was rolling down in waves from the teeming terraces. 'Being there at Wembley that night was absolutely brilliant,' recalls Ian Broudie. 'It didn't feel like my song anymore, but as if it belonged out there, in the country. I guess it's a bit like having a Christmas hit. You get kind of sick of it until Christmas rolls around and then it sounds all right again.'

When the two teams walked on to the pitch, the noise went up another notch. It reached a thunderous crescendo, levelled out and settled at a bated, expectant rumble. 'The feeling of sheer wonder, well-being and optimism will never be bettered in my professional life,' Venables reflected later. 'It confirmed what I always believed: that the English are unbeatable as a nation when they have a common cause. This was the moment I felt I had been born for.'

England took the initiative from the kick-off. McManaman twisted his marker Bogarde this way and that, the Dutch at first caught out by Venables's tactical sleight of hand, and then becoming consumed by self-doubt. The catalyst for each England offensive was Gascoigne. It was not apparent whether Hiddink had detailed someone to man-mark him. If he had, the Dutch coach's appointed guard was not able to get close to Gascoigne, never mind stop him from playing. A seven-minute film has since been posted on YouTube which distils the game to just Gascoigne's touches on the ball. Watching it is instructive and also mesmerising. It reveals that Gascoigne found space whenever he took the ball, and once he had it, never gave it away. Not once did he fail to put his team on the front foot, prodding, popping and measuring his passes across a range of angles, but always moving the ball ahead and with a purpose. Like a conductor leading an orchestra, Gascoigne set and controlled the tempo of the game: slowing it down when the Dutch threatened to press, quickening it up by taking no more than one or two touches on the ball, his passes coming short and quick like arpeggio bursts.

England's first goal arrived in the twenty-first minute, Shearer converting a penalty after Blind had hacked down Ince. The Dutch reeled and England comfortably saw out the rest of the half, keeping them at arm's length, toying with them like a cat with a mouse. After the interval, the home side grew even more in confidence and daring. Six minutes into the half, Sheringham headed in a looping corner from Gascoigne to make it 2–0. Six minutes further on and it was three. Gascoigne, now so dominant he seemed able to bend the game to his will, drove into the Dutch box, tempted defenders to him and then cut the ball back to Sheringham who shaped to shoot, but passed square instead for Shearer to fire into the top corner. It was an exquisitely worked goal, England pulling the Dutch one way and then another, before plunging a rapier through their exposed heart.

'It is possible that one match out of thousands can provide you with everything you believe in as a manager,' Venables mused in 2014. 'It was perfection: my most thrilling moment in football. That performance was the culmination of two and a half years of preparation. In that time I had convinced all the staff and players, not without being questioned, that we had the ability and character to change the style in which we played at international level.

It was intended to be a long-term strategy to take us on to the World Cup finals in France two years later.'

'I was marking Jordi Cruyff,' said Pearce. 'When we went three up, he turned to me and said, "I cannot believe this is happening". I said, "You better fucking believe it". But I thought to myself that he seemed to be abdicating himself of all responsibility.' Cruyff's and his team's dissolution was not an important consideration when Sheringham swept in a rebound off the Dutch keeper, Edwin van der Sar, after sixty-one minutes. Or even when Kluivert, on as a substitute, grabbed a late consolation for the Dutch. That goal ensured that they would eliminate the Scots – who were beating the Swiss 1–0 at Villa Park at the same time – on goal difference and as such was celebrated by the Wembley crowd as if it was a fifth for England. In the relative privacy of the tunnel after the match, Venables savoured the moment, embracing Don Howe, Bryan Robson, Dave Sexton and the other members of his staff. He had measured himself against his benchmark and come up standing tall. 'We had beaten one of the most sophisticated systems in world football,' he said later. 'We had taken the Dutch apart. Wembley was rocking, celebrating like I had never seen or heard it before.'

England's supremo was left with just one issue to resolve from the game. With Ince picking up a booking in the first half, and now suspended for the next match, Venables had withdrawn him on the hour and sent on his likely replacement for the quarter-final, David Platt.

LEFT: All smiles for now: Glenn Hoddle and Terry Venables prior to the London press conference to unveil Hoddle as Venables' successor on 2 May 1996. *© Stu Forster/ ALLSPORT*

ABOVE: (From left) Robbie Fowler, Steve McManaman and Jamie Redknapp visit the Great Wall at the beginning of the England squad's ill-fated pre-Euro 96 tour to China and Hong Kong. *© Popperfoto/Getty Images*

ABOVE: 'An awesome sight': the Tartan Army mass at Euro 96. © *Neal Simpson/ Empics Sport*

ABOVE: Gazza's 'dentist's chair' celebration after his decisive goal against Scotland at Wembley. © *Colorsport/Andrew Cowie*

ABOVE: The brains trust behind the Euro 96 anthem, 'Three Lions': (from left) Ian Broudie, Frank Skinner and David Baddiel. © *Patrick Ford/Redferns*

ABOVE: The aftermath of the IRA bomb attack on Manchester's Arndale Shopping Centre on Saturday, 15 June 1996. © *PA Photos*

LEFT: Alan Shearer's penalty launches England's 4–1 demolition of Holland. Terry Venables said of the game: 'It was perfection, my most thrilling moment in football.' © *Colorsport*

ABOVE: 'Wembley was rocking like I had never seen or heard it before': Shearer and Teddy Sheringham seal the triumph over the Dutch. © *Colorsport*

'A quite dreadful thing': Piers Morgan's *Daily Mirror* front page sets the tabloid tone for England's clash with Germany. © *Mirrorpix*

ABOVE: 'Oh no!'; Gareth Southgate's fateful penalty against the Germans. © *Colorsport*

ABOVE: 'My first reaction was disbelief, then sympathy for Gareth': Venables attempts to console the 'inconsolable' Southgate in the immediate aftermath of the semi-final shoot-out. © *Popperfoto/Getty Images*

LEFT: 'Why didn't you just blast it?': Southgate's mum chastised him after the Germany match. © *Colorsport*

ABOVE: 'This is history!': Oasis at Knebworth, August 1996. © *Mick Hutson/Redferns*

ABOVE: Oasis in their 1996 pomp. 'Everything up to that point was fucking brilliant,' said Noel Gallagher. 'I don't even remember getting a hangover.' © *Brian Rasic/Getty Images*

ABOVE: Gazza's last hurrah. With Ian Wright and Sol Campbell after England had held Italy to a 0–0 draw in Rome that secured their qualification for the 1998 World Cup finals in France. © *Popperfoto/Getty Images*

ABOVE: End of the line: David Beckham's sending off was the prelude to Argentina sending England crashing out of the 1998 World Cup finals. © *Colorsport/Andrew Cowie*

Ince reacted angrily, infuriating Venables. 'Ince always had the capacity to be a nightmare,' Venables recorded. 'When we returned to the dressing room I gave him full vent to my anger at his behaviour. He came and sat next to me on the coach back to Burnham and we sorted out our differences.'

Before boarding the bus, the England management and players met up with their families in the banqueting hall upstairs at Wembley. Venables's dad, Fred, his two daughters, Tracey and Nancy, with grandson Sam, were waiting for him. Ted Buxton told him that Sir Stanley Matthews, Venables's idol as a player, had been at the game. Matthews, Buxton said, had become quite emotional afterwards and stated that it was the best England performance he had seen in years. Venables had come straight up from his press conference, a rare event in that he was afforded a conquering hero's welcome by the contingent of English football writers.

That status would also be reflected in the newspaper headlines the next morning. 'Shades of '66: the glory has returned to Wembley at last,' gushed the *Daily Mirror*. This was the same paper, remember, who three weeks earlier had written off England as 'plonkers'. Writing in the *Sun*, Martin Samuel celebrated 'a sixty-two-minute rollercoaster ride of pure joy. Could it be that Terry Venables has fashioned a team capable of beating – no, thrashing – the best in Europe?' The performance was even hailed across the North Sea in Holland, where the Dutch daily *De Telegraaf* admitted:

'[The Dutch team] was taught a lesson in sharpness, defence, finishing – everything.' Bookmakers William Hill responded by slashing England's odds to win the tournament to three-to-one, installing them as second favourites behind the Germans. 'After the Dutch game, there was the sense that anything was possible,' says Henry Winter. 'The buzz that had been there through Italia 90, and disappeared under Graham Taylor, came back with a vengeance.'

'The road back to Burnham Beeches was lined with supporters waving banners and cheering,' recalled Teddy Sheringham. 'I remember holding the telephone to the window of my hotel room and telling my girlfriend to listen to the singing of the crowd outside.' Thousands more England fans congregated that night in Trafalgar Square to celebrate a famous victory, frolicking in its fountains until nearly dawn. Back at their hotel, the England party also made merry, Venables's players entirely absolved now of their recent sins, though on this occasion they did so away from prying eyes.

'By now, we had settled into an after-match routine which underlined how we had bonded together as a unit,' said Alan Shearer. 'We would all congregate in the hotel bar for a couple of drinks, a few laughs and invariably an impromptu karaoke session. Terry was usually there in the thick of it. It was not unusual to see him leading the singing in the bar, or mixing with the lads if we had a film race night. We usually stayed up until two or three in the morning. It was virtually impossible to sleep after the big games. None of us dared say it for risk of tempting fate, but we knew now we could go all the way in the tournament and win it.'

CHAPTER NINE

'Enjoy it, because it might not get as good as this again'

England's thrashing of the Dutch intensified interest in Euro 96. More than two-thirds of the eighteen million audience for the country's most popular television show, the BBC1 soap *EastEnders*, had reportedly switched over to watch ITV's live broadcast of the game. In the days that followed there was a clamour for the remaining tickets for England's quarter-final against Spain. Thousands queued at Wembley Stadium from five in the morning on 19 June to try and snap up the last of the £75 tickets. Hundreds more English tourists in Spain flooded travel firms with requests to book early flights home for the match.

Elsewhere, various shades of drama accompanied the final quartet of group games which also went ahead on 19 June. At Old Trafford, Germany and Italy ground out a tedious 0–0 draw, but the result eliminated the Italians from the tournament and prompted the sacking of their well-regarded head coach Arrigo Sacchi. It also meant the Germans would be lurking for England if both sides won through to the semi-finals, ruling out a repeat of

1966 in the final. The other decisive game in Group C was at Anfield and turned out to be an unlikely classic. It paired the Czech Republic, needing a draw to see off Italy, with a Russian side playing for nothing but pride. It appeared initially as if the Russians were not going to bother making a game of it as the Czechs raced into a two-goal lead inside the first twenty minutes. However, the Russians fought back, drawing level in the second half and then taking the lead five minutes from time through a thunderous long-distance strike from forward Vladimir Beschastnykh. The Czechs were not finished and in a frenzied climax Vladimir Šmicer pinched a crucial equaliser in the eighty-eighth minute. It sent the Czech supporters and the team bench into a state of delirium.

A degree of controversy attended the resolution of Group D. Croatia had already qualified from the group, leaving Portugal or Denmark, the championship holders from 1992, to fill the remaining berth in the quarter-finals. The Croats fielded a much-weakened team for their match against Portugal at the City Ground, Nottingham, resting seven of their best players. The Portuguese duly cantered to a 3–0 win, Luis Figo scoring their opening goal, and progressed into the next round. In Sheffield, the Danes saw off Turkey by the same score, but were left licking their wounds.

Reaction on the continent to the first stage of the competition had been downbeat. Visiting reporters bemoaned a dearth of magical moments and a shortage of world-class players. Gascoigne for England and Germany's defensive linchpin, Matthias Sammer, were widely viewed as the two outstanding footballers from the group matches. But it was true that there had been no attacker to inspire awe like a Pele, Cruyff or Maradona, players whose feats changed the way one thought about and viewed the game as a whole. Germany's Jürgen Klinsmann and Hristo Stoichkov of Bulgaria were both battling the dimming of their lights. Figo flickered, but was still too gauche to conduct games at the highest level. Karel Poborksý's fleet-footed displays for the Czechs, so far the most attractive team, had caught the eye and would subsequently earn him a transfer to Manchester United.

Once back in Berkshire, Terry Venables and his squad turned their attentions to beating Spain. That, and how best to contain their problem within: Gascoigne. Confined to base for more than two weeks and with expectations mounting on him and England, Gascoigne was wired fit to burst. He had appropriated the look of a country squire at Burnham, parading about in tweeds and enjoying his nightly helpings of brandy and cigar. However, his general demeanour was more like that of a restless child and he appeared inexhaustible. To give the rest of the party a break from having him fizz about the place, David Seaman was detailed to take Gascoigne off on one of his fishing trips. Even in such solitude Gascoigne's capacity for mayhem was not diminished. After a light training session one afternoon, the pair headed out to a nearby lake to fly-fish for trout still attired in their England tracksuits.

Casting off from a wooden jetty, Gascoigne over-balanced and plunged head-first into the murky water. Any passers-by would have heard Gascoigne's panicked shouts as well as the responding gales of laughter from Seaman.

During the lull between games a less pleasant side of English nationalism reared up in the tabloid press. Reverting to Little Englander type, the *Daily Mirror* ran an editorial entitled: 'Ten nasties Spain's given Europe'. Among the examples cited were bull fighting, General Franco and the Inquisition. Quite what any of these had to do with a game of football was not made apparent. In response, the Spanish daily, *El Mundo Deportivo*, concluded that 'not only the cows are mad in England'.

The match was the first of the quarter-finals. The weather had cooled by the afternoon of Saturday, 22 June and slate-grey clouds hung over Wembley, leaden and ominous. All along the route to the stadium from Berkshire, the England squad were cheered as they drove through an ocean of red and white. 'Stuart Pearce turned to me on the team bus and said, "Enjoy it, because it might not get as good as this again",' said Gary Neville. 'In the dressing room before matches, Tony Adams would kick a ball against a wall or the door like he was ready to batter it down. I used to sit next to Pearce and he scared the life out of me the first time I saw him warm up for a match at Wembley. "This is our fucking turf, this is my fucking turf," he kept snarling. There'd be shouting, chest-beating and patriotic roars.'

Knockout football had an extra edge to it anyway, but UEFA were intent on spicing up the decisive games at

Euro 96 further with the introduction of a new initiative for the tournament. The 'golden goal' scenario would apply to any game that went into extra-time with the next goal deciding the outcome. It was a tantalising prospect, two teams being forced to walk a tightrope, one slip bringing sudden death to the side who erred.

England and Spain were inextricably linked by football. The game was first introduced to Spain in the late nineteenth century by visiting sailors and migrant workers from Britain. An Englishman, Walter Wild, was one of the founding players of Barcelona FC and club president from 1899 to 1901. English influence was strongest, though, in the Basque region and most especially in the north-western city of Bilbao. Athletic Bilbao FC was established in 1898 by groups of British miners and shipyard workers and Spanish students returning from Britain. A former Blackburn and Middlesbrough striker, Fred Pentland, had two successful spells as manager of the club in the 1920s and 1930s. Pentland was known in Bilbao as El Bombin, 'the Bowler Hat', because of his choice of headwear. A tradition is carried on to this day in bars across the city for supporters to celebrate a Bilbao victory by stomping on a bowler hat.

The first international fixture between Spain and England took place in Madrid on 15 May 1929. The hosts won 4–3, becoming the first country outside the home nations to beat England. They had met on sixteen occasions since then with England recording ten wins, two of them in the home and away legs of the knockout qualifier for the 1968 European Championship finals. Most recently, Spain had beaten Graham Taylor's England 1–0 in a friendly in Santander on 9 September 1992. Taylor's side that day was captained by Stuart Pearce and also included Paul Ince, David Platt and Alan Shearer.

Though Real Madrid had dominated European club football in the 1950s and 1960s, winning a record six European Cups during that period, the national team was long regarded as one of the perennial underachievers of world football. Despite being blessed as a nation with an abundance of technically gifted footballers, Spain had never finished better in the World Cup finals than the fourth they managed in Brazil in 1950. They had fared somewhat better in the European Championship, winning the fledgling tournament in 1964 and coming runners-up to hosts France in 1984. However, Spain had failed to qualify for the 1992 finals, and the current team had just stuttered through the group stages of Euro 96, winning just one game against a fading Romania side.

All too often Spain had wilted in crunch matches, their teams seeming to lack the collective will and mental strength to back their creative talents. Their present coach, Javier Clemente, a Basque, had been unable to change the perception of them as nearly men. Clemente had led Spain to the 1994 World Cup finals in the United States as genuine contenders, but his side crashed out to a late Italian goal in the quarter-finals. Clemente's stifling tactics were also proving unpopular back in Spain. He had reacted to one bout of vocal criticism of the conservative nature of their win over Romania by getting into an undignified brawl with a Spanish reporter at his post-match press conference. Nevertheless, Spain had gone twenty games unbeaten under Clemente since that defeat by Italy. Clemente and Venables were old adversaries. As coach at Athletic Bilbao, Clemente fashioned a rugged, disciplined team who won *La Liga* in successive seasons in 1983 and 1984. It was Venables, in his first campaign with Barcelona, who wrestled the crown from them in 1985. However, in the two encounters between the clubs that season, Clemente's Bilbao won one and drew the other without conceding a goal. For the next campaign, Clemente moved to take over Barcelona's city rivals, Español, carrying on hostilities with Venables at closer quarters.

'I thought Clemente hated me because he was always having a dig,' Venables reflected at his press conference on the eve of the quarter-final. 'Then I read some of the things he said about Johan Cruyff [Venables's successor at Camp Nou] after I left and realised he must have quite liked me after all. He's a tough customer, [but] a shrewd man and very thorough.'

The clash between the two men's current teams at Wembley was tight and unyielding, a war of tactics and nerve. For England, Platt slotted into midfield to replace Ince in an otherwise unchanged side. It was Venables's opposite number who made an effective adjustment.

Clemente abandoned his preferred four–four–two formation to play with three central defenders, freeing up
left-back, the quick and penetrative Sergi Barjuán of
Barcelona, to attack England's right flank. He also detailed
Barcelona's midfield enforcer, Miguel Ángel Nadal, so combative he was nicknamed The Beast, to shackle Gascoigne.
Nadal's atrocious disciplinary record meant he had been
suspended from Spain's first two games of the tournament,
and he picked up a booking on his return against Romania.
Before the quarter-final, Nadal told English reporters:
'I shall do a job on Gascoigne, he will not worry me. I will
play at Wembley like I always play: hard.' It was no idle
boast. He attached himself to Gascoigne like a virus the
England man could not shake off, smothering him out of
the game. With Gascoigne having his least effective match
of the tournament, England's attacking play lost its extra
dimension and the team toiled. The England players had
been on an emotional rollercoaster these past few weeks
and the harder Spain made them work, the more they felt
its effects. 'I was as tired as I've ever been on the pitch,'
Gary Neville recalled. 'There was such a buzz around the
country that I was hardly sleeping at night.'

The first half of what Venables later termed a 'one-slip-
and-you're-gone' contest was Spain's. Neat and tidy on the
ball, they hogged possession and had two goals disallowed,
the second erroneously for offside as their centre-forward
Julio Salinas had timed his run through England's back
line to perfection. Starting the second period, Venables
pushed Neville further up the pitch in an attempt to stifle

Sergi. It was Spain, though, who continued to threaten. Their sharper cutting edges and better ball-management represented the first serious challenge to England in the tournament. Alfonso Pérez, on as a substitute for Salinas, was booked for diving in the England box when Gascoigne, getting increasingly frustrated, had upended him with a desperate tackle. Defiant, England clung on and the game went into an extra period. The additional time was especially unwelcome for Tony Adams. Since returning from injury Adams had been playing with pain-killing injections in his right knee, and the numbing effects of his latest jab were beginning to wear off. 'I told Doc Crane to stick another one in me,' Adams remembered of the period right before the teams kicked off again. 'I covered it up with his medical bag so that no one watching on TV would be alarmed. He pushed the syringe in again. I had no care about long-term damage right then.'

Rather than being unleashed to claim the 'golden goal', as UEFA had envisaged, both teams now baulked, as if coerced into playing Russian roulette and lacking the nerve to pull the trigger. Wembley went into a nervous silence and the match petered out to an inconclusive end. A penalty shoot-out beckoned.

'There was no mention of penalties beforehand,' said Stuart Pearce. 'The prospect never crossed the minds of the players and I'm not even sure it had occurred to the manager. In that situation you just think about the game and nothing else. Then the realisation dawns.'

Venables had certainly not designated his five penalty

takers in advance. He went round his exhausted players now, many of whom were prone on the pitch, and selected Shearer, Platt, Gascoigne and Sheringham. These four were givens, but picking the fifth candidate presented him with a problem. Pearce, experienced and his club's regular spot-kick taker, would have been the obvious choice had it not been for the spectre of Turin and the shoot-out at the 1990 World Cup semi-final. The spot-kick score between England and West Germany was tied at three-all. Pearce had stepped up to take England's fourth penalty and missed. Venables wanted to spare him more possible anguish, but Pearce volunteered himself. The image of Pearce that still abided was of him leaving the pitch that night in Turin in floods of tears. But he was a resolute, iron-willed character, so strong in the tackle and ferocious in his commitment that he had long ago been christened 'Psycho' by fans.

Born a stone's throw from Wembley, and a former electrician, Pearce was at twenty-one a latecomer to the professional game. He was moulded into a tough, resilient international full-back during the eight years he had spent under the abrasive Brian Clough at Nottingham Forest. Venables had rung Pearce when he first took on the England job, telling him he preferred young Graeme Le Saux of Chelsea at left-back, and offering him the chance to bow out with dignity. He had not anticipated that Pearce would want to be a bit-player. Once again, though, Pearce refused to yield. He reported for duty for one friendly after another, sat uncomplaining on the bench and bided his time. Le Saux broke his leg in December 1995 and Pearce stepped into the breach. Now, Turin was a memory he meant to banish.

'The players gathered in the centre circle, encouraging, showing solidarity for each other,' Pearce recalled of those next, fateful few moments. 'I kept my socks up and shin pads in to stay in game mode. I stayed on my feet, took a drink and kept my mind as sharp as I could.' England won the toss and elected to shoot first, Shearer scoring. Real Madrid's Fernando Hierro went next for Spain and missed, hitting the crossbar. Platt scored again for England and then Guillermo Amor reduced Spain's arrears. Pearce strode forward next. Close to eighty thousand people drew breath all at once. 'I knew the entire stadium was behind me,' Pearce said. 'It was tangible. I was also aware that half of them were thinking, "Oh no, not him again". No one knew I was going to take a penalty that day, not even me. I made a beeline for Terry when he came off the bench. "Are you sure?" he asked. I'd never been surer of anything. You talk to yourself. You tell yourself not to sidefoot the ball to give the goalkeeper a chance. It was now down to the simplest equations – you against him. You try to flood your mind with positive thoughts. There is no searching for the goalkeeper's soul through his eyes: if I look in his eyes that would move the advantage to him.'

Pearce's wife, Liz, was in the crowd, unable to watch. He placed the ball on the spot, on its outermost edge, seeking even the smallest advantage. Walking back to the edge of the penalty area, he kept his eyes fixed on the ball, not once looking up at Andoni Zubizarreta in the Spanish goal. On the referee's whistle, he ran forward again, no hesitation, and shot with his left foot. 'It's like a golf shot,' he reasoned. 'The moment you make contact, you know whether it's good or bad, hit or miss.' It was good contact, driving the ball hard and low, so that it flew into the bottom corner. Pearce turned, punched the air and bellowed at the crowd, his face contorted with the relief of letting go six years of anguish. To see it was to watch a man being exorcised. 'The emotional explosion came up from my boots somewhere,' he said. 'It was like an internal earthquake, a moment of release. I cannot imagine enjoying a euphoric experience quite like that again.'

What followed after that seemed inevitable. Alberto Belsué kept Spain in the contest and then Gascoigne matched it. That left Nadal needing to score to keep his country in the competition. The Beast, though, choked his shot and Seaman saved. Wembley exhaled with the force of a giant pressure cooker being released. The England players retired to the dressing room, relieved, jubilant, sensing an approaching date with destiny.

The country soared right along with them. At Lord's, Seaman's decisive save was replayed on the big screens during the Test match between England and India to a standing ovation. Playing a sell-out show just up the road at Wembley Arena that night, Aussie hard rock superstars AC/DC were made to pause as the crowd sang impromptu choruses of 'Football's coming home' in between songs.

The evening news bulletins and pages of newsprint the next morning also hailed England's win.

The other three quarter-finals were just as fiercely fought and gruelling. France also edged out the Dutch on penalties at Anfield after another goalless draw. The Czechs beat Portugal 1–0 at Villa Park. At Old Trafford, Klinsmann struck an early penalty to give Germany the lead against Croatia, but Davor Suker pulled the under-dogs level just after the interval. For the next eight minutes it seemed as if a shock might be on the cards. Matthias Sammer snuffed that out, restoring the German lead on fifty-eight minutes after which his team put a strangle-hold on the game. They now stood between England and the final.

Venables gave his squad the Sunday off. Pearce had an appointment in north London and took an unsuspecting Gareth Southgate along with him to see the Sex Pistols. In the midst of a seventy-eight-date reunion tour with their original line-up, punk's standard bearers were playing to thirty thousand people in Finsbury Park. The sun shone, the mood was buoyant, and the ageing Pistols promised to roll back the years to another monumental British summer, the one of 1977 when street parties across the country had marked the Queen's Silver Jubilee and an Englishwoman, Virginia Wade, won Wimbledon. For an instant, it appeared as if all the Fates were colliding.

CHAPTER TEN

'Oh, how much I wanted us to win'

More than eighteen million Britons watched England beat Spain, the largest television audience of the tournament so far. Home interest in Euro 96 in general, and specifically the national team, now ratcheted up exponentially in the four days leading up to the semi-final with Germany. 'Three Lions' was racing back up the charts and looking set to return to the number one spot. Terry Venables's star had also risen. Brian Woolnough reported in the *Sun* that the FA was holding 'secret talks' aimed at finding a role for Venables within the England set-up after the tournament. 'Glenn Hoddle would welcome someone in his camp with Venables's experience,' Woolnough claimed with considerable over-optimism. Digesting the very thought of this scenario would probably have caused both Hoddle and Venables to gag on their breakfasts.

More immediate attention focused on the fitness of Germany and England's two star players. Jürgen Klinsmann was reported to be out of the game for Germany with a calf injury, while Paul Gascoigne was struggling with an ankle strain sustained against Spain. As much as any-thing, reaction to Gascoigne's plight illustrated just how abruptly Euro 96 had turned for him and the team. A con-demned man before it, Gascoigne was now seen as being essential to England winning the competition. The media tracked his progress through the week with wringing hands. England would also be missing the suspended Gary Neville. Venables had consoled Neville in the dress-ing room immediately after the game with Spain, telling him he would be back for the final. The head coach's assurance highlighted the conviction running through the England camp that they could and would beat the Germans. It was a view shared by Franz Beckenbauer. A member of the West German side beaten at Wembley in 1966, and their victorious captain in the 1974 World Cup final, the so-called Kaiser made England favourites for the forthcoming game.

In public at least, Venables was more circumspect about the outcome of the contest, but he was nonetheless acutely aware of its extra significance. 'The Germans have this knowledge of how to approach and play games,' he out-lined in his first press conference of the week. 'You always know what system they will be playing because they stick to it, and they also seem to come out on just the right side all the time. We know how hard it is going to be, but we think we can do it.'

'This is too big for any individual,' he expanded. 'We are all selfish and that is normal, but this is a chance, really, for all of us. It is very rare in your life that you can have a special moment where you can forget that selfish side and give something to someone else. We can give something here to a lot of English people who have not felt too good about things for a number of years, for a lot of different reasons. This is bigger than all of us, [but] it would be the greatest moment of my life if we could get to the final.' One reporter lightened the mood, suggesting to Venables that the FA might present him with a clock at the end of the tournament to honour his tenure. 'I bet it's not working,' Venables fired back tartly.

It was also being reported that expectant England fans going home from the Spain quarter-final had struck up one of their favoured chants on the crowded platforms at Wembley Central railway station: 'Two World Wars and one World Cup.' In advance of the semi-final, it was this jingoistic chestnut that staked out the line that was taken by the English tabloid press. On 24 June, the *Sun* looked ahead to the semi-final with a bald exhortation to Venables and his team: 'Let's Blitz Fritz'. The same day, Gascoigne's and Pearce's animated faces glared out from the front page of the *Daily Mirror*. Superimposed on to their heads were British Army Second World War pith helmets and alongside a headline reading: 'Achtung! Surrender! For you Fritz, ze Euro 96 Championship is over.' This was accompanied by an editorial penned by the paper's thirty-one-year-old editor, Piers Morgan, titled: '*Mirror* declares football war on Germany.' The inside pages, purporting to preview the match, contained such pearls of insight as: 'There's a strange smell in Berlin and it's not just their funny sausages, it's the smell of fear.' This was moronic stuff, of course, but also very much in keeping with an established tradition. On the morning of the 1966 final, the *Daily Mail* had trilled: 'If Germany beat us at Wembley this afternoon at our national sport, we can always point out to them that we have recently beaten them at theirs.'

That assertion passed without comment at the time, but the *Mirror*'s xenophobic outburst prompted forty missives to be fired off to the Press Complaints Commission. There was even a letter to *The Times* from one A.P. Millard, headmaster of Giggleswick School in Settle, North Yorkshire. 'Sir,' wrote Mr Millard on 25 June. 'In Assembly this morning I told the school of my deep concern about the extreme and offensive language being used in newspapers with regard to Euro 96 and the forthcoming match between England and Germany. The warlike terminology was a travesty of sport and could damage our relations with European countries . . . I have had the strongest response I can recall in my ten years as headmaster. Staff and pupils alike feel similarly angered and wonder what can be done to redress the situation. A message must be sent to the press concerning their moral responsibility. From whom is it going to come?'

In the short term, the answer was that it came from Piers Morgan's employers. Morgan, reported *The Times*, was 'severely rebuked' by senior executives at Mirror Group for his ill-conceived cover. 'It was intended as a joke,' he pleaded in response, 'but anyone who was offended by it must have taken it seriously and to those people I say sorry. Humour about the Germans has gone back in our history and is reflected in TV programmes like *Dad's Army*.' Morgan refused to comment on additional reports that he had been forced to abandon plans to hire a tank and drive it to Germany and to mount a Spitfire flypast of Bisham Abbey and Burnham Beeches on the morning of the game.

'The *Mirror* cover was a quite dreadful thing,' says Mihir Bose, by then writing for the *Daily Telegraph*. 'I would not go as far as to say it was racist, but it was certainly insensitive. It also gave off that residual feeling that still permeated that we, the English, had been hard done by. Euro 96 was interesting in that respect. In total, it high-lighted that historic angst that we had created football and given it to the world, but they had got better at it than us.'

Wednesday, 26 June dawned overcast and humid. Britons woke to a rum collection of stories in that morn-ing's newspapers. The Prime Minister was being urged by senior ministers to bring forward a Cabinet reshuffle planned for July, and particularly to confirm the fate of his embattled Agriculture Minister, Douglas Hogg. John Redwood, who the previous summer had made an unsuc-cessful attempt to wrestle the Tory Party leadership from Major, was now pressing him to stand up to 'German bul-lying' in Europe. The German Chancellor, Helmut Kohl, object of Redwood's antipathy, was expected at Wembley for the game that evening. 'He [Kohl] offers us the favour of joining Germany's idea of a federal European state before it is too late,' Redwood wrote in *The Times*. 'Britain must say no. Win or lose [the semi-final], it is time for Britain to give some alternative leadership to Europe, based on our mature understanding of the realities of power in our continent.'

In London, talks to avoid industrial action meant to cause a shutdown of the Underground rail network, ground to a halt. Two thousand train drivers were now expected to stage a twenty-four-hour walk-out from midnight on 27 June. Boys from the Temple Church choir, meanwhile, were made to apologise to the Archbishop of Canterbury after an unfortunate incident at Lambeth Palace earlier in the week. A number of the young choristers had locked a toilet in the palace and made off with the keys following a performance. One of England's heroes of 1966 was also on the wrong end of an official reprimand. Jack Charlton, Bobby Moore's partner at the centre of England's defence for that World Cup final, and until recently manager of the Republic of Ireland, was fined thirty pounds by magistrates in Hexham, Northumberland, after being caught fishing without a licence close to his home in nearby Dalton. Charlton's embarrassment was exacerbated by the fact he had not long since appeared in a series of advertisements promoting the self-same licences.

The day's other big sports story was Tim Henman's defeat in the first round of the Wimbledon championships of the reigning French Open champion and number five seed, Russian Yevgeny Kafelnikov. Making his first appearance on the hallowed Centre Court, twenty-one-year-old Henman had prevailed after five gruelling sets and coming from two match points down. The son of a solicitor father and dress designer mother from rural Oxfordshire, the mild-mannered Henman had risen to number sixty-two on the world rankings and was now handed the burden of trying to become the first British man since Fred Perry in 1936 to win a men's singles title at the home of tennis.

Action at Euro 96 recommenced at Old Trafford at five in the afternoon. The Czech Republic, up to that point the most free-flowing side in the competition, took on France in front of a forty-four thousand crowd. In reality, it was a bloodless affair, both sides hesitant and constricted. The Czechs progressed on penalties after another goalless stalemate, their keeper, Petr Kouba, saving the twelfth kick of the shoot-out from the French substitute, Reynald Pedros. Outside of Kouba's homeland, the contest was forgotten as soon as it had finished. To the English and Germans fans, his side did not appear to be an especially imposing barrier between their teams and the title.

England and Germany had first contested a football match in Berlin on 23 November 1899. A representative English team thrashed their hosts' 13–2 and two days later repeated the lesson, beating the presumably punch-drunk Germans 10–2. Before 1966, the most notable game between the two nations was held before one hundred and ten thousand Berliners in the Olympic Stadium on 14 May 1938 as Adolf Hitler primed Germany for war. Two months earlier, Hitler had annexed Austria and even though he did not attend the match, the British Prime Minister, Neville Chamberlain, considered it an ideal opportunity to smooth a path for his doomed 'peace in our time' deal with the German dictator. At Chamberlain's behest, and to the fury of the English press, the England team, Sir Stanley Matthews among them, lined up before kick-off and gave their German counterparts a Nazi salute as a mark of respect. England went on and won the match 6–3, but the result had already been overshadowed.

England, of course, would always have 1966, thanks to the pivotal intervention of an Azerbaijani linesman, Tofiq Bahramov. It was Bahramov who determined that Geoff Hurst's shot against the crossbar in extra-time had come down over the goal-line and awarded England their third goal in a 4–2 victory over West Germany. For thirty years now Germans had argued that Bahramov was wrong. Time and again they had exacted their revenge against England on the pitch. Twice in the next six years the West Germans humbled an Alf Ramsey team in competitive matches. First, in the quarter-finals of the 1970 World Cup in Mexico, they came from two goals down to defeat the defending champions 3–2 in extra-time. Then, they outclassed England on route to winning the European Championship in 1972. Two years on from that triumph, Germany won their home World Cup and they were crowned champions again in 1990, having first ousted England in that penalty shoot-out in Turin. The Euro 96 semi-final was to be the first time the two countries had met in a competitive fixture since German reunification in 1990. Clearly, there was good reason to fear any German team, but the indomitable mood in England had multiplied during the tournament. Indeed, as kick-off approached, it began to seem almost inconceivable that the national team might lose.

Yet for all the belief Venables had instilled in his squad, the Germans were a stronger, more disciplined and better team than any England had faced thus far at the tournament. Self-assurance had been the foundation stone of their success at international football for decades. But the Germans, too, were mindful of the significance of that Wembley date in 1966. Their head coach, Berti Vogts, brought it up at his pre-match press conference which went ahead at his team's north London base, the five-star Landmark Hotel on Marylebone Road. The pugilistic-looking Vogts also emphasised the extra experience his team had gained over England at the highest levels of the game. 'I watched that Wembley final on TV and remember only too well the infamous goal,' said Vogts. 'We just hope history doesn't repeat itself, [but] this German team is used to semi-finals of major tournaments. For us, it will just be a normal match. My players have been out to all the big department stores in London. They plan to finish their shopping next Monday.'

It would not be quite true to suggest that the entire country stopped for the game that night. However, twenty-six million people, half the population of England, did sit down to watch it unfold on television. At a floodlit Wembley, superstars and dignitaries sat next to each other in the VIP seats in the Royal Box. Mick Jagger and Noel Gallagher were in one block, John Major, Tony Blair and their aides in another. The stadium itself was a cauldron of noise, the loudest and most primed it had been during the past month, the sell-out crowd fizzing with nervous energy, but radiating a sense of joy, too.

'Noel Gallagher was sitting four or five rows back from me,' says Andy Saunders, then a press officer at Oasis' record company, Creation. 'I remember going up to see him before kick-off and saying, "This is fucking great, isn't it?" We had this shared sense of amazement. I've never experienced an atmosphere in a stadium like it. There was a sense of peace and love all around. It was an unforgettable moment.' Alastair Campbell was in a less euphoric mood according to the entry he wrote in his diary later that night: 'I had never really supported England, and for political reasons I found myself rooting privately for Germany.'

The minutes ticked by and the extraordinary, tumultuous atmosphere became still more intense, so much so that it felt almost impossibly inflated, as if it must burst. Right there and then, approaching a quarter-to-eight in the evening, it was the case that Euro 96, that summer and the mood of Englishness joined together and reached their highest points, the great gusts of emotion, expectation, hope, optimism and well-being coalescing into a perfect storm.

'It was six or seven minutes before kick-off when they handed over to me from the studio,' recalled Barry Davies, commentating on the game for BBC TV. 'I didn't really say very much in that time because the crowd was singing constantly. It was particularly special. If somebody told me you are going up to heaven and you can take one game

with you, I think it would be that one.' Venables said afterwards: 'I saw no reason to fear the Germans, or anyone
else. 'The moments before kick-off were calm, the players
ready. We walked out to an extraordinary welcome. Oh,
how much I wanted us to win.'

Venables's team took the field in their change strip of
grey. Earlier that week, BBC Radio 1's breakfast show pre-
senter Chris Evans had urged his seven million listeners to
petition the FA to have England switch to the red shirts
the home side had sported at Wembley on 30 July 1966.
Grey was, frothed Evans, 'the world's most boring colour'.
Even so, England could not fail to be lifted by the occasion. Shorn of Neville, Venables reverted to a narrow back
three of Adams, Southgate and Pearce with the returning
Ince supplementing Gascoigne and Platt in midfield. The
extra man in the centre bolstered England and they pressed
forward, winning a corner in the third minute. Gascoigne
swung the ball over, Adams helped it on and Shearer
stooped to head into the German net, his fifth goal of the
tournament. England had struck so fast, Venables had not
had time to take up his seat in the dug-out.

Bedlam broke out inside Wembley, joy unconfined. But
it was short-lived. The Germans quickly cleared their
heads and asserted themselves. They drew level on fifteen
minutes, Stefan Kuntz escaping England's defenders to
score. Parity restored, both sides became more cautious
and the creative spark went out of the match, but not the
tension. The remaining seventy minutes of normal time
passed as a war of attrition, fought out in the centre

ground and with chances at a premium. Like two gun-slingers waiting to draw on each other, Gascoigne and the German's most dangerous player, their captain Andreas Möller, bided their time in midfield, waiting for the optimum moment to deliver the fatal blow.

Into extra-time the match went and now the 'golden goal' was regarded more as a source of salvation than a threat, breaking the chains that had held the teams back. The ball was swept from one end of the pitch to the other, both defences made to stretch and strain. It was the most thrilling period of the entire tournament, pulsating passages of play during which the promise of wonder and peril lurked in equal measure.

England gained the upper hand. Twice they should have scored and won. McManaman got away down the German left and cut the ball back to Anderton, untended in front of goal, but he skewed his shot against the post. Then Shearer broke free and played a pass square to Gascoigne, bearing down on an empty net. The German keeper, Andreas Köpke, made a desperate attempt to reach him and Gascoigne checked his run. The ball slipped beyond Gascoigne's outstretched boot by mere inches. Even then, it felt like a defining moment.

In between times, Kuntz headed in a German corner, but the Hungarian referee, Sándor Puhl, penalised him for pushing, a hairline decision.

The game ended with the teams deadlocked and now facing penalties. Still they could not be separated. Shearer, Platt, Pearce, Gascoigne and Sheringham all scored for

England. Thomas Hässler, Thomas Strunz, Stefan Reuter, Christian Ziege and Kuntz replied for Germany. Venables had prepared for penalties on this occasion, drilling his five chosen takers at Bisham Abbey. But he had not taken into account the possibility that a shoot-out might go beyond ten kicks. Now he was left scrambling about for someone to assume the responsibility for England's next, crucial penalty. Venables turned to Ince. Ince declined. 'The pressure was massive,' Venables reflected later. 'In those circumstances, there is no point arguing. I cannot criticise anyone for not taking a penalty.'

In Ince's stead, Gareth Southgate stepped forward. Southgate had not even taken a penalty for his club, Aston Villa, and he appeared to shrink as he made the long walk from the centre circle to the goalmouth. Wembley fell silent. Deep down, thousands of people could sense, perhaps even know what was about to happen. Southgate took a breath, tried to compose himself but rushed to take his kick. 'The moment is clear in my mind,' Venables recalled. 'When Gareth hit the penalty, it was all wrong.' The ball skewed off Southgate's boot and Köpke easily smothered it on his goal-line.

In his match commentary, Barry Davies let out an anguished cry: 'Oh no!' Just as Bobby Robson had done in Turin six years previously, Venables closed his eyes and looked to the heavens. 'There were so many heads in hands at Wembley,' he said later. 'My first reaction was the same as the fans: disbelief, then sympathy for Gareth. He was inconsolable, but at least he had the guts to take it.'

Möller, so straight-backed and autocratic-looking he was almost satirical, strode up next and finished the contest. High up in the Wembley stands, Labour MP Denis Howell turned to Alastair Campbell, sitting next to him, and said: 'There goes the feel-good factor.' Campbell recalled: 'John Major looked a bit ashen. Just as we had been worrying, however irrationally, about the political benefits to him of England winning, so a part of him must have been banking on this. He looked pretty sick and the atmosphere at the back of the Royal Box was not great. I tried not to let my happiness show as we walked to the car. Once we got in, I said, "Yesss!" and shook my fist. [Blair] said, "Could you save any celebrations until you get home?" I said, "Don't pretend you feel any different".'

Back on the pitch, the dejected England players went on a bittersweet lap of honour. Pearce attempted to comfort Southgate, who looked as if he was sleep-walking. Graham Kelly ran down to embrace Venables on the running track, but Noel White and the other FA mandarins kept their distance. 'I would have expected [Kelly] to be disappointed, maybe even despondent, but no way,' recalled Venables. 'If I remember his exact words, he said, "Fantastic, wonderful, magnificent". He was reacting like the fan he was at heart. I have never asked him, but knowing him he would have wanted to show me support in public when he knew I would be devastated. The result was a disappointment that dug so deep it made me feel sick. I carried on without expression, like a robot.'

Inside the England dressing room, the air was heavy,

funereal. The dejected Southgate sat slumped, staring into space, his team-mates lost in their own thoughts. It was Tony Adams who broke the silence. The captain grabbed a can of lager from a supply laid out in a corner, drank it, took another and drank that, too. Then he moved to go to the shower, stopped, turned to the bereft Southgate and said: 'Well, Gareth, it was a fucking awful penalty.'

The minutes and hours immediately afterwards passed in a kind of bewildered, disbelieving blur. Southgate found the fortitude to step out of the dressing room and face the assembled media. He said he felt as if he had let the whole country down. 'I froze to the spot,' he added, desperately. 'All of that celebrating and feel-good factor and it came down to me in the end. I don't know how I'm going to live with this. All I can say is I'm sorry.'

'I will never forget the look of terrible agony on Gareth's face,' Pearce wrote later. 'Or the emptiness we all felt deep inside at the realisation that our great adventure had come to an end. It was a terrible yet wonderful night for English football. However, the man we felt most sorry for was Terry Venables. We didn't want him to go, but the faceless men at Lancaster Gate had stipulated [otherwise]. Let it be said here and now that the players would have moved heaven and earth to keep him.'

Venables offered his squad the choice of being released to their families or having one last blow-out at Burnham Beeches. The vote was overwhelmingly in favour of the second option. As their bus rolled out from Wembley for the last time, no smiles now on the upturned faces on the other side of the windows, but still the cheering and chanting, Pearce asked Venables if he could address the squad. He got up and told his team-mates it had been an honour to play with them, to share this experience with them, and then announced he was retiring from international football. In a sense, Pearce spoke for all of them. He would soon change his mind, but for all the bravado that sustained him and them that night, he was already reconciled to a cold, hard truth. That this was his, their, moment and it had slipped through their fingers like sand.

Out in the country there were wretched scenes. In London, in stark contrast to the aftermath of the Dutch match, hundreds of England supporters congregated in Trafalgar Square, once again occupying the fountains at the base of Nelson's Column. But this time the mood turned ugly. Police were pelted with plastic bottles and other missiles, shops looted and cars set ablaze. A mob marched on the National Gallery and hurled stones through its windows. There were sporadic outbreaks of violence in other cities and towns and even reports of disturbances outside village pubs. In Brighton, seven drunken men who had watched the game on television jumped off the Palace Pier, and had to be rescued from the sea by lifeboat. Forty-five arrests were made across the capital alone. Soon after, Gareth Southgate received a letter from one of those detained by police. In part, it read: 'I'm inside and it's your fault. I went and attacked a BMW when you missed that bloody penalty.'

At Burnham, there was also a darker, more depressed undercurrent to the proceedings. Adams got drunk, Gascoigne sloped off to his room, and Venables, still beaming on the surface, was underneath succumbing to the dull, deadening ache of defeat and the vision that would haunt him. 'I think about [Gascoigne's miss] most nights, actually,' he admitted in an interview with BBC Radio 5 live in 2014. 'I have nightmares about it. You have a lifetime in football and you think about this one whisker of Gazza missing the ball and not scoring the goal that would have taken us to the final. You wake up and think to yourself, "What could have been?"'

Next morning, the front page of the *Daily Express* focused on the events in Trafalgar Square. 'Our shame,' read its banner headline, above a photograph of the resulting carnage. Other newspapers, though, marvelled instead at the quality of England's performance and mourned the cruelty of the outcome. 'You Lions gave us such pride,' stated the *Sun*, whose match report Martin Samuel presented like a eulogy. 'It is over,' Samuel wrote. 'The dream, the fantasy, that football would come home proud and victorious is gone . . . How sad – how stupidly, ridiculously sad.'

The Prime Minister, meanwhile, was still trying to draw solace from England's loss. He told the Downing Street press corps that 'the team played their hearts out. We could not have asked for more'. Major's words, though, rang hollow, those of another beaten man. Back at Burnham, the paths around the hotel had now cleared of supporters, the England circus packed up and gone.

Four days later Wembley staged the final between the Germans and the dark horses of the Czech Republic. England looked on, a spectator now at someone else's party. Belying the lazy stereotype of the Germans having no sense of humour, their team drove into the stadium singing a chorus of 'Football's coming home'. As expected, 'Three Lions' was back at number one in the UK, but the song also charted in Germany where it was adopted as an anthem, a spoil to the victors.

The final itself was a subdued affair. The underdogs took the lead on the hour through Patrik Berger's penalty. But it was not to be a night for romance. Berger, Poborsky and Pavel Nedvěd, the creative hub of the Czechs team, were otherwise neutralised by a German rearguard marshalled by the excellent Sammer. Oliver Bierhoff equalised fourteen minutes later and sent the game into extra-time. The tournament was settled by the only 'golden goal' of Euro 96, and one that fit the occasion. Bierhoff scuffed a shot, Kouba in the Czech goal got both hands to the ball, but let it slip through his fingers and over the line. Kuntz was flagged offside, but Italian referee Pierluigi Pairetto overruled his linesman. Amid the confusion, the Germans had won.

As they celebrated, Venables looked down from the stands, wondering what might have been. Venables had trooped along to collect a UEFA Fair Play award his team had won for picking up the least number of cautions in the competition. Alan Shearer also received the golden boot for finishing as top scorer. Neither trinket compensated for

England falling short. It was Venables's last official duty as England's head coach. In all, he had taken charge of twenty-four games, of which he had lost just one inside the regulation ninety minutes. On the morning of the final he confirmed to reporters that he had not been approached by anyone at the FA to stay on. 'I go with no bitterness or regret,' he said. 'That's football. I don't want to dump anything on Glenn Hoddle, but I will say that it's not an impossible job, just a hard one. Now there are other things away from football that must be dealt with. They will not be so enjoyable, but they have to be done.'

'Within a week, they were taking down the pictures of Terry at Lancaster Gate and we were sitting down with Hoddle,' says Henry Winter. 'There was always that view of Venables being a nearly-man as a coach. He would have put that to rest if he had taken England to the final. I don't believe that there's a day that he doesn't think about it, or that he's ever got over it.'

England did at least claim one act of retribution at the final. An English spectator, Peter Gibbons, thirty-three, made off with the match ball after a jubilant German player hoofed it into the crowd at the end of the game. 'One bloke, with his face painted in German colours, offered me £50 for it, then another held out £100,' Gibbons told the *Sun*. 'But there's no way the Germans are getting their ball back after they nicked ours in '66. I call it poetic justice.'

PART FOUR:

JULY

CHAPTER ELEVEN

'Shearmania'

Euro 96 provided an immediate legacy, albeit from an unlikely quarter. The English patriotism that had flourished during the tournament, wrapped up in its red-and-white flags, was striking and abundant enough for the Church of England to take notice. On the 1 July, its ruling General Synod announced that it expected to approve plans being put before it to make St George's Day a special 'festival day'. The Reverend Andrew Burnham, a member of the committee who drew up the idea, commented: 'For Euro 96, we all had to learn again what the flag of England is . . . and [in that respect] we have come a long way.'

That same afternoon, Paul Gascoigne and Sheryl Failes were married. Gascoigne had planned a fairy-tale wedding at Hanbury Manor, a baronial-looking hotel and county club set in two hundred acres of prime Hertfordshire countryside. Sixty security guards patrolled the grounds on the day to ward off unwanted press and media attention. The couple had accepted a £150,000 offer from the celebrity magazine *Hello!* for the exclusive rights to coverage of their nuptials, and spent the lot on organising a lavish reception and honeymoon to Miami. The groom arrived for the ceremony in a thirty-two-foot-long Cadillac stretch limousine, dressed like his bride, head to toe in white, his cream frock coat alone costing a reported £1,000. Failes was given a police escort from her family home nearby and the hundred-strong congregation were ferried to the event by a fleet of limousines.

Among the guests were Terry Venables, who was late arriving for the forty-minute service, Bryan Robson and Gascoigne's England team-mates, Paul Ince, Steve McManaman, Jamie Redknapp and David Seaman. In this context, the Arsenal goalkeeper, a bluff Yorkshiremen with a pudding bowl haircut and luxuriant moustache, looked as if he belonged to a vanishing age of the game. Missing was Tony Adams who had set off on a week-long bender. On a Sunday afternoon soon afterwards Adams was involved in a brawl outside a club in Covent Garden where he had been drinking all day. The England captain, the width of a post from emulating the great Bobby Moore, was arrested and put in a police cell overnight to sleep off the effects. 'Next morning I was at the door of my local five minutes before opening time, banging on it to be let in,' he recalled.

At Hanbury Manor, the newly-weds entered their reception to the strains of Gascoigne's favourite song, Van Morrison's 'Have I Told You Lately (That I Love You)', courtesy of their DJ for the evening, Chris Evans. Failes looked radiant, Gascoigne subdued. Then he broke out of their clinch to indulge in a spot of moonwalking *à la* Michael Jackson. Gascoigne's new wife, his family, friends and team-mates laughed right along with him. Euro 96 had been lost, but in that instant it seemed that a happy ending was still within his reach. If so, it was nothing more than an illusion. 'The best part of the honeymoon was the flight,' Gascoigne said later. 'After that, for the whole holiday, we argued.'

Straight after the wedding Venables also flew off to Bali for a short holiday, but he did not intend being idle for long. Now that the curtain had come down on his England tenure, he reverted to his idea of himself being more than just a football coach. He left the country mulling over an immediate offer that gnawed at him. It had come from a well-known source. Martin Gregory, whose father Jim had been his chairman at QPR, was now the owner of Portsmouth and had invited Venables on to the club's board directly after he left his England post.

This was hardly the high-profile appointment Venables craved. The previous season Portsmouth had barely escaped relegation from the second tier on goal difference and the club was deep in debt. However, Gregory played to Venables's ego and, just as importantly, was not asking him to sink any of his own money into the deal. Venables, Gregory told reporters, would instead provide 'expertise and football know-how. If we can get Terry, he would give us the spark which would lift this club up again'.

Intrigued but non-committal, Venables promised Gregory an answer upon his return. By then he might have expected to have other offers to weigh up, though the possible skeletons in his closet so feared at the FA were also still rattling. He had court cases outstanding, which threatened to drag him back through the mire. These were a salutary reminder to him that he had been forced to vacate English football's biggest stage.

Back at Lancaster Gate, the FA was congratulating itself on Euro 96 and aiming still higher. The euphoria that had surrounded England's games, and the surfeit of glamour that attached to them and the players, had encouraged a wider, more socially upwardly mobile audience into football. On 28 June, Graham Kelly announced plans to redevelop the old, fraying Wembley into a £160 million 'space-age super-stadium' with a retractable roof and top-class corporate facilities. A venue fit, in other words, for football's new, more affluent audience. England's biggest clubs would soon follow suit, either redeveloping their existing stadiums or moving to gleaming new palaces. In *The Times* on 2 July, Kelly cited a total attendance figure for the tournament of 1.3 million spectators and ventured that 'nobody can question any longer England's ability to stage the biggest sports events in the world'. The FA, Kelly continued, had therefore decided to take 'the logical next step' and was preparing a bid to host the 2006 World Cup. They were assured of government support with the beleaguered Prime Minister still eager to hitch his fortunes to the England team's bandwagon. Later that day, John Major's National Heritage Secretary, Virginia Bottomley, told the House of Commons that the government would support the FA initiative 'in every possible way'.

Flush with hubris, the FA believed it had an unbeatable enticement. Who could resist the ideal of bringing football home yet again, and this time on the fortieth anniversary of England's singular triumph? In due course, the boys of '66, Geoff Hurst and Bobby Charlton, were wheeled out once more to summon up the old ghosts and press the flesh of visiting Fifa dignitaries. Between them the Major and Blair governments sank an estimated £10 million into boosting the bid, but it was to end in abject humiliation. The fatal blow was struck by Egidius Braun, chairman of the German Football Federation. Not long after the England bid was formally confirmed, Braun revealed details of a meeting that had taken place in Las Vegas between himself and Bert Millichip. In return for having supported England's bid for Euro 96, Braun claimed the two of them had reached a gentleman's agreement that the Germans would be given a clear run at the 2006 World Cup. Millichip raced to deny the claim, but the substance of it was well-known among the powerbrokers of international football.

With Euro 96 over, and in the lull before the football season started, the other, familiar sports of an English summer took over. Rain lashed down at Wimbledon on 3 July and the covers were out on Centre Court as a packed crowd huddled beneath umbrellas. Suddenly, Sir Cliff Richard stepped into the Royal Box to deliver an apparently impromptu performance. Sporting a mullet hairdo, check jacket and armed with a microphone, the self-styled 'Peter Pan of Pop', fifty-five years young, began by singing an unaccompanied version of his 1963 hit, 'Summer Holiday'. It was almost as if pop, rock, punk, New Wave, Acid House and Britpop had never happened as the crowd were transported back through three decades to an age of light entertainment, big bands and easy listening standards. Richard, naff but enduring, was like a Pied Piper leading on his audience. It was the older spectators who succumbed first, clapping along and mouthing the familiar words. Soon, younger and overseas visitors, too, were complicit. Encouraged, Richard continued to plunder his back catalogue for 'The Young Ones' from 1961 and 1962's 'Bachelor Boy'.

'It happened to be the first year I was a member of Wimbledon,' Richard told the *Guardian* in 2009. 'The club secretary wanted a word with me. His wife had suggested that he ask me to sing something . . . Well, I'm a professional. If I'm put on the spot, I can't really say no. It was a wonderful accident.' In total Richard soaked up more than twenty minutes of airtime on the BBC, which was broadcasting live. As he pressed on, he was joined by a troop of champion women tennis stars, among them Martina Navratilova, Pam Shriver and Virginia Wade, Britain's last Wimbledon winner. 'I never dreamed I would play Centre Court,' Richard announced at one point, beaming, before the rain stopped, the covers came off, and the whole surreal episode was brought to an end.

It did not prelude British glory on the court, either. Two days later, Tim Henman, who had progressed through to the quarter-finals, was beaten in straight sets by the big-serving American Todd Martin, the thirteenth seed. There was a further unscheduled interruption before the men's singles final on Sunday, 7 July. The two finalists, Richard Krajicek of Holland and American MaliVai Washington, had just completed their warm-up when a streaker ran across the now sun-bathed Centre Court. Melissa Johnson, twenty-three, was working as a catering assistant at the tournament. A statuesque blonde, she had left her work station and stripped down to nothing but a white apron, which was tied and now flapping around her midriff. She ran, smiling, past the players as they posed for photographs and into the arms of two policemen. Krajicek went on to win the final in three sets. Johnson subsequently graduated from Manchester University with a degree in graphic design.

It was also a mixed summer for England's cricketers. Their third and final Test match against India ended on 9 July in a draw at Trent Bridge, Nottingham, despite captain, Michael Atherton, scoring a handsome century in the first innings. The result was enough to secure England a one-nil victory in the series. A fortnight later they began a second three-match series at Lord's against a potent Pakistan side. The tourists romped to a 164–run win and went on to take the series two-nil with their fast bowlers, Wasim Akram and Waqar Younis, dominating the English batsmen.

The Open golf championship was staged at Royal Lytham & St Annes on the Lancashire coast, but Nick Faldo was unable to repeat his triumph at The Masters. Faldo finished in fourth place, three shots behind the champion, American Tom Lehman. A twenty-year-old American was the only amateur to make the cut. Tiger Woods, from Cypress, California, shot a three-under-par 281 to tie for twenty-second place.

Damon Hill, though, was still dominating the Formula One season, and went into the British Grand Prix at Silverstone on 14 July as hot favourite. Hill had won the two previous races in Canada and France and scorched to pole position in his Williams-Renault car. Born in Hertfordshire in 1960, Hill was the only son of Graham Hill, Formula One world champion in 1962 and 1968. The senior Hill was killed in 1975 when the light aircraft he was piloting crashed in fog at a golf course on the outskirts of north London. His teenaged son had already resolved to follow in his father's footsteps as a racing driver. He proved to be good enough to make the leap into the rarefied, high-pressure world of F1 and in 1993 was named number two driver to three-time world champion Alain Prost at the British-based Williams team. The next season Hill was paired with the brilliant Brazilian, Ayrton Senna. Their partnership, though, was brief and came to a tragic end at the 1994 San Marino Grand Prix when Senna was killed in a crash. Senna's shocking death forced Hill out of the shadows and he came within a point of winning the title that year, beaten by the German Michael Schumacher. His efforts earned him the BBC's

Sports Personality of the Year award, but he slipped further behind Schumacher in 1995 and seemed destined to always be in someone else's slipstream.

That had all changed during the course of the 1996 season. Hill was handed the keys to an outstanding car, the Williams-Renault FW18, a triumph of engineering that was faster and more reliable than Schumacher's Ferrari. He had won six races by the time of the British Grand Prix, and surged ahead of both Schumacher and his closest challenger for the title, his team-mate, the young Canadian driver Jacques Villeneuve. More than one hundred thousand supporters were bated for a Hill victory at Silverstone, where Union Jack and St George flags were as prominent as at Wembley. But Hill was sluggish off the start-line and never recovered. At half-race distance he spun off the track when attempting a passing manoeuvre and was forced to retire. Villeneuve claimed victory with the Scot David Coulthard and Hill's fellow Englishman, Martin Brundle, fifth and sixth respectively.

The result barely put a dent in Hill's championship tilt, though. He still led Villeneuve by fifteen points with just six races to go. Hill was even feeling confident enough to publically float the idea of demanding a bumper £12 million contract from team owner Frank Williams for the next campaign. However, on 25 July *The Times* ran a story headlined: 'Hill to be sacked by Williams team'. According to the report, sources at Williams claimed a deal had already been struck to promote Villeneuve to number one for the 1997 season and replace Hill with Heinz-Harald

Frentzen. The German driver had not finished higher than third in forty-two starts at Formula One, but *The Times* had their facts right. Hill went on to win the next Grand Prix in Hockenheim, Germany, on 28 July, and secured the title at the Suzuka circuit in Japan on 13 October, but that was the last race he drove for Williams. 'When Damon was good, he was very good,' Williams' co-founder, Patrick Head, told *Motorsport* magazine in 2008. 'When he was there, he was top level. But those days didn't come along often enough.'

On 19 July, the world's greatest sports gathering opened in Atlanta, Georgia. A record 197 nations, represented by more than ten thousand athletes, came together to compete at the twenty-sixth summer Olympic Games. Britain had to wait ten days to celebrate a gold medal when Steve Redgrave and Matthew Pinsent won the coxless pairs rowing. Remarkably, it was Redgrave's fourth Olympic gold medal, but it was also Britain's last of a disappointing Games. Tim Henman, in the men's doubles tennis, Roger Black on the track and sailor Ben Ainslie were among the team's eight silver medallists while cyclist Chris Boardman claimed one of six bronzes. In the final medal table, though, Britain placed behind Norway, North Korea and Kazakhstan.

However, it was not the sport but an incident that occurred at Centennial Park in the centre of Atlanta that was to set these Games apart. Twenty minutes after one o'clock local time on the morning of 27 July, a pipe bomb hidden beneath a park bench exploded, killing two and injuring one hundred and eleven people. The perpetrator, Eric Robert Rudolph, a handyman working in the city, escaped capture for seven years and committed three more bombings before his arrest on 31 May 2003.

In the midst of this tumult, the English football revolution was accelerating. It was boosted by the thrust of Euro 96 and the vision of an international, multi-cultural game that it had been put on display to English supporters and club owners. Until now, players from overseas had trickled into the Premier League, but the floodgates were opened. Bryan Robson began the deluge at Middlesbrough on 5 July by signing the Italian international striker Fabrizio Ravanelli for £7 million from Juventus. Despite his grey hair, Ravanelli was just twenty-seven years old and at his peak, having won the Champions League with the Turin club that May. Robson then paid Porto of Portugal £4 million for Brazilian midfielder Emerson, who linked up with his compatriot Juninho at the Riverside Stadium.

Ruud Gullit was also making his Chelsea team more international. Glenn Hoddle's replacement at Stamford Bridge picked up veteran Italian target man Gianluca Vialli from Juventus on a free transfer and shelled out a club record £4.9 million to bring his compatriot Roberto Di Matteo from Lazio. To this pair he then added the French centre-half Frank Leboeuf, signed from Strasbourg for £2.5 million. West Ham snapped up two players who had represented their countries at Euro 96, Romanian striker Florin Răducioiu and defender Slaven Bilic of Croatia. The Upton Park club also recruited a Portuguese forward, Paulo Futre, and Răducioiu's countryman Ilie Dumitrescu from Spurs. At Old Trafford, Alex Ferguson had picked out Karel Poborský from the summer tournament and snapped up the Czech winger from Slavia Prague for £3.6 million on 16 July. That month Ferguson had already added two Norwegian players to his ranks: defender Ronny Johnsen and a promising young striker, Ole Gunnar Solskjaer. Liverpool, meanwhile, were reported to be chasing Poborský's international team-mate, Patrik Berger, who they would eventually sign in August from Borussia Dortmund.

Ravanelli was set to earn a minimum of £4 million over four years at Middlesbrough. His contract was symptomatic of the new riches pouring into the game. A decade earlier a top-flight English footballer could expect to earn £24,934 a year, two and a half times the national average. During the 1996–97 season, the average salary of a Premier League player leapt almost three hundred per cent to £175,066 – more than eight times the national average. By 2014, even jobbing Premier League footballers were raking in that sum each month.

The boom in salaries was accelerated by the exposure Euro 96 had given to football in England, and the platform it had afforded foreign players. It was funded by a lucrative new deal the Premier League had struck with BSkyB. But the actions of an unsung Belgian footballer were instrumental in making this great wealth available to the players. Jean-Marc Bosman had shown enough promise as a teenager to be made captain of the Belgian youth team and had turned out for two of the country's top clubs, Anderlecht and Standard Liège. However, he did not kick on and by 1990, aged twenty-five and at the end of his contract, Bosman was consigned to Liège's reserves. A French club, Dunkirk, offered him the chance to start afresh. However, under the rules then governing the game, the selling club to all intents retained ownership of an out-of-contract player. Liège set Dunkirk an inflated fee for him of £500,000 and the deal collapsed. Bosman was left with no option but to re-sign with Liège, but on greatly reduced terms.

That would have been the end of the matter in countless transfer dealings conducted across Europe for many decades. Bosman, though, was the exception and was determined to fight his corner. He took legal action to free himself from his contract with Liège and committed to a process that would last five years. A Belgian court ruled in his favour, but too late for him to resurrect his move to Dunkirk. Bosman dropped into the lower leagues in Belgium and France. He went bankrupt, his marriage fell apart, but he pressed on, seeking damages. Finally, at the end of 1995, Bosman's case was heard at the European Court of Justice in Strasbourg.

It was there that what soon became known as the Bosman Ruling was passed. In the simplest terms, it decreed that footballers should be free to move to another club when their contracts expired. This had the immediate effect of transferring power from the clubs to the players, and was potentially of huge financial benefit. Free-agent footballers were enabled to negotiate greatly inflated signing-on fees on the basis that the clubs they were joining had not paid a transfer fee for them. The clubs were also now more likely to secure them on lucrative long-term contracts. This meant rich pickings for football agents who could hawk their clients to the highest bidder. The clubs were compensated as well. Since it tacitly endorsed the principle of freedom of movement, the ruling effectively ended restrictions applied by UEFA on the number of foreign players clubs were permitted to field. And it was now, six months on and in the wake of Euro 96, that all parties started in earnest to exploit the advantages that the Bosman Ruling had afforded them.

Ironically, the one person who was not able to reap the rewards was Bosman himself. Forced to retire from the game in 1990, no longer able to make a living from it, he proceeded to lose all the compensation he had won from the case. In December 2011, twenty-one years after he took up his fight, Bosman hit bottom. He was arrested by Belgian police following a violent altercation with his girlfriend, during which he punched her in the face and also struck her fifteen-year-old daughter. He was sentenced to a year in prison. One of his failed investments was a bespoke line of T-shirts that bore his name. Bosman had thought these might be snapped up by the countless footballers he had effectively made rich. In the event he sold just one.

The pre-season transfer frenzy made the Premier
League a truly cosmopolitan and, by extension, more
marketable product. However, the influx of foreign talent
was not universally welcomed. Gordon Taylor, chief executive of the players' union, was concerned about the
damaging effect it might have on the chances of a future
England side surpassing the performance of Venables's
team. 'There is now an awful lot of money going out of
our game and clubs need to be reminded of their respon-
sibilities,' Taylor told *The Times* on 6 July. 'The success of
England in Euro 96 shows that we have to put more
resources into youth development. I wouldn't want that
momentum to be lost.' Nor would it be that this pick-and-
mix free-for-all was a guarantor of success. For all the
reserves of talent they had accumulated, Bryan Robson's
Middlesbrough were relegated from the Premier League
at the end of the season.

The biggest transfer story of that hectic summer,
though, involved an English player. Alan Shearer's goalscoring feats at Euro 96 had secured his status as an elite
player and made him a wanted man. Potential suitors
were encouraged by his reluctance to commit his immediate future to Blackburn. The Italian giants, AC Milan,
were the first club to be linked with him at the start of the
month. Then Manchester United entered the fray, but in
unusual circumstances. Alex Ferguson was rumoured to
be readying a £12 million bid for Shearer as his squad
prepared to fly out to Europe for a pre-season friendly. On
10 July, several newspapers carried a story that Shearer's

name had appeared on the club's travel documents and that United's travel agents, Travel Management Limited, had suspended a member of staff as a result. United's solicitor, Maurice Watkins, reasoned to inquisitive reporters: 'I suspect this was over-optimism on the part of someone, or else a sense of humour.'

United's supporters, though, believed the cat was out of the bag. Within hours of the story breaking they had snapped up the club's allocation of seven thousand tickets for the Umbro Tournament, a curtain-raiser for the new season that was due to be staged in Nottingham on 3 and 4 August. Tournament organiser, Roger Broomhall, perhaps having first had the word put in his mouth by a tabloid reporter, was moved to describe the rush for tickets as 'Shearmania'. Mania it might have been, but there were more twists to come in the Shearer saga.

CHAPTER TWELVE

'He hits the ball as if he means to kill it'

The transfer merry-go-round went on turning. Coventry City smashed their transfer record to sign Gary McAllister from Leeds United for £3 million. Leeds manager Howard Wilkinson invested their windfall from the sale of the Scotland captain in Crystal Palace's goalkeeper, Nigel Martyn. Returning from his fractious honeymoon to pre-season training with Rangers, Paul Gascoigne found himself paired up with a new midfield partner. Manager Walter Smith had just splashed out £4 million to sign Jörg Albertz from Hamburg. Albertz was on the fringes of Berti Vogts's German squad, but had not made the cut for Euro 96. Jordi Cruyff became Alex Ferguson's fourth signing of the summer at Manchester United. The young Cruyff had been made surplus to requirements at Barcelona by the sacking of their manager, his father.

It was Alan Shearer, though, who was Ferguson's main target. AC Milan's city rivals, Inter, along with Juventus and Barcelona, were now circling the England man, but Shearer had made it known he would not uproot his family and move abroad. Arsenal, Everton and Liverpool were among the other Premier League sides tipped to come to the negotiating table. But Ferguson knew his biggest challengers would be Shearer's hometown team, Newcastle. The chairmen of the two clubs, Martin Edwards at United and Freddy Shepherd at Newcastle, were neighbours in Majorca and were in contact with each other over the terms of their chase for Shearer. Both men agreed not to offer Blackburn more than £10 million for him, and they would inform the other in advance if they meant to break that ceiling.

Ferguson had tried to sign Shearer once before, in 1992, when he was on the point of leaving Southampton for Blackburn. He had intended to gazump that deal, even calling Shearer to tempt him, but was forced to wait three weeks while the United board scrabbled to get the money together. By the time they did, Shearer had pledged himself to Rovers' then-manager Kenny Dalglish and their steel magnate owner, Jack Walker. The Lancashire club had reaped the rewards of having him. Shearer scored 112 goals in 138 Premier League games for Rovers, so prolific a strike rate as to seem outlandish, and fired them to the league title in 1995 ahead of United. Admiring him from a distance, it was Ferguson who best described Shearer's approach to hunting down goals. 'He hits the ball,' Ferguson considered, 'as if he means to kill it.'

On 22 July, the race for Shearer began in earnest, and in Crewe of all places. Still under contract to Blackburn, Shearer meant to keep the negotiations secret and had arranged to use the house of his England team-mate David Platt's mother-in-law as the venue. On that particular Monday morning, eagle-eyed residents of the old railway town would have seen Kevin Keegan and Alex Ferguson, one after the other, trooping in and out of their neighbour's modest terrace. 'Fergie came in,' Shearer told *FourFourTwo* magazine in 2015, 'and the first thing he said was, "Am I first or has Keegan got you?" I told him I had already spoken with Keegan, and he said, "That's me fucked then".'

In fact, Shearer was leaning towards United. They were the bigger club, the more successful and as title holders offered the lure of Champions League football. Shearer left Crewe with his wife, Lainya, and the couple drove up the M6 and went house-hunting around the leafy Cheshire towns and villages that ringed the southern approaches to Manchester. Ferguson, meanwhile, pressed Edwards to act and to go in high. Edwards called Shepherd and informed him that United were going to bid above £10 million. Shepherd got straight on to Walker, who viewed Shearer as a kind of surrogate son, and asked him to name his price. Brought up as an ardent Rovers supporter, Walker was schooled to disdain neighbours United for their perceived airs and graces and was rich enough now to repel them. He told Shepherd: 'It's £25 million to Manchester United, but for you it's £15 million.'

Keegan went back to Shearer that night, asking to meet with him again the next evening. At the age of twelve, Shearer had queued for five hours to stand and watch

Keegan's goalscoring debut for Newcastle against QPR from the Gallowgate End of St James' Park. He readily agreed to the request. The venue on this next occasion was the McAlpine Stadium in Huddersfield and under the smokescreen of a concert by the Canadian soft-rocker Bryan Adams. Secreted together in an executive box, Keegan made a typically effusive last pitch to Shearer. Newcastle, he told him, were the coming club in Europe, boundless in their ambitions, and he would be their totem and idol. Shearer asked if he would be able to claim the number nine shirt, worn by such giants of the club's history as Hughie Gallagher, Jackie Milburn and Malcolm Macdonald. No matter that Shearer's Euro 96 squad-mate Les Ferdinand was his current number nine, Keegan readily acceded. Ferdinand could like it or lump it. Shearer left the McAlpine with his mind made up. He was going home.

First, though, Shearer wanted to square things with Walker. They met the next morning at Walker's home. Desperate to keep hold of his most cherished asset, Walker played all his aces. He offered Shearer a bumper contract, unprecedented in English football at the time, and to make him player-manager at just twenty-five. He had already fixed it so that the incumbent manager, Ray Harford, would step down to a coaching role. Shearer, however, was as unbending off the pitch as he was on it.

On 29 July, Newcastle announced they had signed him for £15 million on a five-year contract. It was an astonishing fee: almost doubling the amount Liverpool had paid

Nottingham Forest for Stan Collymore in 1995 to set the previous British transfer record. It was also £1.5 million more than the existing world record, which had been established just two days earlier by Barcelona when they signed Brazilian striker Ronaldo from PSV Eindhoven. Shearer's fee stood unchallenged for three seasons until Real Madrid paid Arsenal £22.5 million for their French striker, Nicolas Anelka. It was Shearer's transfer, though, that truly set off the era of football's super-deals. Over the next two decades the sums changing hands among Europe's biggest clubs reached astronomical proportions. Manchester United, Chelsea and Manchester City all smashed the record in the coming years, but even their largesse was dwarfed by that of the Spanish giants Real Madrid, who handed over a combined £165.3 million to lure Cristiano Ronaldo from Manchester United and Gareth Bale from Spurs in 2009 and 2013 respectively.

Shearer was understood to be pocketing a £1.5 million signing-on fee and stood to make at least £7 million more in wages. Newcastle, *The Times* claimed, 'had pulled off one of the most breath-taking deals of all time . . . sending out tremors that were felt all over the country'. Keegan told reporters it was 'a signing for the people of Newcastle. It just shows you . . . we are the biggest thinking team in Europe right now'.

There was a wild, delighted reaction to the news in Newcastle. A sports shop in the city centre sold five hundred Shearer number nine shirts in just two hours, and ran out of letters to print up more. In Manchester, United's power-brokers were left bristling with frustration. 'There was no way that Blackburn were prepared to let [Shearer] come to us,' Martin Edwards bemoaned to the *Independent*. The dust would not settle on the battle for a while yet, but when it did, even the indomitable Shearer would have cause to doubt himself.

'Three Lions' finally slipped off the top of the UK charts on 13 July. It was replaced a week later by the anodyne 'Forever Love', the first solo single from Gary Barlow. Until their split the previous February, Barlow had been the principal member and sole songwriter with Take That, the omnipotent British pop group of the decade until Oasis happened along. 'Forever Love' was in turn knocked off its perch by an altogether spikier, spunkier pop song. 'Wannabe' was the first single from the Spice Girls and sounded as if it had been brewed up in a laboratory test tube with its gleeful gait, route-one chorus and liberal use of a meaningless but curiously captivating hook-line: 'Zig-a-zig-ah'. The five Spice Girls had been hand-picked from hundreds of applicants to an advert placed in the trade magazine *The Stage* by pop impresario Simon Fuller. Geri Halliwell, Melanie Chisolm, Melanie Brown, Emma Bunton and Victoria Adams were banded together in a recording studio with teams of songwriters.

Going on to become the biggest-selling single of all-time by an all-girl group, 'Wannabe' romped to number one in thirty other countries and telegraphed a tilt in the pop zeitgeist away from skinny boys with guitars. That same month, the *Top of the Pops* in-house magazine bestowed off-hand nicknames on the girls as shorthand for identifying them. They stuck fast. Thereafter, Ginger Spice, Sporty Spice, Scary Spice, Baby Spice and Posh Spice were household names. However, by a quirk of fate, it was Posh, and not Sporty, who would soon become inextricably linked with football.

The five other most recognisable faces of the time adorned a series of instantly iconic posters that launched the defining British movie of the decade. The posters consisted of black-and-white photographs, framed in orange, and alongside a simple instruction to 'Choose Life', they were the film's lead characters: Renton, Spud, Diane, Sick Boy and the psychopathic Begbie. *Trainspotting* had opened in UK cinemas to rave reviews back in February and crossed the Atlantic on 19 July. The fact that it was a British film showcasing the sort of technical flair and bruised glamour more normally associated with American directors such as Martin Scorsese and Hollywood's new *enfant terrible*, Quentin Tarantino, was not lost on critics in the United States. The *Washington Post* was quick to hail it: 'The most provocative, enjoyable pop-cultural experience since Tarantino's *Pulp Fiction*.' Irvine Welsh was thirty-five and a recovering heroin addict at the time of writing *Trainspotting*, his first novel, in 1993. The book was set in the tough Edinburgh port district of Leith where Welsh was born and raised by his dockworker father and waitress mother. Essentially a collection of short stories,

Trainspotting chronicled the lives of a group of disparate, desperate characters linked by heroin. Written by Welsh in the local dialect and peppered with jet-black humour, it presented a brutal, hellish vision of inner-city existence among an underclass of addicts and Aids victims whose lives were defined by boredom, poverty and random violence. Its anti-heroes encapsulated all the hopelessness and despair felt by certain sections of Thatcher's Britain, but also a kind of unbreakable spirit. Within three years of being published it had sold half a million copies.

Producer Andrew Macdonald read Welsh's book on a plane and brought it to the attention of his creative partners, director Danny Boyle and scriptwriter John Hodge. The trio had made their film debuts together two years earlier with *Shallow Grave*, a taut thriller set in Edinburgh and starring a callow young Scottish actor, Ewan McGregor. Boyle, thirty-nine, cut his teeth in regional theatre and helming episodes of the popular television detective drama, *Inspector Morse*. He also cast McGregor in the central role of Mark Renton for *Trainspotting*. Filmed almost entirely in Glasgow, as opposed to Edinburgh, Boyle's version nevertheless retained the hallucinogenic and lacerating qualities of its source material. Such scenes as McGregor being sucked down a filthy toilet, and imagining a dead baby crawling across a ceiling, burnt themselves into audiences' minds. *Trainspotting*'s pulsating soundtrack also moved to the beat of the time, corralling together the likes of Blur, Elastica, Pulp and two trailblazing electronic acts, Underworld and Leftfield.

The tendrils of *Trainspotting*'s influence ranged out far and wide across pop culture, further than any other single British art work of that decade. Before its release the British film industry was churning out period dramas like *Room with a View* or else such rom-coms as *Four Weddings and a Funeral*, the smash hit of 1994. *Trainspotting* cut a swathe for tough, gritty independent films that showed Britain in a more unforgiving and contemporary light. In 1996 alone it paved the way for such coruscating offerings as Mike Leigh's *Secrets & Lies*, *Brassed Off*, also starring McGregor, and *Small Faces* which respectively examined in unflinching details working-class attitudes to race, the after-effects of the miners' strike of 1984–85 and Glasgow street gangs of the 1960s. Similarly, Welsh's book inspired a new wave of hip young gunslingers into British literature, most notably that summer with the publication of twenty-six-year-old English author Alex Garland's debut novel, *The Beach*.

By the end of the month Terry Venables was pre-occupied with reclaiming his elevated position in the football firmament. He had made a decision about his immediate future. Returning from Bali, he was courted by Jack Walker with a view to replacing Ray Harford at Blackburn. It was no more than a team manager role, though, and since Alan Shearer had just been sold, the club was a busted flush when it came to chasing the biggest honours. The Portsmouth job nagged at Venables as being something bolder and more able to satisfy the pioneering ambitions that drove him on. He accepted Martin Gregory's offer and was installed as the First Division club's director of football, overseeing a rookie first-team manager, Terry Fenwick, who had played under him at QPR and Spurs, and charged with leading Portsmouth into the Premier League. At the same time, Venables was also negotiating with the chairman of the Australian FA, David Hill, with a view to replacing Scotsman Eddie Thomson as their national team coach and taking the country to the 1998 World Cup finals. This was an opportunity Venables could not resist. It gave him both a route back to the high-wire act of international football and the shot at the World Cup that the English FA had deprived him. It also carried an annual salary of £200,000. Venables accepted this second role in November 1996. He was again empire-building and chasing the glory that would preserve his legacy.

Portsmouth began to mount a promotion challenge and as the season developed also had a run to the quarter-finals of the FA Cup. However, the club was losing £150,000 a week and was in a perilous state. Torn between two continents, Venables was able to be no more than a fleeting presence at Fratton Park, sighted in midweek before weekend matches but otherwise invisible. Nevertheless, in February of the following year he took up an offer from Gregory to buy a fifty-one per cent controlling stake in the club for just £1 and appointed himself chairman. It was only on paper that this looked a gift. 'By the time I arrived at the club, they were on death row,' Venables recalled in

2014. 'The bank had control of the debt, which effectively meant I had fifty-one per cent of nothing.'

The dream soon soured on the pitch, too. Portsmouth faltered and finished the season seventh in the league, one place short of the promotion play-offs. With Venables unable to attract investors, forced into hocking the club's assets and struggling to pay the wages of the players and staff, the team had a wretched start to the next campaign and slumped to the bottom of the division. England's Euro 96 hero was now cast as a villain. As the crisis engulfing the club worsened, it emerged that Portsmouth had paid Venables's own company, Vencorp, a one-off 'performance-related' bonus of £300,000. His discredited tenure was finally ended in January 1998 when Gregory paid him a further £250,000 to buy back his shares. Venables's pupil, Fenwick, followed him out of the club, a terse statement from Gregory noting: 'The time is right for Venables to go . . . I realise I'm not the most popular person in Portsmouth, but things were never this bad [under me].'

In Australia, Venables also enjoyed a honeymoon period. Constructing his squad on a strong foundation of English-based players, including three from Portsmouth, John Aloisi, Craig Foster and Robert Enes, he won his first twelve games in charge of the Socceroos and led them to a two-legged play-off with Iran for a place in the World Cup finals. The first leg went ahead in Tehran on 22 November 1997 and was drawn 1–1. A week later, a record eighty-five thousand crowd packed the Melbourne Cricket Ground for the return fixture. Australia took a

2–0 lead, but then their resolve crumbled. Iran scored twice in the last fifteen minutes and won through to France on away goals. It was, said Venables, like being 'kicked in the teeth'.

Venables flew back to England intending to fight a case being brought against him by the Department of Trade and Industry. This eventually reached the High Court in January 1998 and was expected to run for three weeks. In the event it was closed in just five minutes. Venables decided not to contest the nineteen allegations the DTI had ranged against him, accusing him of serious business malpractice with regard to his time at Spurs and his running of Scribes West. Venables also accepted the subsequent High Court ruling that he be barred from holding a directorship for seven years. Commenting on the verdict, Nigel Griffiths, the Competition and Current Affairs Minister, told the BBC: 'We recognise Mr. Venables's great achievement in football, but even our national heroes cannot be allowed to fall below accepted standards of probity when they enter the business world.'

For Venables, it was the end of a sharp, steep fall from grace after the heady days of the summer of 1996 when all of England had sung his name.

PART FIVE:

AUGUST

CHAPTER THIRTEEN

'Everything was rosy until I began to
turn into a bastard again'

The after-effects of Euro 96 spread out through the rest of that summer like ripples across water. Anticipation for the forthcoming football season was reaching fever pitch. There was a sense that people wanted to participate in, and celebrate at, the type of mass communal events which had been forged at Wembley back in June. Premier League clubs enjoyed record season-ticket sales. In London, Chelsea, Spurs and Arsenal all reported significant increases from the previous season. Chelsea, boosted by Ruud Gullit's appointment and their transfer splurge, saw theirs go up by a whopping fifty per cent. In the North East, Bryan Robson's pre-season spree and the imminent arrival of Alan Shearer had led to close on advance sell-outs at both the Riverside Stadium and St James' Park. Match-day admission prices were being hiked at the same time. It was the influx of the more well-off supporters tempted to Wembley to watch England who sparked the gentrification of the game and Premier League club owners raced to capitalise. That season, just three of the twenty Premiership clubs announced price freezes: Leeds, Wimbledon and Manchester United. At Old Trafford, the cost of seeing a game remained £18 or £12. For £8, meanwhile, one could get a seat in the lower west stand at Hillsborough to watch Sheffield Wednesday. This benevolence did not endure. Ticket prices shot up in the seasons ahead. Between 1990 and 2014, the cost of watching a match at Old Trafford soared by almost eight hundred per cent. By the start of the 2015–16 Premier League season, the most expensive season tickets at Spurs, Chelsea and Manchester City were well over £1,000. To see Arsenal from the best seats at the Emirates, supporters would have to fork out an eye-watering £2,039. In the four years up to that point, even the price of the cheapest match-day tickets rose at almost twice the cost of living. It was true that Euro 96 had united the country and extended football's tentacles. It was also the case, though, that the net effect of this was to encourage the game at the top level to be priced out of the reach of the working-class supporters who had once been its lifeblood.

However, on the pitch English football could still claim to have a genuine folk hero in its midst. On 6 August, eighteen thousand Newcastle supporters turned out in drizzle to witness Shearer being paraded at St James' Park. Flanked by Kevin Keegan and Freddy Shepherd, both beaming like cats with cream, and sporting his number nine jersey, Shearer was led up on to a makeshift platform erected in front of the main stand.

A rapturous chant went up from the crowd, 'Shearer, Shearer'. On and on it went. It was not just the club's riches that had been invested in one footballer, but so much hope, so many dreams. 'I've always wanted to play here, I've never hidden that fact and it's a dream come true for me,' Shearer told a scrum of reporters at his press conference. 'To play in front of these supporters, and to play in front of my mum and dad at Newcastle as well, is something else. We just need to win that first trophy and if we get that one, then who knows, I think this place will be alight.'

Four days later, Shearer made his debut for Newcastle in a pre-season friendly at Lincoln City. A full house of ten thousand at the Third Division club's ramshackle Sincil Bank ground witnessed his first goal for his new team, a thirty-third-minute penalty, in Newcastle's 2–0 win. Shearer's mere presence illustrated the widening gulf in realities and expectations between those at the top and bottom of the game. 'Without this match,' Lincoln manager John Beck said afterwards, 'we couldn't have run the club this year.'

The following weekend, attention turned to Wembley again and the season's annual curtain-raiser, the Charity Shield. Manchester United, the Double winners, versus Newcastle United, runners-up last time out. But more pointedly, Shearer meeting Ferguson so soon after snubbing him. Heavy, ominous clouds hung over Wembley and these were portents for Shearer and his team. Keegan went with his customary bold, attacking line-up with Shearer and

Les Ferdinand, now wearing the number ten shirt, at its head. Frenchman David Ginola and Peter Beardsley supported them from the flanks with David Batty and Rob Lee left to guard the midfield. Ferguson had Eric Cantona as captain and David Beckham, Paul Scholes, Nicky Butt and Phil Neville in his team. Goalkeeper Peter Schmeichel aside, he kept his Euro 96 players, Gary Neville, Karel Poborský and Jordi Cruyff on the bench. Seventy-three thousand spectators looked on as Shearer toiled against his markers, David May and Gary Pallister, and Manchester United ran rampant.

Cantona and Beckham were handed acres of space and led the assault. Beckham slid the Frenchmen through for United's first goal. Cantona, with an impudent back-heel, and Beckham a sweeping cross, combined to tee up Nicky Butt for the second. Then Cantona returned the favour, setting Beckham free to chip in the third. Roy Keane's long-range strike rounded off a chastening afternoon for Newcastle and Shearer, jeered throughout by the red-clad supporters. Beaten 4–0 and left chasing shadows. 'Manchester United outpaced, outplayed and outwitted the pretenders from the North-East,' ran a match report in *The Times*. 'It was Cantona, around a twelfth of the cost of Shearer, who inspired the Double winners to such an emphatic victory.'

Among the first of the new wave of overseas imports into the English top flight, precursor to the legions recruited and welcomed into the thriving domestic game post-Euro 96, Cantona was also one of, if not *the* best of them. So insouciant and self-assured on the pitch, playing with the collar of his shirt turned up, preening like a peacock, he was the complete modern footballer. Not blessed with a sprinter's turn of pace, but so much quicker in thought and more skilful than the average player, Cantona had a painter's eye for the crucial small details of a game and was able to exploit them with unerring precision. He joined United midway through the 1992–93 season for just £1.2 million from Leeds, where he had won the league title. He had become the touchstone of Ferguson's team and had helped them to three Premier League titles and two Doubles. Cantona was dashing, brilliant, but also unpredictable and untameable. The kung-fu kick at Selhurst Park in January 1995 was his most notorious eruption in England, but playing in his native France he was once banned for three months for throwing a ball at a referee and then telling the disciplinary committee that they were idiots. Yet Cantona was a devoted trainer, too, forensic about honing his fitness and technique. It was this that had rubbed off on Ferguson's young blades and, at thirty, he was still in his pomp, a footballer and sportsman supreme.

At the same time there was a storm brewing at Highbury where Bruce Rioch was an unreconstructed manager of the old school. A strict disciplinarian, this son of a regimental sergeant-major was intolerant of having to nurse the fragile egos of players now being handed million-pound contracts. The previous season, his first at the club, Rioch had clashed with Arsenal's star striker, Ian Wright, and fractured the dressing room. This was compounded during the summer by a rift that opened up between him and the club's influential vice-chairman, David Dein. The Arsenal board, swayed by Dein, negotiated the club's transfers and rejected Rioch's list of English-based targets. The resulting Mexican stand-off had rumbled on all through pre-season, but came to an abrupt halt on 12 August when Rioch was sacked. Dein was known to favour a fresh, more cerebral and continental approach to football affairs and Johan Cruyff, ousted from Barcelona in May, was immediately installed as favourite for the Arsenal vacancy. The dark horse, though, was Arsène Wenger, little known in England outside football circles and still the man Glenn Hoddle hoped to tempt to Lancaster Gate.

Tony Adams had been one of Rioch's staunchest supporters. The Arsenal captain was then negotiating a new, improved contract with the club, but he was barely functioning, physically or mentally. Adams reported for pre-season training looking gaunt and wan, having hardly eaten a proper meal in the weeks since Euro 96. His troublesome knee injury had flared up again and while Rioch was dangling Adams was absent, visiting the club's Harley Street doctors, or else drunk or hungover. Towards the end of July, he underwent a second bout of surgery on his knee and vanished altogether from Highbury and the club's training complex at London Colney. 'As I sat at home with my leg in a cast,' he recalled in 1999, 'and was thus forced out of the pub routine, I began to get a bit of self-respect back, just for odd periods. I became obsessive about drawing and painting . . . Some days I couldn't manage it and would struggle out on crutches for a session. One day I was in a pub in the West End, a fight broke out and I smashed a crutch over someone's head. It was another of those incidents where I was in blackout.'

On the eve of the new season starting, Adams was due to report to London Colney and then travel with Arsenal's physiotherapist, Gary Lewin, to a hospital appointment in Whitechapel. He was expected to have his knee examined and be given the all-clear to resume full training. 'Instead, I was in a hotel room at the Holiday Inn in Kensington,' he admitted. 'I had set out on a bender with a friend on the Wednesday . . . The dying stages of alcoholism are not pretty. After taking in a strip club, I picked up a girl for the night and took her back to the hotel.'

The previous day, on 15 August, Arsenal's board had sanctioned the signing of two new players: thirty-year-old Rémi Garde, on a free transfer from Strasbourg, and Patrick Vieira, a beanpole twenty-year-old who had made just two appearances in *Serie A* for AC Milan and cost £3.5 million. Since both were French, and Vieira unproven, the obvious deduction was that Dein had secured his continental manager and that Wenger was already influencing recruitment policy at Highbury. For Arsenal, and English football as a whole, Wenger's imminent arrival would herald the changing times.

* * *

The sight and sound of the vast, roaring Wembley crowds at Euro 96 continued to impact on English sport and culture in general. In the years ahead, support for the national cricket, rugby union and even the European Ryder Cup golf teams became notably more boisterous and brazenly patriotic. That summer, though, it was no more evident than at two rock concerts held on the same weekend as the Charity Shield just up the road from London Colney at Knebworth House. Oasis had set off on a victory lap around the country and a week earlier played two shows to a total of sixty thousand people at Balloch Castle on the shores of Loch Lomond. The band's two Knebworth dates, though, were on a different scale altogether, dwarfing these and even the great tribal gatherings at Wembley.

First built in 1490, and redeveloped in a Tudor Gothic style by the architect Henry Edward Kendall Junior between 1843 and 1845, Knebworth House was a classic English stately home set in acres of verdant Hertfordshire countryside. In previous decades its grounds had been used as venue for massive gigs by the Rolling Stones, Led Zeppelin, Pink Floyd and Queen. Prog-rockers Genesis had been the last superstar band to play there in 1992 and Oasis' appearances were set to elevate them to the pantheon of British rock royalty. By that summer, (What's the Story) Morning Glory? had sold more than three million copies in Britain alone and there was unprecedented public demand for the Knebworth gigs. More than two and a half million people submitted postal applications for the 250,000 tickets on sale. Priced £22.50, these tickets were soon changing hands for fifteen times their face value. On the weekend itself, temperatures soared into the mid-twenties (°C) and miles-long caravans of traffic snaked down and up the main A1 arterial road from the North and London. On site, queues for the toilets and beer tents stretched for hundreds of yards. The guest-list numbered seven thousand and included Kate Moss, Jarvis Cocker of Pulp and what seemed to be the entire British music industry. They were entertained backstage in Creation's hospitality tent, the size of an aircraft hangar and with a self-aggrandising banner strung across its gaping entrance that read: 'Creation Records – World Class.'

Spread over the two days, Oasis' hand-picked supporting cast showcased the key elements of British popular music through the mid-1990s. Britpop infantrymen such as Ocean Colour Scene, Cast and Kula Shaker lined up alongside more established guitar bands such as the Manic Street Preachers and the Charlatans. The Prodigy and the Chemical Brothers carried the rave flag. John Squire of the Stone Roses joined Oasis for their encore, a triumphant, euphoric reading of 'Champagne Supernova'. Each night, a huge, sprawling multitude, delirious and tumultuous, greeted Oasis like deities, just as the England team had been met at Wembley two months before.

Opening the second night, rain lancing down from the heavens, Noel Gallagher regarded the great sea of humanity laid out before him and proclaimed: 'This is history!

This is history!' It was that. But it was also an orgy of excess and the point at which cracks began to show in and around the band as their spirit became corrupted and then drained out of them. In this respect Oasis could be viewed as being symbolic of the more general air that pervaded as the country rushed towards a new millennium. 'Everything up to that point was fucking brilliant,' Gallagher opines. 'Every day was different. I don't even remember getting a hangover, not once. I down a pint of Guinness now and get a headache. Afterwards, that's when the phone calls all came to be about sales figures. I still didn't own my own house when we played at Knebworth. Admittedly, I was renting a nice place in St John's Wood, but I didn't feel like a rock star then. I had butterflies all the time. We flew into Knebworth in a helicopter, but we were all wearing Adidas trainers. It was still a little bit unprofessional. Once [guitarist] Bonehead and [bassist] Guigsy became millionaires, I think they wanted out. I don't think they believed they were good enough to be in a band that big. On stage at Knebworth, Liam and I both felt like we were in our backyard. Whereas the pair of them were going, "How the fuck did we get here?"'

'Knebworth was silly, ridiculous,' says Creation Records press officer Andy Saunders. 'There were people going around backstage on golf carts and helicopters landing. I went there in a limousine. It was a really good gig, but I remember not feeling part of it at all. Alan McGee said the same thing. He couldn't even get a Diet Coke in the hospitality tent and he was paying for it.

Literally, that was the tipping point for the company. From then on, the vibe was never as good and McGee was losing interest. We had to have security guards on the doors of the offices in Primrose Hill because crazy people were coming in and claiming Noel had stolen the lyrics to 'Wonderwall'. One night in the office, the phone rang and it was Ronnie Kray. He wanted Noel and Liam to go and visit him in prison.'

It would be another four years before McGee shut up shop at Creation, but things started to unravel for Oasis within a fortnight of Knebworth. On 23 August they were scheduled to shoot an *MTV Unplugged* performance at the Royal Festival Hall on London's South Bank. Liam Gallagher pulled out on the morning of filming as a result of laryngitis and left his brother to take over lead vocal duties for the show. The younger Gallagher still turned up to watch on the night, though, peering down from a perch in the dress circle where he was sat alongside his girl-friend, the actress Patsy Kensit, chain-smoking cigarettes. Four days later, the band gathered at Heathrow Airport to fly out for an American tour. Liam Gallagher announced he would not be joining them as he and Kensit had an urgent need to go house-hunting.

It was not perhaps the best period for the band to be working on a new record, but Noel Gallagher ploughed on regardless. At the start of June, Noel had settled down to writing new songs at a house he was renting from Mick Jagger on Mustique. He and Meg Matthews were holiday-ing on the Caribbean island with Kate Moss and Johnny

Depp. Oasis' regular producer, Owen Morris, was summoned from England and Gallagher began setting down
demos of his new tracks. It was the last time he would
find the experience of being in Oasis carefree. In keeping
with the general mood of abandon, Depp played guitar
and Moss tambourine on one of the songs. 'The Mustique
session was the last good recording I did for Noel,' Morris
later told Keith Cameron of Q. 'We were recording in a
shack, drinking rum, smoking quality weed, and outside
Kate Moss was swimming naked in the pool. Life doesn't
get much better.'

Six months later, Oasis repaired to Abbey Road studios
to start tracking the album in the same room the Beatles
had once used. The sessions were strained from the start,
not eased by having paparazzi camped outside the famous
old studio or the mountains of cocaine being consumed
behind its walls. The operation lurched from there
to Ridge Farm Studio in West Sussex and then back to
London at AIR Studios, the record getting more over-
blown. 'We should have let ... *Morning Glory?* and
Knebworth settle and fade into the distance and never
made that album,' Noel Gallagher admits. 'Everybody in
and around the band at that point – we were all just drug
buddies.' Morris said: 'As far as I could tell, the only reason anyone was there was for the money. Noel had decided
Liam was a shit singer. Liam had decided he hated Noel's
songs. I got badly into cocaine and lost the plot. So on we
went. Massive amounts of drugs, big fights, bad vibes and
shit recordings.' The result of their labours would not

emerge until the following August, but when it did, *Be Here Now* was to prove ruinous for Oasis and pretty much the entire Britpop era as well.

Paul Gascoigne's fall from the pedestal he had been put on after Euro 96 was even more jarring. Oasis' first Knebworth show coincided with the start of the new season in Scotland. Forty-six thousand supporters turned out at Ibrox to watch Gascoigne's Rangers narrowly beat Raith Rovers 1–0. Two weeks later Gascoigne struck his first goal of the campaign in another 1–0 home victory over Dundee United. Outwardly Gascoigne appeared becalmed and settled. On the pitch he was playing with the same panache and freedom he had shown at Wembley, the centrifugal force from which his team was powered. Off it, Gascoigne had moved his new wife and family into his latest acquisition, a rambling old lodge house built on the shores of Loch Lomond and in the heart of the Trossachs National Park. It seemed it might be his own personal oasis. It was half-an-hour's drive from Glasgow but half the world away from the hustle and bustle of the city. To begin with he indulged the same fantasy as he had at Burnham Beeches. Attired now like a Scottish laird, he went fishing in the abundant waters and bestrode his grounds, the lord of all he surveyed. The idyll, though, was not to last.

'Everything was rosy until I began to turn into a bastard again,' he told his biographer, Hunter Davies. '[It was] for various reasons, most of them stupid.' Gascoigne tried to shut them out, he always did, but the demons were back. They were like a nest of vipers in his head, poisoning his thoughts and unleashing all his irrational fears and paranoias. He brooded over the state of his marriage, disintegrating no sooner than it had started, and as the season progressed, on his own apparently dwindling football powers. With the exception of the Old Firm games against Celtic, the pace of the Scottish Premier League was slower and the quality of opposition lower than in its English counterpart. And Gascoigne was a marked man in his second campaign north of the border. He was kicked, goaded, ruffled, and as a result of a spate of niggling injuries, increasingly not as quick to escape the close attentions of tormenting defenders. He started to drink heavily again, trapped once more in a hellish, vicious cycle.

One afternoon, Gascoigne turned up drunk for a game. Walter Smith told him to put his suit back on and ordered him out of the dressing room. At such times, Gascoigne would plead forgiveness from his manager and swear off the booze, only to hit the bottle again. He was running off the rails, hellhounds on his trail, and Smith snapped again when he rolled into training on another morning still stinking of the night before. 'Walter picked me up by the scruff of the neck,' Gascoigne remembered, 'and said, "Get out, go home and never come back". I was starting to let him and his assistant, Archie Knox, down on a regular basis. All of the rows and fights with Shel made it worse.'

In October, Gascoigne took his wife and their children to Gleneagles for a weekend break before a Champions League game against Ajax in Holland. It was meant to repair damage, but Gascoigne was twitchy, distracted. The first night at the hotel, the couple went down to dinner, leaving his adopted daughter Bianca, ten, and son Mason, seven, up in their room with a nanny. Gascoigne started to become dangerously unwound and was mixing his drinks, whisky on top of Champagne. An argument started between the two of them, by whom and over what he would not remember, but it got loud and ugly. Eventually, Sheryl Gascoigne fled the restaurant, escaping her belligerent husband and the appalled stares of their fellow diners. Possessed now, Gascoigne took off after his wife, chasing her into their room and then lashed out. Afterwards, he would dimly recall the awful sequence of events of the next few seconds. By his own account, Gascoigne headbutted his wife, knocked her to the floor, breaking her finger. The children heard their mother's screams from the adjoining room.

'The next day, Shel took the kids and left,' Gascoigne related to Davies. 'I did nothing to stop her. I just accepted it. I had pushed her around before, but nothing as bad as this . . . Perhaps I had done a bit more in the past than pushing her. I had twisted her arm once and, yes, there was the time I banged her head on the floor in Italy. But I paid dearly, because it all came out and Shel and I separated, and I lost my wife.'

Gascoigne flew off to Amsterdam with Rangers. The

following evening he was sent off after just ten minutes as his team slumped to a 4–1 defeat. Back home, his estranged wife went to the newspapers and bared the details of his abuse. Gascoigne drifted further into the blackness. He started smoking with the zeal of an addict and was soon getting through a packet of cigarettes a day. He took pills to help him sleep, pills to numb the pain and the dark thoughts in his head. His insomnia got worse. He began pilfering batches of the sedative Zimovane from Rangers' medical supplies and skulking back to his lodge. The house empty and silent now, and with just his nightmares for company, Gascoigne felt trapped, hunted. 'Everywhere I went,' he said, 'on the pitch and off it, rival fans would shout, "Wife-beater" at me.'

Somehow he still managed to function as a footballer. His instincts were dulled, and he was again making himself susceptible to knocks and strains, but he would nevertheless be able to play thirty-four games and score seventeen goals for Rangers during the course of the season. With him at the helm of their midfield, steering their course, the club went on to win a second consecutive league title and also the League Cup. Walter Smith, too, had not yet grown weary of having to bully, cajole and nurse Gascoigne from one week to the next. Smith understood that it was only football that could now keep Gascoigne balanced on a precarious even keel. And most of all, it was the idea, however vague it might have been to Gascoigne during his bleakest moments, that he might yet be able to recapture English hearts that soothed him

most of all. Whenever he stepped out of line, or lost control, Smith cautioned him: 'Be careful. Hoddle will want
to make his name.'

CHAPTER FOURTEEN

'My soul was screaming out for help'

Nothing highlighted the rapidity of the changes Euro 96 was ushering into English football better than how suddenly Paul Gascoigne was usurped as the nation's most famous footballer. More than any other English player, Gascoigne was restored and built up during the tournament. Yet the overall furore that surrounded Euro 96 had also accelerated footballers towards a more heightened form of celebrity. This was as a result of the game having for the first time reached an audience that bridged class, gender and generational divides. On the back of this came a deluge of sponsors and marketing gurus and they were looking for younger, cleaner-cut models to sell football. And hawk their wares. The perfect vehicle for this burst into bloom on the opening Saturday of the 1996–97 Premier League season.

Britain sweltered through a heatwave on 17 August. Temperatures across the country soared to ten degrees above the seasonal average. The mercury touched 31°C in Birmingham, Nottingham and Leeds. Coastal roads were gridlocked and beaches teemed with holiday-makers and day-trippers burning crimson. In the North East, Alan Shearer made his home debut for Newcastle against Everton. Fourteen years earlier, Shearer had presented himself at the club's training ground as a schoolboy for a two-day trial. He had told the coaches he was a centre-forward, but they foisted a goalkeeper's jersey on him and he stood disconsolate between the posts on both days. Shearer had gone off to Southampton instead. His homecoming was just as inglorious. Everton made Newcastle look toothless, Shearer impotent and won 2–0.

Elsewhere that baking afternoon, Fabrizio Ravanelli opened his account for Middlesbrough with a hat-trick against Liverpool. The Riverside Stadium was almost full a good half-an-hour before kick-off, two samba bands working up a sunshine beat from either end of the ground. Liverpool almost spoiled the party, three times taking the lead, Robbie Fowler pinching their third with a typical predatory goal. Ravanelli, the 'White Feather', pulled the home side back into the game on each occasion: a penalty and two poacher's strikes. The Tottenham of Teddy Sheringham and Darren Anderton won 2–0 at Blackburn, while Gareth Southgate's Aston Villa were beaten 2–1 at Sheffield Wednesday.

At the same time, Stuart Pearce's Nottingham Forest won 3–0 at Coventry. It was to be an eventful, rollercoaster season for Pearce and his club. Going off on holiday to Zimbabwe in July, Pearce had watched the victorious German squad file through Heathrow Airport with the

European Championship trophy. It tweaked him enough that when Glenn Hoddle called soon after, Pearce had not taken much persuading to recant his decision to retire from international football. He would be back in an England team within a fortnight and player-manager of Forest by that December following the resignation of boss Frank Clark, himself a former Forest left-back. Clark left the club rooted to the bottom of the Premier League. Pearce went on to galvanise the team, leading by example, winning four of his first six games in temporary charge and landing a Manager of the Month award. Pearce hauled Forest out of the relegation zone before the board brought in the former Wimbledon and Sheffield United manager, Dave Bassett, on a full-time basis. Pearce returned to the trenches. But under Bassett, Forest failed to win any of their last eleven games and ended up relegated to the First Division.

However, the moment that stood out like a beacon on that opening day occurred three minutes from the end of the game between Wimbledon and Manchester United at Selhurst Park. United were coasting to victory after Eric Cantona and Denis Irwin had given them a 2–0 lead. Then, David Beckham picked up the ball in space and approaching the halfway line. He looked up, spotted Wimbledon goalkeeper Neil Sullivan standing off his line and let fly. The ball sped from his right boot covering the fifty yards to goal in a long, fast, vicious arc, clearing Sullivan, desperately back-pedalling now, and crashing into the back of the Wimbledon net. 'Oh!' gasped John Motson, commentating on the game for *Match of the Day*.

'That is absolutely phenomenal.' It was, and still is. In that instant, the twenty-one-year-old Beckham not only became the newest and brightest star in the English game, but it also marked the beginning of his ascent towards an entirely new kind of football super-being.

Beckham grew up in Leytonstone, east London. His dad, Ted, was a kitchen fitter and mum, Lorraine, a hairdresser, both of them ardent Manchester United supporters. In 1986, the Beckhams enrolled their eleven-year-old football-mad son on a week-long summer course at a Bobby Charlton soccer school in Manchester. He won a skills competition there, the prize being a trip to Barcelona to visit Camp Nou, then the domain of Terry Venables. The young Beckham, slight and looking bashful, even had his picture taken with El Tel on the training pitches outside the grand old stadium. Coaches at Charlton's school also tipped off scouts from Manchester United about Beckham and he went on to sign schoolboy forms with the club at fourteen. Alex Ferguson shepherded him around the place that summer.

'We were training when the boss himself walked over, his arm around the shoulder of this skinny kid with gel in his air,' Gary Neville recalled in his autobiography. 'He was wearing a brand-new United tracksuit and his best trainers. We were thinking, "Who's this flash git?" He was so slim he looked like he'd be blown over in a gale, but when we started training, he could deliver a ball better than anyone I'd ever seen. He could hit a brilliant pass off any part of his foot – spinning, dipping, a low grass-cutter or whipped into the box. And game after game, you've never seen anyone cover so much ground.'

Alongside Neville, Ryan Giggs and Paul Scholes, Beckham was part of the Manchester United team who won the FA Youth Cup in 1992, and again the next season. He made his first-team debut in September 1992, coming on as a substitute during a League Cup tie at Brighton. Ferguson loaned him out to Preston to be toughened in the blood and thunder of the Third Division, before handing him his Premier League debut, aged seventeen, in a home game against Leeds on 2 April 1995. He was a fixture in the side during the following, title-winning season, and had just been taken on by an agent, Tony Stephens, who also looked after the affairs of Alan Shearer and David Platt. '[Stephens] had sorted out some major commercial deals for Shearer and Platt,' said Neville. 'It was obvious that Becks would be appearing on adverts before long with his looks and talent. It just seemed logical: Becks was always going to be a star.'

Platt's Arsenal, under the stewardship of caretaker manager Pat Rice, won their first game of the campaign 2–0 against West Ham at Highbury. Not fit for selection, Tony Adams reported to the ground with the rest of the squad that lunch-time, wished them luck and then went home to bed to dry out. He had reached the end of his long, dark road. Adams's last port of call had been a working men's club near his home in Hornchurch late in the afternoon of Friday, 16 August. He arrived there still wearing the clothes he had slept in the night before and

reeking of booze, sweat and stale piss. 'The club was closing, but I knew the steward, Jack, would let me have a
drink,' Adams related in his memoir. 'I ordered a pint of
Guinness. It was five o'clock, I noticed, when Jack came
over to the table in the corner where I was sitting alone
with an empty glass. "You all right, Tone?" he asked. "No,
I'm not," I said and started to cry. Five p.m., Friday,
16 August 1996: I took, I hope, God willing, my last drink
of alcohol . . . I just wanted to stop drinking. I felt I was
beaten. My soul was screaming out for help.'

Adams got up and went home, picking up fish and
chips on the way, his first meal of the day. He could not
eat, though, his stomach cramping, so crawled into bed
instead and sweated and fever-dreamed through a terrible
night and into the next morning. Obeying club rules, he
managed to haul himself off to Highbury, to hold himself
together, and then went back to his wretched vigil.

'Over the next thirty-six hours or so, I alternated
between hot sweats and cold shivers,' he recalled, 'getting up only for small portions of nourishment: cereal,
toast, soup, scrambled eggs. Dehydrated, I drank jugs of
water. And I wept as I had never wept before. At times,
my body demanded a drink, but I ignored it, though I'm
not sure how.'

On the Monday morning Adams got up and reported
for training at London Colney. He was physically diminished and mentally exhausted. In the car park he bumped
into a friend of Paul Merson's, Steve Jacobs, a counsellor
who had helped the Arsenal striker battle his own

addictions. 'It was surely meant to be,' Adams reflected. 'I blurted out, "I've got a drink problem and I need to go to Alcoholics Anonymous". It was the first time in my life that I had asked another person for help.'

'Tony had drunk himself stupid, basically,' says Ian Ridley, Adams's ghost writer. 'I got to know him ten days later. I'd always thought he was a pretty boorish sort of character, very ungracious. However, he grew as we worked on his book over an eighteen-month period. He was finding himself and became a very different character. I was also a recovering alcoholic and we got on well. In many ways, the change he was going through at that time was reflective of how English football was changing. Both went hand in hand.'

One of the ironies of the huge swell of patriotism set off at Euro 96 was that it coincided with a period in which the public's affection for the Royal Family took a dip. Up until that June, it had been the great royal state occasions when the Union and St George flags were displayed *en masse* and with such pomp and pride. However, the Royal Family's popularity had begun to dwindle four years earlier as a result of two failed marriages and an entirely symbolic inferno.

The course of 1992 was indeed a sorry one for the House of Windsor. During it, The Queen's two eldest sons, Princes Charles and Andrew, separated from their wives, revealing in the process very human foibles that had hitherto been kept hidden. Added to this, on 20 November 1992, a fire swept through the royal castle at Windsor, causing damage amounting to £36.5 million. When it initially seemed that the public purse was going to have to fund the restoration works, a treasonous mood swelled, compelling the Queen to foot the bill.

This new mood of antipathy towards the Royal Family had hardly abated by 28 August 1996 when the Prince and Prince and Princess of Wales, Charles and Diana, were granted a *decree nisi*, officially ending their fifteen-year marriage. The terms of the divorce provided for joint custody of their two young sons, William and Harry. The Princess surrendered her 'Royal Highness' title, but would continue to reside at Kensington Palace and retain offices at St James's Palace. Furthermore, Diana was awarded a reported £17 million lump sum and £350,000 a year to run her private staff. Charles also announced he had no intention of re-marrying. The cold, hard facts of the divorce were a far cry from their fairy-tale wedding on 29 July 1981, when a worldwide television audience of close to a billion watched the thirty-two-year-old Prince and the then twenty-year-old Lady Diana Spencer marry at St Paul's Cathedral.

The slow, tortuous unravelling of Charles and Diana's marriage had been a cancer eating away at the heart of the monarchy. Diana, establishing for herself the role of victim, sucked up from the House of Windsor the respect and devotion of its subjects. England supporters had sung the National Anthem at Wembley that summer more for their team than their Queen, and in any case, they had imbued 'Three Lions' with greater gusto and meaning.

The royal couple's disentanglement began in the tawdriest of circumstances. In August 1992, the *Sun* got hold of a private telephone conversation between Diana and a male friend, James Gilbey, taped eighteen months earlier by seventy-year-old Cyril Reenan, an amateur radio operator and retired bank manager from Abingdon in Oxfordshire. Gilbey referred to Diana as 'darling' and 'squidgy' throughout the thirty-minute recording. The latter endearment gave the story its name when the tabloid published the transcripts: 'Squidgygate'. Diana in turn expressed her concern to Gilbey that members of the Royal household would find out about their recent tryst and that she might be pregnant. At one point, she claimed to have burst into tears while having dinner with Charles. 'I just felt so sad and empty,' she confided to Gilbey, 'and thought, "Bloody hell, after all I've done for this fucking family".'

To lay bare both a member of the Royal Family's intimate secrets and its inner workings was almost unthinkable, and the *Sun*'s exclusive went off like a bomb. Buckingham Palace rushed to limit the damage, announcing Charles and Diana would separate. However, there was another, still more revealing phone conversation lurking in the wings. This was a six-minute bedtime chat between Charles and Camilla Parker-Bowles, an old debutante flame of his, who, since 1973, had been married to an Army officer, Andrew Parker-Bowles. Dating from

18 December 1989, it was also understood to have been captured by an amateur radio scanner. Four years later, the contents of 'Camillagate' also became explosive when they were rehashed in full by an Australian tabloid and German magazine. Soon after, on 17 January 1993, two British tabloids, the *Sunday Mirror* and *Sunday People*, published excerpts of the transcript simultaneously.

At the time of the call, Charles was visiting the dowager Duchess of Westminster in Cheshire while Parker-Bowles was at home in the West Country. Rumours that the two of them were conducting an affair were rife in Establishment and media circles, but the tabloid revelations were nonetheless shocking, not least because the heir to the throne was, of all things, found to be talking dirty to his mistress. 'I want to feel my way all along you,' Charles began one exchange, 'all over you, and up and down you, and in and out.' 'Oh, Charles,' Parker-Bowles cooed. '*Particularly* in and out,' the Prince confided as if reciting from the pages of a bodice-ripping novel. This was, as both of the British papers might have put it, sensational, salacious stuff.

Charles waited eighteen months before attempting to recover his dignity. He consented to a television interview with Jonathan Dimbleby, broadcast on ITV in June 1994. The programme aimed to present a revealing, yet sympathetic portrait of the Prince. But the public fixated instead on Charles's admission to Dimbleby of his infidelity. What was now a royal soap opera carried on becoming more lurid and riveting with each instalment: Diana was exposed again in March 1995 with the publication of a new book, *Princess in Love*. In this, another British Army officer, Major James Hewitt, spilled the details of a long-running, but doomed affair with Diana to journalist Anna Pasternak, who regurgitated his revelations in the frothing style of a Mills & Boon. By that summer, Diana was also being linked with the England rugby captain, Will Carling, a *Boys' Own* figure who frequented the same west London gym as the Princess. Diana declined to comment, but Carling and his wife were later to divorce.

All of this, though, was nothing compared with the impact of a television interview granted by Diana. Conducted by Martin Bashir of the BBC's *Panorama*, it gripped an audience of twenty-three million on the evening of 20 November 1995. The Princess chose this as the moment to set out and pick over the bones of her marriage to Charles. It was on her part an unprecedented tilt at the buttoned-up conventions of royal decorum as well as a cold, calculating act of revenge. Comporting herself as if gravely wounded, Diana revealed that she had suffered post-natal depression, eating disorders and had self-harmed. She, too, admitted to her infidelity with Hewitt, but also made repeated, jabbing references to Parker-Bowles and her estranged husband, locating their relationship as the source of her own ills. 'There were three of us in this marriage,' she told Bashir, sharpening her blade, 'so it was a bit crowded.' Towards the end of the hour-long broadcast, sat amidst the emotional wreckage she had brought crashing down, Diana was asked by

Bashir what future role she imagined for herself. Her answer was vainglorious. 'I would like,' she said, 'to be the queen of people's hearts.'

Directly after the *Panorama* broadcast, and still clinging to long-established, stiff-upper-lipped Royal formalities, the Queen wrote to both her eldest son and daughter-in-law imploring them to divorce. The Queen meant the divorce to staunch the wounds from their shattered marriage. These, though, were still pouring out a year later as the British press chewed over revelations of Diana's relationship with Dodi Al-Fayed, eldest son of the Egyptian entrepreneur and Harrods owner Mohamed Al-Fayed.

August 1996 was almost out before Alan Shearer recovered a semblance of the form he had shown during Euro 96. Shearer opened his Premier League account for Newcastle with two goals in their next two home matches. The first was a late, clinching strike in a midweek clash with Wimbledon. The second a penalty against Sheffield Wednesday on Saturday, 24 August, though it was not enough to prevent his team crashing to a 2–1 defeat and prolonging their stuttering start to the season.

There was a more unexpected scorer in the midweek game at Villa Park as Gareth Southgate notched the home side's winner against Blackburn. Southgate managed just seven goals in his six years with Villa, but none was cheered as much as this one by supporters, hoping their acclaim might rid him of the memory of his penalty miss. Southgate himself underwent another form of public exorcism. Later in the year, alongside Stuart Pearce and Chris Waddle, who had also missed from the spot in Turin in 1990, he was paid £40,000 to appear in a television advert for Pizza Hut poking fun at their shared failure.

Terry Venables's Portsmouth, meanwhile, lost their first two games of the season in the First Division against Bradford City and QPR. Looking on as his team toiled at Bradford's Valley Parade ground, chimney stacks and rows of soot-stained terraced houses on the horizon, Venables must have felt the dull, hard thud of coming back to earth. 'A trip to Moldova with England a week tomorrow suddenly looks an attractive proposition,' sniped a reporter from *The Times* after the QPR defeat. 'Perhaps he should not have stood down.'

On Monday, 24 August, Venables's successor gathered his first England squad together at Bisham Abbey to prepare for the game in Moldova, their first qualifier *en route* to the 1998 World Cup finals. Glenn Hoddle called up the core of Venables's Euro 96 group: Gascoigne, Ince, Seaman, the returning Pearce, Gary and Phil Neville, Barmby, Ferdinand and others were all present. Shearer was made captain in Adams's absence. The new manager also had his own men in mind. He recalled Gary Pallister of Manchester United and David Batty of Newcastle, and brought into the squad Beckham, Everton full-back Andy Hinchcliffe, Mark Draper of Aston Villa and Matt Le Tissier, fitful but capable of dazzling feats at Southampton.

There were new expectations of the national team manager now that the England team was once again perceived to be a potent force. A number of newspaper editorials had been published directly after Euro 96 emphasising the scale of Venables's achievements and the extent of the shadow he cast over his replacement. Hoddle was charged not so much with making England competitive, which previously would have been enough, but to go on and win the biggest prize in the game, the World Cup. What is more, he was given little more than a week to prepare for the start of this mission.

From the outset, the mood Hoddle established in the England camp was very different to the relaxed set-up that Venables had encouraged. Hoddle believed in strict conditioning and monitoring of his players. Ribald sessions in the Burnham Beeches bar were to be replaced by lectures on vitamin supplements and the finer points of refuelling given by Hoddle's old Monaco contact, Dr Yann Rougier. Hoddle meant his new broom to sweep out attitudes to the game that had endured for decades in England, but had made their last stand at Euro 96. His players were still to grasp as much, though. It was also the case that Hoddle's manner could be abrasive and unsettling. In short, he was the very antithesis of Terry Venables.

'I detected a change in tone right from the first meeting,' said Gary Neville. 'I went to book a car to go down to the local shop to buy some magazines. An FA official told me it wasn't allowed under the new management. Then I tried to order a sandwich in my room. Again, it was forbidden. Glenn wanted to know exactly where we were, what we ate and precisely when we went to bed. This was a culture shock. He possessed a great football brain. He's a guy who can spot a player and read the nuances of a game. When it came to strategy he was excellent in laying out what he wanted and in a very detailed way. The trouble was that Glenn never had Terry's ease around the players. He felt a need to exert control. I always got the impression he was disappointed that we didn't have the flair and skill of European players. If you failed to control a ball, or a pass wasn't true, you would often hear him tut. There was one occasion when Becks was asked to go through a free-kick routine and didn't quite take it right. "I'm not asking too much of you, am I?" Glenn said.'

'Hoddle's handling of Beckham was very strange,' affirms Matt Dickinson. 'He had technical ideas about the game and a clear vision of the type of England team he wanted, but his undoing in a football sense was undoubtedly his man-management. That was a flaw that is quite intrinsic to him. That Manchester United cabal grew to be very strong in the squad. So if you mishandled Beckham that would affect your relationships with the Nevilles and later with Scholes and Butt. Hoddle had a very fractious relationship with Alex Ferguson, too. Gary Neville talks of the two of them being on the phone and Fergie screaming down the line at Hoddle.'

Like Venables, Hoddle also had a strained relationship with the media. However, Venables, though excessively pre-occupied with how he was perceived and portrayed, was cute enough to nurture a band of football reporters who acted as his loyalists in print. Whereas Hoddle could have cared less about what the England press pack thought of him, never mind cossetting them on to his side. Eventually, this would be to his great cost. 'I was quite struck by Hoddle's absolute arrogance,' says Matt Dickinson. 'I know that football managers are always sure of themselves, but he seemed surer than most. He was pretty intolerant of questioning.' Ian Ridley agrees: 'That was Glenn, really – never quite there. He was curious with us. There was always this coolness, this distance and he was a little bit disparaging. That was why when the end came for him, he had very few allies. No one leapt to his defence.'

PART SIX:

SEPTEMBER

CHAPTER FIFTEEN

'She's the one for me. I've got to go out with her'

On 1 September England were in the Moldovan capital of Chişinău for their opening World Cup qualifier. Back home in England interest in the humdrum-looking fixture was heightened because it was Glenn Hoddle's first game in charge, but also due to the greatly enhanced support thanks to their exploits earlier in the summer. Indeed, the country as a whole had benefited from Euro 96. A report estimated the tournament was responsible for a quarter of the growth in the British economy recorded between April and June 1996. This was credited to the additional revenue from overseas supporters and to dramatic increases in the amounts spent in supermarkets on lager and takeaway pizzas during the tournament. 'Whatever the true impact, it is certain it would have been larger had England gone on to win Euro 96,' noted economist Jonathan Loynes from HSBC Markets, who had compiled the report. 'Gareth Southgate has a lot to answer for.'

One of the former republics of the Soviet Union, the tiny Eastern European country of Moldova is encircled by

Romania and Ukraine and had declared its independence just five years earlier. The Moldovan national team was ranked by Fifa down among the international footballing minnows, but the fixture still presented England with challenges. Late summer temperatures in Moldova were hot, humid and the playing surface at the worn-looking Republican Stadium was agricultural, the grass long and the ground bone-hard. Hoddle also knew that he could ill afford a slip up with Italy and a potentially tricky trip to Poland lurking in England's qualification group.

The mood in the England camp appeared to be good. During an open training session held at the stadium on the eve of the match, Paul Gascoigne amused the watching press pack by yanking down Paul Ince's shorts. Hoddle, though, was irked by having his predecessor criticise the way he meant to set up his team for the game. Just as Venables had on occasion, Hoddle was going with a three–five–two formation. Southgate, Gary Pallister and Stuart Pearce made up the backline, but with Steve McManaman and Darren Anderton both declaring themselves unfit to travel, Hoddle deployed two conventional full-backs on the flanks, Gary Neville and Andy Hinchcliffe. Speaking in his role as a television analyst, Venables suggested that this was a more negative version of his own default line-up. 'If it's that negative,' Hoddle retorted, 'my answer is that Germany play exactly the same system.'

England's return to action came just nine weeks after the Germans had sent them crashing out of Euro 96.

Hoddle's other tweaks were to pair Nick Barmby with Alan Shearer in attack and to hand David Beckham his debut on the right-hand side of Gascoigne in midfield. In front of a small crowd in the tight, open stadium, England struggled to get into a rhythm. However, their second-rate opponents barely troubled them and Ince and Gascoigne gave them a commanding lead within two first-half minutes before Shearer finished the tie off after the restart. It was a routine victory, but a perhaps more significant event occurred at the team hotel on the morning of the game. 'Becks and me shared rooms,' recalled Gary Neville. 'We were lounging on our beds watching MTV when the Spice Girls came on the telly. Victoria [Adams] was wearing a tight, shiny cat-suit and Becks just said, almost matter of fact, "She's the one for me. I've got to go out with her". Not long after that, he did – I think it took him about three weeks. You could never fault Becks for his single-mindedness.'

At the time still callow and gauche, Beckham was to end that season being voted PFA Young Footballer of the Year by his fellow players. However, it was his burgeoning relationship with Posh Spice that greased his ascent to a level of stardom that was then unprecedented for a footballer. It turned out that Jamie Redknapp and Louise Nurding had been nothing more than a dry run for a better player, a more successful pop star and a more glamorous coupling. 'Redknapp and Louise were the Marks & Spencer version of what Beckham and Posh became,' says Anthony Noguera, a former editor of *FHM*. 'Louise, God bless her, was lovely, but not in the biggest girl band of all time, and both of them were terribly lacking in real glamour.'

Beckham and Adams were subsequently married in July 1999 with Gary Neville as best man. The couple were already self-regarding enough by then to have their own coat of arms designed for the event and greeted their guests seated on two matching gilded thrones. The following year Beckham unveiled a new crop haircut at a Premier League game at Leicester City and sparked an instant trend across Britain among other footballers and young men in general for the 'Beckham buzz cut'. In 2003, and having just joined Real Madrid, Beckham signed up with Simon Fuller's 19 Entertainment group. Fuller, the Spice Girls' manager, was a long-standing Manchester United season ticket holder and helped to make Beckham Britain's highest earning sports star and transformed the couple into a jet-setting global brand – the Beckhams.

Fuller negotiated Beckham lucrative contracts with such blue-chip fashion brands as Armani and Police sunglasses. On one occasion, Beckham pocketed £12 million for undertaking a ten-day tour of the Far East on behalf of a car manufacturer. He progressed to being England captain, the country's most capped outfield player and ended his career as a trailblazer for Major League Soccer having joined LA Galaxy in a reported $250 million deal brokered by Fuller. The Beckham's marriage survived his alleged fling in 2004 with his then-personal assistant, Rebecca Loos, and they went on accumulating wealth on a staggering scale. By 2015, their combined earnings from football, pop music, endorsements and their own bespoke fragrance and clothing lines was estimated at being as much as half-a-billion dollars. Not even England's best footballer, Beckham was nonetheless the first to become bigger than the game itself and a global icon in his own right. The shift from Gascoigne to Beckham, begun during the summer after Euro 96, marked the English game's leap from one era into the next.

'Beckham's emergence coincided with the next age of English football,' opines Ian Ridley. 'He was an incredibly dedicated player, wanted nothing more than to be remembered for his football. However, he was also a good-looking man who had the notion of making the most of his talents both on and off the pitch. Beckham was charming and emotionally intelligent as well, smart and savvy, and unlike Gascoigne he was also balanced and looked good on TV. He was the perfect player for his time.'

For the rest of that summer, echoes of the Euro 96 feel-good factor continued at a range of events taking place far outside football stadiums. The annual London Fashion Week opened with a fanfare on 24 September. The 1996 jamboree was significant in the ongoing renaissance in British fashion. For years, home-grown design talent had been forced to leave Britain to gain work and notice. But noted exiles like Katharine Hamnett and Vivienne Westwood, the *grande dame* of punk, were now returning to show at London. A British designer, Gibraltar-born

John Galliano, was then heading up the prestigious French house, Givenchy. Such factors, in tandem with the omni-presence of Kate Moss, combined to make British fashion again vital and vibrant, and London was swinging as it had not swung since the 1960s.

The most significant reverberation, though, occurred at the Labour Party Conference, which kicked off in the rather less chic environs of Blackpool on 30 September. With a General Election due the following spring, and opinion polls giving Labour a seemingly impregnable lead over the Tories, there was a giddy, exultant air rush-ing around the Lancashire coastal town all that week. On the eve of Conference, Creation Records sponsored a fringe event, the Youth Experience Rally, at which two hundred local youngsters had the dubious pleasure of being entertained by one of the label's lesser lights, 18 Wheeler, and Alan McGee presented Tony Blair with an Oasis platinum disc.

The rally was good PR for Blair and the Labour Party, but of minor importance next to the main event, Blair's leader's speech to Conference on Thursday 1, October. Before an attentive but excitable audience, Blair began his address by stating: 'This year we meet as the opposition. Next year, the British people willing . . . we will meet as the new Labour government of Britain.' Blair, much more than Major, was able to tap into the mood running through the country that summer. At Conference he went on and attached his party to the single most evocative sentiment of the moment. 'Labour,' he told hundreds of cheering delegates, 'is coming home.'

'I saw that as central to [Blair's] speech and probably one of the main headlines out of it,' Alastair Campbell wrote in his diary. 'It got such a good reception, better than I thought it would . . . it went down a storm.' Come General Election day on Thursday, 1 May 1997, the forecasters' prediction that Labour would win by a landslide proved accurate. At forty-two, the still-then fresh-faced Blair was the first Prime Minister to be born after the Queen was crowned, and seemed to represent a decisive break with tradition. The huge intake of Labour MPs changed the make-up of Parliament at a stroke. The number of women sitting in the House of Commons was more than doubled from fifty-seven to one hundred and twenty. New Labour's ranks were also swelled by greater numbers of MPs from varied social and ethnic backgrounds, and with different declared sexualities. Like the narrative suggested at Euro 96, and dispensed by BSkyB and the Premier League for English football, Blair's election was purported to have swept Britain out of a dark age to become a better, more optimistic, rainbow-coloured nation.

This impression was further embellished by television footage the next morning of Blair setting off to see the Queen at Buckingham Palace. His route from Downing Street was lined by cheering, jubilant crowds, basking in the sun and waving Union Jack and St George flags, still more reminders of London from the previous summer. A year on from Euro 96, Blair hosted a glittering reception at Number 10 to celebrate British attainment and this new golden era. One hundred celebrities and high achievers filed into the Downing Street state rooms to quaff Champagne with the Prime Minister, among them actors Ian McKellen and Maureen Lipman, comedians Eddie Izzard and Lenny Henry, Vivienne Westwood, Alan McGee and Noel Gallagher. In advance of the party, Blair fretted that Gallagher might be trouble. '[Blair] felt he was bound to do something crazy,' wrote Campbell. 'Gallagher arrived with his [new] wife, Meg, McGee and his girl-friend, [and there were] loads of photographers outside. Cherie met them and took them upstairs . . . Gallagher said he thought Number 10 was "tops", that he couldn't believe there was an ironing board in there. He was very down to earth, very funny.'

However, along with Gallagher's compliance, and much else about the post-Euro 96, post-election glow, all was not quite as it appeared to be at the time. Not long after, Oasis' leader claimed to have snuck cocaine into the Prime Minister's official residence and snorted it in the WC especially reserved for the Queen's use.

Following England's win in Moldova, midweek action resumed on 4 September. A glut of goals and the Euro 96 factor were being held up as the catalysts for a forty per cent year-on-year increase in attendances at Premier League games. Hoddle, meanwhile, was reported to have 'raised his eyebrows' upon hearing that Robbie Fowler, McManaman and Anderton, all of whom had begged off international duty, were turning out respectively for

Liverpool and Spurs at Coventry and Wimbledon. In response, the FA was said to be considering a rule change stopping players who withdrew from England duty from competing for their clubs up to a week afterwards. Nothing, though, came of their deliberations.

Even at this early stage of the season, it looked likely that the title race would be between four dominant teams: Manchester United, Newcastle, Arsenal and Liverpool. Ferguson's team drew 1–1 at Derby and at the weekend put Leeds to the sword 4–0, Karel Poborský scoring his first goal for the club. Leeds manager Howard Wilkinson paid for the result with his job. His replacement, appointed on 9 September, was George Graham, who had served his punishment after the 'bungs' inquiry. Liverpool beat Coventry 1–0 and then crushed Middlesbrough 4–0. Newcastle also started to work up a head of steam, recording back to back 2–1 victories over Sunderland in the Tyne-Wear derby and at Tottenham, Les Ferdinand scoring three of their goals as Shearer drew blanks. Arsenal were held at Villa and Chelsea and remained in a holding pattern under Pat Rice.

The week after, the three European club competitions began in earnest, providing a litmus test for the evolving Premier League. Results in the UEFA Cup were inconsistent, inconclusive. Arsenal lost 3–2 at home to Borussia Mönchengladbach, Villa were held 1–1 by Helsingborgs of Sweden, and Newcastle demolished another Swedish side, Halmstads, 4–0 at St James' Park. Neither Arsenal nor Villa survived their first-round ties, but Newcastle reached the quarter-finals where they were pummelled 4–0 on aggregate by Monaco. Liverpool opened their Cup-Winners' Cup campaign with a 1–0 win over MyPa in the industrial heartland of Finland. They made it the semi-finals before losing 3–2 on aggregate to Paris Saint-Germain after trailing 3–0 from the first leg in the French capital.

The Champions League, though, provided the most telling yardstick. It was still then restricted to the title holders from each country, and Manchester United were grouped alongside Juventus of Italy, Fenerbahçe of Turkey and Rapid Vienna, the Austrian champions. On 11 September, United were in Turin for their first and most daunting-looking fixture of the group stages. Juventus were managed by Marcello Lippi who, like Ferguson, was a tough, resilient, unremarkable player, but an outstanding coach and master tactician. Lippi had arrived at Juventus from Napoli two years earlier and was in the process of building his own empire at the Stadio delle Alpi. His side boasted the considerable talents of French internationals Zinedine Zidane and Didier Deschamps, Croat striker Alen Bokšić, a world-class defender in the Uruguayan Paolo Montero, and two contrasting but dangerous Italian forwards, Christian Vieri, a battering ram, and the darting Alessandro Del Piero.

Juventus dominated from the start. Pressing and pressuring the ball from the English side and then almost taunting them with it. Bokšić scored in the thirty-fourth minute and though the Italians were unable to add to their tally, they kept their opponents at arm's length for the rest of an uneven contest. 'If you give the ball away at this level, you cut your throat,' Ferguson reflected afterwards. He had withdrawn Ryan Giggs for erring too often and watched Beckham and Butt overrun in midfield. 'They must take a lesson from Eric Cantona,' Ferguson admonished. 'He never gave the ball away once.' No one at Old Trafford, least of all Ferguson, could possibly have foreseen it then, as United mounted their assault on a fourth Premier League title in five years, but this was to be Cantona's swansong. At the end of the season he unexpectedly retired from playing the game that he had adorned, unfathomable to the last. Cantona shunned football to start with, setting out instead to forge a career as an actor. He had a degree of success, too, appearing as the imperious French ambassador to Tudor England in a 1998 biopic of the Virgin Queen, *Elizabeth*, and as himself in Ken Loach's well-regarded 2009 movie, *Looking for Eric*. He was eventually coaxed back into the sport and coached a French national team to victory in the inaugural Fifa Beach World Cup staged in Rio de Janeiro in 2005. In January 2011, Cantona was appointed director of football at New York Cosmos, but was dismissed four years later after a scuffle with a photographer on a visit to London.

In the period immediately following Cantona's retirement, English football's horizons expanded further. The glamour and enhanced technical flair of the continental game showcased at Euro 96 served to inflate the appeal of the Champions League. English television embraced the new order, and viewers who had lapped up the European

Championship now grew accustomed to feasting on live Champions League games twice weekly as well as following battles for the titles in Spain, Germany and Italy. The riches offered by the Champions League also meant it usurped the domestic cup competitions in the clubs' priorities. By 2005, and with a quartet of Premier League teams able to qualify for an enhanced Champions League, finishing fourth in the race for the Premier League title became of much greater consequence to English clubs than winning the FA Cup. Eventually, Alex Ferguson was twice able to match the feat of Sir Matt Busby and bring the European Cup back to Manchester. The first occasion was on a memorable night in 1999 in Camp Nou against Bayern Munich when the Germans were the better team, but United pinched the title at the death. Liverpool and Chelsea have also lifted the famous trophy in the intervening years.

That 1996–97 season, though, Juventus repeated both the 1–0 scoreline and lesson in the return game at Old Trafford. It seemed then, as the long, hot summer slipped into autumn, that English football's ventures into Europe were destined to have the same chastening ending. Writing in *The Times* after United's defeat in Turin, Rob Hughes summed up the essence of it: 'The best team in England were outplayed, considerably more so than the scoreline suggests. A young Juventus team, cunning in movement and design, is being built. It is technical, it is tactical, and it continues to hurt.'

* * *

The international game continued to exert a magnetic pull in the two years after Euro 96. England's matches at Wembley retained the same fervent, populist and impassioned feel that they had at the tournament. But where Terry Venables's team had approached Euro 96 playing to half-full, apathetic houses, Hoddle's side enjoyed the full wattage support that had been switched on that June. On pre-Euro 96 evidence, Wembley might have been expected to be at best two-thirds full for England's World Cup qualifier against Poland. In the event, the match on 9 October attracted a near-capacity, seventy-five thousand crowd. The England team, though, was not boosted on the night in the same way it had been against Scotland, Holland, Spain and Germany. Tentative and nervous-looking, England edged the game 2–1 with goals from Shearer.

It was when the squad had met up at Burnham to prepare for the game that Hoddle sprung his most far-out idea on his players: introducing them to his friend and faith healer, Eileen Drewery. Hoddle had first become acquainted with Drewery in 1976 when he was seventeen and going out with her daughter, Michelle. A south Londoner, Drewery had moved with husband Phil to Essex, where they ran a pub. Drewery turned to healing at thirty-two, claiming to have cured a friend of arthritis simply by holding her hand and asking God to remove the pain. By her account, would-be patients were soon trooping into the pub and asking Drewery for her miracle cure. At the time the young Hoddle was on the verge of breaking into Spurs' first team when he suffered a hamstring injury. Drewery offered to treat it, but since Hoddle was reticent about having his girlfriend's mum 'lay hands' on him, she used instead a technique she called 'distant prayer'. According to Hoddle, his strain was healed overnight. 'It was incredible,' he wrote later. 'There was no more pain [and] the experience had a profound effect on me.'

In the years that followed, Hoddle became increasingly interested in spiritualism and continued to see and consult Drewery. He had her treat his players at Swindon and also Chelsea. He told the England squad that Drewery was available to them, that he recommended they visit her, but that he was also not making such appointments compulsory. Nevertheless, Paul Gascoigne would subsequently be packed off to Drewery on three separate occasions. 'She put her hand on my head,' Gazza told Hunter Davies, 'gave it a lot of soft chat . . . and then said demons were coming out of my head and into her house.' Matt Dickinson says: 'It was clearly an amazing story that Eileen Drewery was involved with the England team. The fact that Hoddle was into this stuff wasn't just a side-issue, but part of his whole football philosophy. You had international players being ushered in to see someone who thought she could cure injuries through celestial power.'

'Tony Adams was sober and looking for new experiences when he returned to the England set-up,' Ian Ridley notes, 'but even he thought Drewery was crackers. You used to see her in the bar at Wembley with a cigarette and a gin and tonic. Tony always felt that wasn't a sign of someone who was at peace with themselves. Some players did swear by the fact they felt muscle injuries healing under her and others thought it was mumbo jumbo. Tony's Arsenal team-mate, Ray Parlour, went along to see her when he got into the squad, because I think he believed it would be held against him if he didn't. He was with a couple of the other England players in her front room. Drewery put her hands on Ray's head and he said, "I'll have a short back and sides, please".'

For all the oddities of Hoddle's preparations, England won again the following month in Georgia, 2–0. The result bolstered Hoddle for his first serious test as an international manager: the visit of Italy to Wembley on 12 February 1997. The Azzurri had flopped at Euro 96, but history was on their side. England had not beaten an Italian team since winning another World Cup qualifier at Wembley in November 1977. Even then, the game was a dead rubber and Italy had already progressed at England's expense.

The afternoon of the match, a delegation of Fifa officials was wined and dined in central London on the FA's tab, the first move in its doomed tilt for the 2006 World Cup. Anyone at the time looking for omens about how the bid would ultimately fare might have found one in that night's game. England began purposefully and to choruses of 'Football's coming home'. But the Italians soon reined them in and silenced a packed crowd. Gianfranco Zola, Chelsea's latest signing, gave the visitors the lead in the nineteenth minute and though England toiled for an equaliser, Italy had their measure. The hope stirred during those glorious days of the previous summer seemed in danger of fading and a familiar theme re-emerged instead. 'England showed abundant effort,' ran a match report in the next morning's *Independent*, 'but lacked both the Italians' class and fortune. The crowd drifted away. Uncertain whether to boo or cheer, they did neither.'

CHAPTER SIXTEEN

'He was like a man possessed'

Two days before Arsenal beat Sheffield Wednesday 4–1 at Highbury, Tony Adams called a team meeting after training at London Colney. He sat before his peers in the first-team dressing room and told them he was an alcoholic, but that he had not had a drink for almost a month and was attending regular Alcoholics Anonymous meetings. The crux of what Adams said was also released to the newspapers. There was a sense of disbelief among the Arsenal players that Adams, their leader on the pitch and ringleader off it, had a drink problem. Captain Tony: the first to the bar, the last to leave.

The following Saturday afternoon, Adams made his return to first-team action at Middlesbrough. Arsenal won 2–0, Bryan Robson's team wilting as they would do all too often that season. Pat Rice was again in charge of Arsenal, but prepared now to step down. On 23 September, the club finally unveiled Arsène Wenger as their manager. At his first press conference Wenger revealed he had also been deliberating over Glenn Hoddle's offer to join the England set-up.

'We had an agreement for him to call me back in August,' Wenger explained. 'It was then I told him I would take over at Arsenal. I love to work on the field and I had the feeling that I am not yet of an age to work in administration.'

Wenger was also questioned about Adams and his recent confession. His response was thoughtful, measured. 'My special message to Adams will be: respect,' he said. 'I know that what he did needs a lot of courage. When people are brave and honest, you always have to respect them.' It was clear even from these initial exchanges that Wenger, dressed in a well-cut, charcoal-grey suit and looking more like a college professor, was not only a breed apart from his immediate predecessors, Bruce Rioch and George Graham, but that he represented something very different for English football.

Forty-six at the time, Wenger was born in Strasbourg on France's north-eastern border with Germany. He graduated from the city's university with a degree in economics and went on to a singularly unremarkable playing career in French football. A midfielder, but short of pace, he played mostly in the lower leagues and managed just eleven games in the French First Division for RS Strasbourg. He was, though, a deep thinker about the game. By the time he hung up his boots in 1981, Wenger was coaching the club's youth team. He graduated to senior management at Nancy-Lorraine in 1984, and three years later was appointed coach to France's glamour club, AS Monaco, where he won a league title. Hoddle was among the players he signed during his seven-year spell on the French Riviera before moving on to work in Japan.

It was not until 12 October, and a 2–0 victory at Blackburn, that Wenger officially took up his duties at Arsenal. By then he had already begun to implement changes that would have a profound and revelatory impact at both his new club and on the Premier League as a whole. The personal battles fought by Adams and Paul Merson at Arsenal, and by Paul Gascoigne, might have been extreme cases, but as a general rule beer, chips and curry were still integral parts of the average British footballer's diet. Wenger arrived in north London preaching the value of nutrition and sports science. He prescribed his Arsenal team grilled fish, raw vegetables and fruit and issued them with vitamin pills and supplements. Up to that point, Adams, Merson and others would gobble a Mars bar at half-time to boost their energy levels. To train under Wenger was also to experience a new kind of thinking to the boot camp mentality that had been prevalent in the British game. His sessions were short, often no more than forty-five minutes' duration, and Wenger conducted them with a stopwatch and clipboard.

'We had stretching and a warm-up, then played a ten-minute each way small-sided game and finished with a run around the pitch,' Adams revealed later. 'We also had regular massages, and once a month Arsène would fly a guy in from France who was a mixture of osteopath and masseur to realign the players' bodies. [Wenger] was certainly different from anything the boys had experienced before. He has a lot of qualities. He is a thinker, a listener and he cares a great deal about the welfare of his players. I think he knows professional footballers inside out. He can tell just by how a player runs if he is fully fit or not.'

'If Adams had still been drinking he would not have lasted two minutes under Wenger,' says Ian Ridley. 'Wenger told him he didn't know how he had managed to drink and sustain a career at that level. Tony had to tell him that all English players were like that at the time. Arsenal had been a dour team, but now all of a sudden they were about pace, movement and sharpness. At that point, Wenger was ahead of everyone else in British football and a huge catalyst for change. His success with Arsenal was why a vogue developed for overseas managers, whether they were any good or not. In many respects he was presented with an open goal in this country because of the money that was exploding in the game. Wenger was able to convince the English players at Arsenal that if they embraced his methods it would add a further two or three years to their careers. That would mean an extra million pounds a year for them all and that made sense to footballers.'

Wenger's appointment, of course, was reflective of the new mood in English football to advance the game using methods and technical expertise imported from the continent. It was an ideology that Terry Venables had introduced to the England team ahead of Euro 96 and which Hoddle continued to practise. Arsenal and Chelsea, with Wenger and Ruud Gullit, were in the vanguard of a pronounced shift at English clubs towards appointing overseas managers. Wenger's compatriot, Gérard Houllier, who had overseen the French FA's highly successful development academy at Clairefontaine, followed him to England to take over at Liverpool in 1998 and won the UEFA Cup with the Merseyside club. By the 2015–16 season, twelve of the twenty Premier League clubs had an overseas manager. The practice was even extended to the national team via the appointment of a Swede, Sven-Göran Eriksson, and an Italian, Fabio Capello, as England managers in 2001 and 2008 respectively.

In his first season at Arsenal, Wenger guided the club to third place in the Premier League, qualifying them again for the UEFA Cup. He had begun, though, to rebuild the Arsenal team around quick, tall, athletic footballers, establishing a benchmark for the rest of the Premier League. Arsenal won the title the next season and again in 2002 and 2004, wrestling Ferguson and Manchester United for domestic dominance. Wenger's 2003–04 team, his so-called 'Invincibles', managed a feat unparalleled in Premier League history, and unlikely to be equalled, by going through the season unbeaten. They finished fifteen points clear of the trailing United.

Adams had then retired, but this was perhaps the Premier League's perfect team. One with the strength and raw power of Sol Campbell, Patrick Vieira and the Brazilian, Gilberto Silva, the quick feet of Robert Pirès, Dennis Bergkamp's guile and in French striker Thierry Henry, thirty goals in thirty-seven Premier League games during the campaign, a player to rival his compatriot Eric Cantona as the best to grace the league. Wenger could not, though, conquer Europe. The best he has managed to date with Arsenal was reaching the 2006 Champions League final, a game they lost in Paris to Barcelona. Nonetheless, his imprint on English football is indelible. 'I came to like, respect and admire [Wenger] more and more,' said Adams. 'I needed to work with people like that, but I never thought it would be someone who had never played the game at the highest level.'

Arsène Wenger, though, was not to be the first manager from overseas to win a major trophy in England. That honour went to Ruud Gullit whose Chelsea team claimed the FA Cup in May 1997, easing past relegated Middlesbrough in the Wembley final. In the race for the title, Manchester United had an autumn wobble, losing three consecutive games, the most damaging of which was a 5–0 reverse at Newcastle on 20 October. Alan Shearer scored the fourth and as his team eviscerated their rivals, it seemed possible that the order of English football was changing right there on the St James' Park pitch. However, the swiftness with which this was proved wrong was breath-taking. As United recovered and kicked on, Newcastle went into an instant slump, winning just one of their next nine league games. Kevin Keegan resigned in January, his vision of building the club into a European powerhouse turned to rubble. His replacement was Shearer's old Blackburn boss,

Kenny Dalglish, more pragmatic, less of a dreamer, who guided Newcastle to a second runners-up finish in successive seasons, but this time well adrift of United and with their moment already racing past. Shearer finished the season with twenty-five Premier League goals and once again as the PFA Player of the Year. However, in the ten years he was to spend leading the line for his hometown club, he was not able to win a single trophy. In the same period, Manchester United, the club he had spurned, won nine: five Premier League titles, two FA Cups, a League Cup and that crowning Champions League in 1999.

'I did a dinner with Fergie a couple of years ago,' Shearer told the *Daily Telegraph* in 2010, still defiant. 'He got up and said, "Can you imagine the number of things you would have won if you had come to Manchester United?" I said, "Yeah, I can imagine you'd have won a lot more as well".' Ferguson admitted in an interview with the same newspaper two years earlier: 'Alan Shearer is one player I wish I had signed.' However, it was another Geordie he had tried to sign from Newcastle and failed, who was a bigger source of regret for Ferguson. 'The most disappointing one for me was Paul Gascoigne,' he said. 'He was the best player of his era, a breath of fresh air because he played with a smile on his face. Around 1987, Newcastle were bobbing around the relegation zone. We played them at St James' Park and my midfielders were Bryan Robson, Norman Whiteside and Remi Moses. All great footballers and he tore them apart. They couldn't get near him. When he nut-megged Moses and patted him on the head, I was out of the dugout shouting, "Get that fucking so-and-so!" I think not coming to United was a bad mistake [on Gascoigne's part]. We had Robson, a Geordie, Steve Bruce, a Geordie, and Gary Pallister from Middlesbrough. We had a structure of players who could have helped him and it would have given him discipline.'

Back in September 1996, Gascoigne scored a hat-trick for Rangers at Kilmarnock, and then the winner in an Old Firm game against Celtic at a packed, febrile Ibrox. These were almost his last hurrahs for the club before he slipped his moorings altogether. He missed England's defeat by Italy at Wembley the following February, and also the 2–0 win over Georgia in April, injured and otherwise out of sorts. He was back, though, for the match in Poland in May, but the game finished goalless. However, England's World Cup qualifying group was turned on its head on the evening of 10 September 1997. That night, Georgia held Italy to a draw in Tbilisi and England strolled past Moldova once more, 4–0 at Wembley. Suggesting their toothless showing at Euro 96 was not, in fact, a momentary aberration, the faltering Italians had also failed to win their previous match in Poland to allow England to move ahead of them going into the last group match in Rome. A draw in the Olympic Stadium on 11 October would qualify England for the finals as group winners. Robbed of the injured Shearer, Hoddle obsessed over the details of his team selection and most particularly about Gascoigne. He worried that Gascoigne was too hot-headed and would be agitated even more by returning to what had been his old stomping ground with Lazio. Gascoigne was desperate to prove himself to the doubting Italian press but, thought Hoddle, without the mental resolve and in no physical condition to be able to make his point.

In fact, Gascoigne sat deep with Paul Ince in the central areas key to Hoddle's game-plan of taking the Italians on at their own game and containing them. Gascoigne broke up Italian attacks, linked play for England and managed a disciplined, focused performance that belied his manager's fears. England recorded the draw they required and Gascoigne, smiling, triumphant, celebrated on the pitch with Hoddle and his team-mates. Freeze-framed there, he still seems impish, boyish, yet able to bring the world to his feet.

The World Cup gave Gascoigne something to aim for, to hold on to, but his grip was never more than tenuous at best. Returning from Rome to a more uncomfortable reality at Rangers, he crashed again. He was already absenting himself from the club during his frequent injury lay-offs, going off to London to carouse with Chris Evans and other friends and hangers-on. Now he was also facing divorce proceedings and was unravelling at a frightening rate. Warming up as a substitute for another Old Firm clash at Celtic's Parkhead Stadium on 2 January 1998, and being barracked by the home support, he mimed playing the flute. A sectarian gesture he had picked up from Rangers' supporters, almost certainly without grasping its deeper significance, it referred to the Protestant Orange Order marches that were flash points in Belfast each summer and a particular source of fury in Celtic's Catholic strong-holds. The splenetic reaction of the Celtic supporters inside the stadium was mirrored across tracts of Glasgow, the Scottish media and also in Northern Ireland. Gascoigne was hit with a £20,000 fine by Rangers and received death threats. It was the breaking straw for the club.

In February 1998, Gascoigne was again on England duty for the first of a batch of friendlies leading up to the World Cup finals. Hoddle's team were beaten comprehensively 2–0 at home by Chile. However, the England manager was more concerned with Gascoigne's evident decline and left him on the bench. 'He was not playing regularly for Rangers,' Hoddle wrote in his World Cup diary, 'and I was still worrying about his fitness and some of his habits and actions off the pitch. I'd bent over backwards to help him in the past, but hadn't seen him for several months when the squad met up . . . and knew he needed a jolt. Luckily, I know how to treat him – with the right mixture of love and discipline.'

Walter Smith had taken a similar approach with Gascoigne at Rangers and been able to eke two seasons out of him. Smith, though, had announced the previous October his intention to retire at the end of the campaign. Not long after the incident at Parkhead, Rangers confirmed Dick Advocaat as Smith's successor. Gascoigne was tipped off by Smith that Advocaat, a forthright disciplinarian, meant to drum him out of the club and in March he agreed to be transferred to Middlesbrough for £3.45 million. The move reunited him with Bryan Robson and also with England colleague, Paul Merson, inevitably shipped out of Arsenal by Wenger.

Gascoigne moved into a six-bedroom mansion at Seaham on the North-East coast, sharing it with his new team-mate, Andy Townsend. He was able to play in six of Middlesbrough's last seven games of the season as the club won promotion back to the Premier League, but looked ragged and frail. At the end of April, England hosted Portugal at Wembley. Gascoigne turned up at Burnham Beeches the Sunday before the game in such poor condition that Hoddle sent him home. 'I wrote a pro-file of Gascoigne around that period in which I revealed he was smoking a packet of fags a day,' says Ian Ridley. 'That became a huge tabloid story. Drink and everything else was ruining what was left of his career. He'd had his day. Now that Wenger had come in, you could no longer survive at the top level in England as a drunk.'

Even then Gascoigne might have been able to go to the World Cup and salvage something. To give a glimpse of all that he had been just two years earlier, like a light bulb that was near exhausted but was still flickering in the dark. He was, though, too far gone even for that, unable to stop or contain himself. Hoddle named him in his provi-sional thirty-man squad for the finals before the last Wembley warm-up against Saudi Arabia. In the interim, Gazza was pictured in the tabloids being helped out of a

London restaurant and gorging on a kebab in the early hours of the morning in Soho.

The Saudi game was a dire affair and ended goalless. Immediately afterwards Hoddle whisked the squad back to Burnham Beeches and their Bisham Abbey training base. He flew in Dr Yann Rougier from France and had him blood-test each of the players to evaluate their fitness and then put them on personalised diets. It was an altogether different regimen to the one Venables had presided over before Euro 96 and something that Gascoigne was in no way capable of adhering to. Two days later he set off on what would be his valedictory trip as an England player.

The England party's destination was located on a finger of coastline poking out into the Mediterranean from southern Spain. According to its own blurb, the La Manga Club resort was 'a privileged setting bordered by natural parks and unspoilt beaches, offering luxury, leisure and sport with wonderful weather all year round'. Two further warm-up matches were scheduled in a low-key tournament in Morocco and Hoddle chose the base ostensibly because it was just a hop by plane from north Africa. An avid golfer, he was also swayed by the fact La Manga boasted three championship courses.

Hoddle and his squad occupied a wing of the resort's lavish, five-star Hyatt Regency Hotel, the manager lording it in the opulent Royal Suite. He continued to keep a tight check on his charges. Alcohol was forbidden and the dutiful Dr Crane charged with ensuring that none of the players spent more than forty-five minutes each day sunbathing. At the end of the week Hoddle had to name his final twenty-two-man squad for the finals and was still stewing over unresolved issues. But none was more vexing to him than that of Gascoigne.

England's first game of the King Hassan II International Cup tournament was against the host nation on 27 May. As they arrived at the Stade Mohamed V in Casablanca on a scorching afternoon, the players and staff were showered with water and spit by a section of a partisan, eighty thousand-strong crowd. England won 1–0, Liverpool's Michael Owen becoming his country's youngest goalscorer at seventeen. Arsenal's Ian Wright suffered a torn hamstring that ruled him out of the World Cup. On his thirty-first birthday, Gascoigne managed a full ninety minutes, but looked sluggish and out of breath. He had always been able to starve excess weight off in two weeks or less, but now he was lacking muscle tone and basic stamina. Two years on from the infamous Cathay Pacific flight from Hong Kong, he was presented with a birthday cake on a more subdued journey back to base.

'The next day, I could see he wasn't right,' Hoddle recalled in his diary. 'A picture of his wife Sheryl with a new "friend" had appeared in a newspaper that by early afternoon was floating around the hotel.' Despite Sheryl having already instituted divorce proceedings when the piece ran, Gascoigne obsessed over the substance of this story all that day and into the next when the England team was set to face Belgium. He kept Hoddle, his staff and the rest of the squad waiting at La Manga on their airport bus while he hectored his estranged wife on the phone. He called her again from pitch-side in Casablanca and Hoddle was forced to dispatch one of his assistants, Glenn Roeder, to haul him into the dressing room for the team-talk. The match itself, which went ahead in a near-empty stadium, ended with neither team able to score and with Belgium winning in a penalty shoot-out. Gascoigne, distracted, disengaged, lasted fifty minutes before being forced off with a dead-leg and a cut to his head. These, though, were just his surface wounds.

Back at La Manga, Hoddle relaxed his no-drinking rule and gave the players a night off. There would, though, be no repeat of the Dentist's Chair Incident. The hotel's Piano Bar was reserved for their exclusive use and sheets hung across the windows to preserve their privacy. Gascoigne was intent upon drowning his sorrows and by the time Tony Adams belatedly joined the party with Paul Merson at ten in the evening, he was in full swing. 'We called it the Blue Oyster bar after the comical gay club of that name in the *Police Academy* film,' Adams recorded later. 'When [Merson] and I walked in, Gazza was on the karaoke machine singing the old Elvis Presley song 'Wooden Heart', among other things. Nobody could get the microphone off him. There was sadness about him for me as he was obviously worse for wear from drink. "Come on, Tone, give us a song, you boring bastard", he shouted at me. I just said to Merse, "Come on, let's get away from this crap", and we went and had a coffee and a sandwich some-where else before bed.'

Soon after Adams and Merson departed Hoddle arrived on the scene. Gascoigne was still hogging the karaoke, bleary and sweat-drenched. 'As I walked down the stairs and saw him there, I knew I couldn't take him to France,' Hoddle recorded. 'He was ushered up to his room by David Seaman. I ignored him.'

First thing next morning, the players were informed that Hoddle would see each of them in turn at five-minute intervals in his room from four-fifteen that afternoon. The appointments were fixed on a notice board in the hotel. Though none of the players knew it, Hoddle meant to do his blood-letting quickly and had scheduled the unfortunate six among his first eleven meetings. 'For many people, all that day was an excruciating experience and not one I believe they should have been subjected to,' Adams opined. 'Nobody at that stage really expected Gazza to be left out, although the evidence on the pitch was mounting against him.'

To kill time, most of the players headed out on to the golf course. Gascoigne took several cans of lager with him and swilled them throughout his round. He returned to the hotel in mid-afternoon, slurring and unsteady on his feet. Adams and Merson persuaded him into the pool and then plied him with coffee in a last-ditch attempt to sober him up. Upstairs, Hoddle had begun. First to face the axe was Ian Walker and then Phil Neville, Andy Hinchcliffe, Nicky Butt and Dion Dublin. In an attempt to soothe them, Hoddle had one of his Kenny G CDs playing in the background. The American saxophonist's outpourings failed to placate Walker and Neville, both of them leaving Hoddle's suite distraught and in tears. Soon it was Gascoigne's turn. 'Gazza said, "I don't know if I can do it anymore. I'm not going to go, am I, Tone? Am I going to go?"' Adams related. 'Then he steadied himself to go upstairs for his meeting.'

It was five-fifteen when Gascoigne trooped off. Hoddle's right-hand man, John Gorman, was waiting for him in the corridor outside the Royal Suite. Gorman put his arm round Gascoigne's shoulders and forewarned him of the news Hoddle was about to deliver. Gascoigne snapped. 'I already knew that the next few minutes were going to be stormy,' said Hoddle. 'I had received a phone call from one of my staff, just before David Seaman had come in, marking my card that Gazza was half-cut again. There was a bang on my door. I knew it was Paul. He was drunker than I thought he would be.'

The confrontation that ensued lasted less than five minutes. Gascoigne launched a kick at Hoddle's wardrobe door. He overturned a glass coffee table, smashing a vase and cutting his leg in the process. Blood from the wound splashed on to the floor and furniture. 'He was like a man possessed,' said Hoddle. 'I thought he was going to hit me. There was a lamp to his right and he just punched it. The glass shattered all over the room.'

Alerted by the commotion, Gorman and Roeder burst into the room and man-handled Gascoigne out and back downstairs to his room. Seaman and Ince joined them there. Gascoigne was inconsolable, screaming invective about Hoddle and sobbing. Seaman summoned Dr Crane who got Gascoigne to take a Valium. The others started to pack his bags. 'I heard shouting down the corridor,' remembered Gary Neville. 'I walked outside and one of the lads said that Gazza had been left out. I didn't blame him for blowing his top. The whole experience felt brutal.'

Within an hour, Gascoigne and the five other outcasts were being driven the twenty miles to Mercia Airport. A private plane was waiting to fly them home via Birmingham. Gascoigne, just as he had done in Turin, and again in the summer of Euro 96, left the scene in tears. This time, though, there would be no comeback for him, no great third act. He was heading off out of the sunset and into a long, black night.

AFTERMATH

'I can't die! I've got to water the plants!'

'Three Lions' was re-released in May 1998 as '3 Lions 98' and to send Glenn Hoddle's England squad off to the finals of the 98 World Cup in France. Unfortunately, the newly-written set of lyrics made a premature claim that 'Gazza' was as 'good as before'. Once again it topped UK charts, but it was nonetheless overshadowed by an altogether more unconventional anthem. It was titled 'Vindaloo', and despite the fact it amounted to little more than the constant repetition of the title word and was shunned by Radio 1, it sold more than half a million copies and soared to Number Two on the charts. It was the work of a haphazard collective known as Fat Les and made up of Alex James from Blur, Damien Hirst, the *enfant terrible* of the British art world, and Keith Allen of 'World in Motion' fame. James and Allen wrote the song in just thirty minutes. To promote it, the trio appeared on the cover of the *Guardian*'s *Weekend* supplement dressed in items of women's lingerie they had taken from Hirst's next-door neighbour's clothes line.

'They were party animals and basically uncontrollable,' says the man employed to be their publicist, Phill Savidge. 'I would arrange for them to do a photo session at ten in the morning and they would still be up at the Groucho Club, stinking. Keith owned a black London cab and employed a tramp who slept outside the Groucho as his driver. His name was Outside Dave and the trouble was he stank, but he ferried Keith all over. All Damien ever said to me was, "You're in the art world now, mate". He was quite mad. At one point he told me he liked me and handed me a shopping bag filled with fifteen grand in cash to work the record with.'

Buoyed by the success of 'Vindaloo', James, Hirst and Allen subsequently invested their considerable proceeds in a follow-up festive single, 'Naughty Christmas' (Goblin in the Office)', and lost the lot when it flopped. James estimated he had also at that point 'spent about a million pounds on Champagne and cocaine. It sounds ridiculous,' he mused, 'but I don't regret it.'

Not that 'Vindaloo' heralded the team to glory. England went to France having risen to sixth in the Fifa world rankings and handed a soft-looking passage through a group also comprising Tunisia, Colombia and the ageing Romanians. Glenn Hoddle, like Terry Venables before him, meant his side to play with the precision of the other top international sides, possessing the ball, sucking opponents in and striking at them with pace. England, though, stumbled through their opening games, beating Tunisia in the heat of Marseilles, but coming undone against Romania in their next match, losing to a late sucker-punch goal.

Although they went on to beat Colombia, Beckham scoring with a deft free-kick, England only qualified for the knock-out stages as runners-up in their group, which left them to face a strong Argentina side in the last sixteen. This was a stern test earlier in the tournament than Hoddle would have wished or anticipated. In the build-up, there was an undignified repeat of one of the lowest points of Euro 96. Back in England, the tabloid press fired off jingoistic broadsides about the Falklands conflict. This was made worse by the fact that Mariana, wife of Hoddle's full-back Graeme Le Saux, was Argentine, and much to the player's consternation their family home was besieged by reporters.

The game itself went ahead on a warm 30 June evening, a Tuesday, at Saint-Étienne in central France. Argentina had won all three of its group games without conceding a goal. The current team included no one as mercurial as Diego Maradona, but was powerful, skilful and its prime movers were drawn from Europe's premier leagues. Central defender Roberto Ayala, playmaker Juan Sebastián Verón and dashing forward Gabriel Batistuta were all playing in *Serie A*. Batistuta's strike partner, Ariel Ortega, had spent the past season with Valencia in Spain. Hoddle set England up pairing Manchester United's Paul Scholes with Paul Ince in central midfield and young Michael Owen up front with Alan Shearer.

As the contest progressed, no one could have failed to recall England's encounter with Germany in that Wembley semi-final. Again, this one was an epic played out under floodlights and pregnant with drama. Kicking off at nine o'clock local time, it began at a breakneck pace that barely let up for the next two hours. Argentina drew first blood. In the sixth minute, Batistuta converted a penalty after Seaman felled Diego Simeone. England drew level within four minutes, Owen going down in the box under the slightest contact and Shearer scored from the spot. Six minutes later, England went ahead with the goal of the game. Seizing on Beckham's through ball, Owen burst between Ayala and José Chamot in the middle of the Argentine defence and arrowed a shot into the top left-hand corner of the net. The details of it remain as indelible as those of Paul Gascoigne's goal against Scotland. Soon after, Scholes had a glorious chance to extend England's lead but poked the ball wide from six yards. England were made to pay on the stroke of half-time. England dozed at a free-kick and Batistuta slipped the ball past their defensive wall for Javier Zanetti to score.

Two minutes after the restart the game turned on an innocuous-seeming incident. Simeone hacked down Beckham close to the touchline. As he lay prone on the pitch, Beckham raised his right leg and clipped his assailant on the thigh with the studs of his boot. The Argentine let out a scream and fell as if shot. Danish referee Kim Milton Nielsen showed Simeone a yellow card. But he pulled out a red for Beckham, reducing England to ten men for the remainder of the contest.

Hoddle's immediate response was to revert to one of the training drills he had used at Bisham Abbey, playing ten against eleven and getting his two main strikers to

shuttle back into midfield. With Shearer and Owen covering the extra ground, England contained Argentina for
the rest of the half and into extra-time where the 'golden
goal' once again applied. England even appeared to have
won the game at the death as Sol Campbell headed in a
corner, but Nielsen penalised Shearer for raising an arm
against the Argentine goalkeeper, Carlos Roa. Just as it
had with Germany, the contest was decided by a penalty
shoot-out. This time, England went second. Sergio Berti
struck first for Argentina, then Shearer for England.
Hernán Crespo missed, but so did Ince. The next five
kicks all found their target and it fell to substitute David
Batty to score and keep England in the competition. Batty,
like Gareth Southgate before him, had never taken a penalty for his club. It was a last, sorry echo of England's
decisive sudden-death duel at Euro 96 and the result was
the same. Batty shot tamely and England went out in the
cruellest circumstances.

Like the Euro 96 semi-final, the England dressing room
afterwards was desolate. But on this occasion the stakes
had been even higher. There would be no more World
Cups for Tony Adams or Shearer, both of whom sat staring into the distance as if shell-shocked. Neither would
there be for Hoddle, though he could not have known it at
the time. His next task was to qualify England for the
finals of the 2000 European Championship. However,
England began that campaign falteringly with a 2–1 defeat
by Sweden in Stockholm and a home draw with Bulgaria
in the autumn of 1998.

As he was coming under increasing pressure, Hoddle chose to give an interview to Matt Dickinson of *The Times*. Asked to expand on his religious convictions, Hoddle talked to Dickinson about his belief in reincarnation and karma. 'Karma has been around for thousands of years,' Hoddle ventured. 'You have to come back to face some of the things you have done – good and bad. You and I have been physically given two hands and two legs and half-decent brains. Some people have not been born like that for a reason. The karma is working from another lifetime.'

It was not the first time Hoddle had expressed the view that disabled people were being punished for sins in a previous life, but his team had been winning at the time and his comments were not picked up. Published on 30 January 1999, Dickinson's interview prompted an hysterical outcry from both the media and public. It extended to the Prime Minister, Blair criticising Hoddle if the reports were true, whilst appearing on ITV's *Richard and Judy* daytime show on 1 February. Two days later, and after claiming he had been misrepresented, Hoddle was dismissed by the FA.

'My first thought when I came off the phone to Hoddle following our interview was that he was a bit of a weirdo,' says Dickinson. 'It wasn't, "Wow, this is a major story", but, "My God, he actually believes this stuff". I certainly didn't think he would automatically lose his job. I thought the FA's PR machine would crank into action and he would come out and apologise. People underestimate the fact that there had been a lot of disgruntlement and niggles in the

England squad about Hoddle's management. So the fact that the FA didn't support him has to be put into context.'

It was a year before Hoddle returned to management with Southampton, who he saved from relegation and then left to take over at Tottenham in March 2001. He was sacked again after just eighteen inglorious months at White Hart Lane and lasted no longer in his next posting in the First Division with Wolverhampton Wanderers. In 2008 he founded the Glenn Hoddle Academy in Spain with the aim of giving young players released from English clubs a second chance at a professional football career. The academy has had at best mixed results and so far failed to unearth an overlooked gem. Most recently, Hoddle served as first-team coach at QPR, but left after nine months along with manager Harry Redknapp and before the club was relegated from the Premier League.

Euro 96 had promised a gilded new age for the England national team, but this never quite materialised. The FA pressed on with its bid to host the 2006 World Cup and sunk to grubbing around for support from such unsavoury characters as Fifa vice-president Jack Warner, who along with other senior Fifa officials was arrested in an FBI sting operation in 2015 and charged with fraud, racketeering and money laundering offences, which he denies. In 1998 the English governing body also reneged on a commitment by the fifty-one European football associations to vote in UEFA president Lennart Johansson as the new chief of Fifa and instead backed his rival, Sepp Blatter, wrongly believing he would endorse an English World Cup.

Four years to the month after it was first unveiled with a flourish, England's 2006 bid was dragged like a beaten dog along to Fifa headquarters in Zurich for the decisive vote. By then a Fifa inspection report had rated England's proposed facilities below those of Germany and another of the candidates, South Africa. In the event, England polled no votes from the twenty-four strong Fifa executive committee assembled. Even the rank outsiders, Morocco, managed one endorsement. Inevitably, the Germans saw off the South African challenge, but by just a solitary vote. It appeared to be just as Venables said in the heat of battle at Euro 96: the Germans always won and at any price.

Since firing Hoddle, the FA has appointed a further five full-time England managers: Kevin Keegan, Sven-Göran Eriksson, Steve McClaren, Fabio Capello and latterly Roy Hodgson. In eight subsequent major championship campaigns, the England team have not progressed beyond the quarter-finals of any, and failed to even reach the finals of the 2008 Euros in Austria and Switzerland when they were dumped out in the qualifiers by Croatia at Wembley. The image of the hapless McClaren sheltering from rain under a golf umbrella as his team was reeling in that match – the 'wally with a brolly' as the tabloids termed it – summed up how far England had drifted off course since dismantling Holland at Euro 96. It was a sad fact that McClaren's assistant that night was Terry Venables, tempted back into the England fold but in a toothless role.

Hodgson's England lost all three of the group games at the 2014 World Cup finals in Brazil to Italy, Uruguay and Costa Rica. It was the worst performance at the tournament by the national team, and the sight of Hodgson's men being out-passed by the Italians and dismembered by Uruguay's fleet-footed striker, Luis Suárez, emphasised the gulf that had again opened between England and the heavyweights of international football.

Nevertheless, the FA's chairman, Greg Dyke, set a target of England winning the World Cup again by 2022. In order to mark out a path to this point, the FA opened the doors to its National Football Centre on a three-hundred acre site at St George's Park, Burton-upon-Trent, in October 2012. Costing more than £105 million, the centre was modelled on the Clairefontaine Academy outside Paris, which groomed the generation of French footballers who won the 1998 World Cup for the host nation. The National Football Centre was established with the intention of doing the same thing for England. Two years later, the FA's Director of Elite Development, Dan Ashworth, published a blueprint for how young English players were going to be developed to win major tournaments. The next summer, the England under-21 team, under manager Gareth Southgate, failed to win a match at the European finals in the Czech Republic. Ashworth was compelled to announce that his plans would take at least a decade to come to fruition.

Ever since Euro 96, the top-flight English clubs have recruited players from overseas in growing numbers, which has served to shrink dramatically the pool of talent available to an England manager. On Boxing Day 1999, Chelsea, then managed by Gianluca Vialli, became the first English club to field a team with no British players in it for a Premier League fixture at Southampton. During the 2015–16 season, just thirty-one per cent of players representing Premier League clubs were English.

Manchester United's Champions League win in 1999 announced the Premier League's arrival as an international force. However, in more recent seasons European club football's premier competition has been dominated by sides from *La Liga* in Spain and the German *Bundesliga*, notably Barcelona, Real Madrid and Bayern Munich. This has not prevented Richard Scudamore, chief executive of the Premier League, or Sky TV's marketing blitzes, from routinely hailing England's elite division as the world's best league. Nor have reservoirs of cash stopped from pouring into the Premier League and its clubs. In February 2015, Sky and BT Sport together forked out £5.1 billion for the exclusive rights to screen Premier League games for the three seasons from August 2016.

The changes to English football sparked by Euro 96 came quicker and have been more sweeping than anyone at that time could possibly have envisaged. Almost at a stroke, the domestic game was made cosmopolitan, gentrified, moved into state-of-the-art stadiums and available to view, along with the cream of European football, seven days a week on one subscription service or another. Gascoigne, Shearer, Adams *et al* begot Beckham, Cristiano Ronaldo, Gareth Bale and a new generation of superstar footballers, trained and conditioned to a peak of fitness, fêted like rock stars and paid like kings. The vast sums of money swilling around the game also attracted investors from overseas. By 2015, more than half of the Premier League clubs had foreign owners, among them oil-rich sheikhs and multi-millionaire American venture capitalists. Football in England is bigger and wealthier now than it has ever been. Whether or not it is better is much more open to question.

A more starkly defined two-tier system between the haves and have-nots has opened up in the domestic game. The race for the Premier League title, and qualification for the Champions League gravy train, is now monopolised by four or five of the biggest and richest clubs. The rest face a desperate battle each season just to cling on to their Premier League status. Losing this can be ruinous. The owners of Leeds, Portsmouth, Blackburn, Bolton, Derby and more drove their clubs into financial meltdown trying and failing to stay in English football's top flight.

Premier League football is also now faster, more athletic and higher-profile than it was twenty years ago. But it is also more expensive to watch and less inclusive, too. From this distance, and as memory fades, England's march to the semi-finals of Euro 96 might just be as good as it gets. It was, for certain, a defining moment for the top-class game in this country.

'People talk about 1992 and the founding of the Premier League being a turning point, but it wasn't,' says John Motson. 'It was Euro 96 that was pivotal. It was only after it that a new kind of football reality dawned in England and we were able to see where the game was going in the future.'

'There was a genuine sense of excitement at, and immediately after Euro 96,' maintains Ian Ridley. 'English football was still then predominantly about English footballers and we were producing good players. There is a certain cynicism about the game now. This isn't English football, but football being played in England. This country is the setting for the movie, but it's a Hollywood-style production and the punters are treated as the extras rather than its lifeblood. I'm not suggesting English football is dying, but I do believe that it is seriously struggling to stay in touch with its soul. It's drunk on the excesses of money and celebrity. Euro 96, and the 1990s overall, felt to me like a much less cynical time.'

At all events, it seems unlikely that any time soon the English national team will come as close as did Terry Venables and his boys of '96 to ending all those years of hurt. Certainly, Venables himself never again reached such heights. After his ill-fated tenures at Portsmouth and with Australia, he passed through a series of short-term appointments at Crystal Palace, Middlesbrough and Leeds United, chasing one last hurrah but with diminishing returns and a blotted reputation.

In 2006, he accepted Steve McClaren's invitation to return to the England set-up as his assistant. Both men were sacked in November 2007 after England's ignominious defeat by Croatia. It was Venables's last job in football. He turned seventy in 2013 and the following year opened a boutique hotel in the Alicante region of Spain. A former hunting lodge dating from 1881, La Escondida has ten bedrooms and is set in five hundred acres of olive and almond groves and in the middle of the Font Roja National Park.

Eight of Venables's Euro 96 mainstays have also tried their hands at football management: Tony Adams, Gareth Southgate, Stuart Pearce, Paul Ince, David Platt, Teddy Sheringham, Alan Shearer, and most surprisingly of all, Paul Gascoigne. Not one of them could claim to have been an unqualified success in the endeavour and the majority have failed.

Adams retired from playing in 2002, having won sixty-six England caps. He had managerial stints at Wycombe Wanderers, Portsmouth and in Azerbaijan with Gabala, none of them lasting for more than a season. Much more enduring has been his Sporting Chance Clinic. Founded in 2000, and based in Hampshire, it provides treatment and counselling to sportsmen and women suffering from drink, drugs and gambling addictions.

Southgate hung up his boots in 2006 at Middlesbrough and then took over as manager at the Riverside. The club was relegated from the Premier League in 2009 and he was sacked five months later. He signed a three-year contract to manage the England under-21s in August 2013 and is now charged with leading them to the finals of the 2017 European Championship in Poland.

Pearce won his seventy-eighth and last England cap at the age of thirty-seven in a Euro 2000 qualifier against Poland on 8 September 1999. He also managed the under-21 national team for six years from 2006 after a turbulent two-year reign at Manchester City. Pearce was made caretaker manager of the senior England team for one match before Hodgson's appointment, a 3–2 defeat by Holland at Wembley in March 2012. After leading the Great Britain team to the quarter-finals of the London 2012 Olympic football tournament, he returned to Nottingham Forest as manager at the start of the 2014–15 domestic season, but was dismissed after six months with Forest twelfth in the Championship.

Platt was also unable to restore Forest to the Premier League during his spell as manager at the City Ground between 1999 and 2001, and was another to have helmed the England under-21s. After serving on the coaching staff at Manchester City for three years, he began the 2015–16 season as head coach at FC Pune City in the Indian Super League.

Ince became the first black Englishman to manage a Premier League club when he took over at Blackburn in 2008. His tenure lasted a mere seventeen league games, of which the Lancashire club won just three. Ince was sacked as manager of Blackpool in the Championship in January 2014 after his team had gone two months without a win.

Sheringham won the Champions League with Manchester United in 1999 and was the oldest player in all four divisions of English football at the time of his retirement at Colchester in 2008, aged forty-two. He worked as attacking coach at West Ham during the 2014–15 season before taking up his first managerial job at Stevenage in League Two in May 2005. Sheringham was dismissed from this post in under nine months.

Shearer played his last international game under Kevin Keegan at the finals of the 2000 European Championship, a defeat by Romania which knocked England out of the tournament at the group stage. He bagged thirty goals for his country in sixty-three appearances, and also finished up breaking the great Jackie Milburn's all-time goals record for his beloved Newcastle. The pull of the Magpies was enough to tempt Shearer into management in April 2009 when he took over at St James' Park for the last eight games of the Premier League season with the club in a relegation dogfight. Shearer's team won just one of his games in charge and were relegated after which he returned to his regular role as a pundit on *Match of the Day*.

Steve McManaman, who left Liverpool for Real Madrid in 1999 and won two Champions Leagues with the Spanish club, now works for BT Sport as a pundit, as does Darren Anderton on television in North American where he retired to in 2008. Gary Neville ended his playing career in 2011 with eighty-five England caps and fifteen major trophies in nineteen years at Old Trafford. He has since straddled both media and coaching, working as an analyst for Sky Sports and serving as a member of Hodgson's England staff before becoming head coach at Valencia in 2015.

David Seaman left Arsenal in 2003 after thirteen years at the club and retired following one more season with Manchester City. In 2004, he was the winner of the ITV TV show *Dancing on Ice*.

Robbie Fowler's itinerant playing career took him to eight clubs after his departure from Liverpool in 2001, including spells in Australia and Thailand, before a return to Anfield for a single, unremarkable season in 2006. Fowler quit the game in 2012 having built up a bulging property portfolio. He now conducts motivational seminars on how to become a millionaire out of dealing in real estate.

It is Paul Gascoigne, though, who remains the most totemic of his era, and particularly that summer of 1996. He epitomises how the hopes and dreams that were conjured up, then withered and died. He had a year left on his contract with Middlesbrough when the club released him on a free transfer to Everton in 2000, reuniting him with his old Rangers manager, Walter Smith. He began the new season well on Merseyside, but at thirty-three his body was betraying him and making him susceptible to injuries. Unable to play regularly, he sunk back into the old cycle of black depressions and epic bouts of self-destruction.

The slow, drawn-out death of his football career continued through a short spell at First Division Burnley and from there to Gansu Tianma in the Chinese B-League and Boston United in the English basement. He was able to play just four competitive games for Boston and retired in summer 2004, at which point he was also receiving treatment for both bulimia and Obsessive Compulsive Disorder. Writing at the time, Gascoigne listed his addictions as including alcohol, chain-smoking, gambling, exercise, energy drinks and junk food. He was nonetheless appointed manager of non-league Kettering Town on 27 October 2005, but held the job for just six weeks.

He had still not hit his rock bottom. In February 2008, Gascoigne was sectioned under the Mental Health Act following an apparent suicide attempt at a Newcastle hotel and hospitalised again the next September after trying to overdose on alcohol and drugs. More bizarrely, on 9 July 2010 he turned up at a stand-off between police and gunman Raoul Moat. Thirty-seven-year-old Moat had gone on a shooting spree, killing three people, including his ex-girlfriend, and sparked a six-day manhunt. It concluded with police marksmen cornering him outside the Northumberland town of Rothbury. It was to this scene that Gascoigne arrived unexpectedly, carrying a can of beer, a fishing rod, a Newcastle United shirt, a dressing gown and some fried chicken – all of which he intended to hand over to the fugitive who he had met briefly when Moat was working as a nightclub bouncer in Newcastle. Police, though, denied Gascoigne access to Moat, who shot himself in the early hours of the next morning.

Things became still more desperate for Gascoigne at the beginning of 2013. He was being treated for alcoholism at a rehab centre near his home in Bournemouth, but sinking fast. The alarming details of his decline were made public when he turned up to fulfil a speaking engagement on 31 January. Billed as 'An Evening with Paul Gascoigne', it went ahead in the unglamorous surroundings of the Park Inn Hotel, Northampton, where he relived his past glories and indiscretions before a gawping, beery crowd of five hundred. At forty-five, he looked like an old man, frail, wizened and wracked by uncontrollable shakes. He appeared to be drunk and was mostly incoherent.

Camera-phone footage of the event emerged and his agent, Terry Baker, went on BBC Radio 5 live to plead that his client required urgent help. Gascoigne was broke, but in response to Baker's appeal, friends and supporters, among them Chris Evans, Piers Morgan, Alan Shearer, and his former Spurs team-mate Gary Lineker, clubbed together to send him to the Cottonwood Clinic in Arizona to dry out. Arriving in Tucson, he was photographed at the airport bar with a pint of beer. Once at the clinic he suffered a severe, critical reaction to alcohol withdrawal and was rushed into the intensive care unit at the nearby Tucson Medical Centre and put into an induced coma for the next eighteen days. Strapped to a hospital bed, a mess of tubes and drips, Gascoigne remembered later drifting towards wakefulness and hearing his attending doctor speculate that his patient might not pull through. 'I can't die!' he recalled shouting out. 'I can't die! I've got to water the plants!'

Less than five months after he was discharged, Gascoigne was arrested at Stevenage railway station for assaulting a train guard and being drunk and disorderly. He submitted himself again to a detox treatment, his eighth attempted rehabilitation from alcohol and other addictions. He has since admitted that he was then consuming up to four bottles of whisky and snorting sixteen lines of cocaine a day.

Twenty years on, Gascoigne is still a troubled soul. He has, though, retained the affection of the English public. This was forged with his tears at the Italia 90 World Cup, but cemented by the magical impudence of his goal against Scotland and the uplifting sight of him bamboozling opponents during Euro 96, the twilight of his prime when he bordered on genius for the last time.

'He is the touchstone of that whole period,' says Ian Ridley. 'This wonderful figure with the freshness of youth at Italia 90 who had wept and turned a whole generation of men – and women – on to the game. We have, all of us, watched him decline and in all honesty, we worry that we are going to wake up one morning, turn on the news and find out that he is dead. Bobby Robson once told me that he loved Gazza to bits, but worried every day about him.'

'Pele, at his best, would not have bettered that finish against Scotland,' Terry Venables said in 2014, summing up what had made Gascoigne the player of the tournament and also of his generation. 'There have been many occasions when I have watched his genius. You couldn't explain it – it just happened.' Venables concluded that, right there, right then, at Wembley in the midst of the glorious summer of 1996, 'you could sense the depth of empathy' that all of England had for Gascoigne and for the England team. Together, they had made the nation dare to dream.

ACKNOWLEDGEMENTS

This book could not have been written without the help and input of:

Matthew Hamilton (consigliere, agent *extraordinaire*, friend, sage and AOR guru); a 'golden boot' for Melissa Smith, Martin Smith and the good people at Aurum Press; Robin Harvie, who set the ball rolling; the great Bill Bryson for invaluable inspiration; Matthew Bannister; Mihir Bose; Martin Carr; Johnny Dean; Matt Dickinson; John O'Farrell; Sheryl Garrett; Johnny Hopkins; Michael Craig Martin; John Motson; Anthony Noguera; Ian Ridley; Andy Saunders; Paul Stewart; Tim Southwell; Stephen Twigg; Henry Winter; Noel Gallagher, who spoke to me at length and bought dinner in 2009; the staff at the newspaper reading room at the British Library.

The good stuff in this book is a result of their combined contributions. It goes without saying that any mistakes in it are mine alone.

A further doff of the hat to the 'Boy' Arnopp, Dave Everley, Fishy, Scarlet and all those who sailed and served with me on the good ship *Kerrang!* through the mid-1990s – among the best of times; Anton Brookes, who was with me in Rome; and last but never least, the Rees and Jeffrey clans and most especially Denise, Tom and Charlie for bearing the brunt of things with unending patience and with much love.

BIBLIOGRAPHY

Among the invaluable source material for this book were the following:

BOOKS

Adams, Tony with Ridley, Ian – *Tony Adams: Addicted*, CollinsWillow, 1998

Callahan, Maureen – *Champagne Supernovas: Marc Jacobs, Alexander McQueen, Kate Moss and the '90s Renegades Who Remade Fashion*, Simon & Schuster, 2014

Campbell, Alastair – *The Blair Years: Extracts from the Alastair Campbell Diaries*, Arrow Books, 2008

Cavanagh, David – *The Creation Records Story: My Magpie Eyes are Hungry for the Prize*, Virgin Books, 2001

Collin, Matthew – *Altered State: The Story of Ecstasy Culture and Acid House*, Serpent's Tail, 1998

Collings, Matthew – *Blimey! – From Bohemia to Britpop: the London Art World from Francis Bacon to Damien Hirst*, 21 Publishing, 1997

Folkenflik, David – *Murdoch's World: The Last of the Old Media Empires*, PublicAffairs, 2013

Garratt, Sheryl – *Adventures in Wonderland: A Decade of Club Culture*, Headline, 1998

Gascoigne, Paul with Davies, Hunter – *Gazza: My Story*, Headline, 2004

Gould, Philip – *The Unfinished Revolution: How New Labour Changed British Politics Forever*, Abacus, 2011

Haines, Luke – *Bad Vibes: Britpop and My Part in its Downfall*, Windmill, 2010

Harris, John – *The Last Party: Britpop, Blair and the Demise of English Rock*, Harper Perennial, 2004

Hoddle, Glenn with Davies, David – *Glenn Hoddle: My 1998 World Cup Story*, Andre Deutsch, 1998

James, Alex – *Bit of a Blur,* Abacus, 2008

Mathur, Paul – *Take Me There: Oasis, the Story*, Bloomsbury, 1996

Neville, Gary – *Red: My Autobiography*, Corgi, 2012

O'Farrell, John – *Things Can Only Get Better: Eighteen Miserable Years in the Life of a Labour Supporter, 1979–1997*, Black Swan, 1999

Pearce, Stuart – *Psycho: The Autobiography*, Headline, 2000

Rawnsley, Andrew – *Servants of the People: The Inside Story of New Labour*, Penguin, 2001

Shearer, Alan – *Alan Shearer: The Story So Far*, Hodder & Stoughton, 1998

Sheringham, Teddy – *My Autobiography*, Little, Brown, 1998

Southwell, Tim – *Getting Away With It: The Inside Story of Loaded*, Ebury Press, 1998

Sugar, Alan – *The Way I See It: Rants, Revelations and Rules for Life*, Pan Macmillan, 2011

Turner, Alwyn W. – *A Classless Society: Britain in the 1990s*, Aurum Press, 2014

Venables, Terry – *Born to Manage: The Autobiography*, Simon & Schuster, 2014

Wener, Louise – *Just For One Day: Adventures in Britpop*, Ebury Press, 2011

SELECTED ARTICLES

Benson, Andrew – 'Damon Hill's fall from grace at Williams', *Motorsport*, July 2008

Bevan, Chris – 'Davide Gualtieri: the man from San Marino who shocked England', BBC Online, 11 October 2012

Burton, Mark – 'Who is Jean-Marc Bosman?' *Independent*, 21 September 1995

Fordyce, Tom – '10 Years since Bosman', BBC Online, 14 December 2005

Millward, David – 'Germany leaves England's world in ruins', *Daily Telegraph*, 7 July 2000

Unless otherwise stated, the quoted material in the book was sourced from my own original interviews or else the aforementioned autobiographies and published diaries of Terry Venables, Glenn Hoddle, Paul Gascoigne, Tony Adams, Stuart Pearce, Gary Neville, Teddy Sheringham, Alan Shearer, Alex James and Alastair Campbell.

INDEX